DEDICATION

MY PARENTS

MY SIBLINGS

MY FRIENDS

MY FAITHFUL FIFTEEN

Thank you for warring for me and with me. Thank
you for celebrating with me.

Thank you for entering into my story and knowing
that this is not my only story.

Thank you for loving me. I love each of you.
Your prayers and your presence have made all
the difference.

I love the Lord more because of each of you.

GETTING OUT

HOW I GOT INTO A
LESBIAN RELATIONSHIP AND
HOW GOD GOT ME OUT

CARLY HOPE

GETTING OUT
HOW I GOT INTO A LESBIAN RELATIONSHIP AND HOW GOD GOT ME OUT

ADDITIONAL RESOURCES FROM CARLY HOPE:

- Paperback
- eBook
- Audio Book
- And More

AVAILABLE FOR ORDER AND DOWNLOAD AT:
www.gettinghope.com

GettingOutBook

GETTING OUT

HOW I GOT INTO A LESBIAN RELATIONSHIP AND HOW GOD GOT ME OUT

PROLOGUE

Dear reader, I am writing this book for you and for me because there is hope.

For eleven years, I was *in*—what some would say are the prime lesbian years of life. I fell in love with one woman my senior year of college and had a mostly monogamous relationship, a relationship that my friends envied. Solid commitment, passionate, financially successful, loyal, and free of drama. We were well-travelled, well-liked, pretty, athletic, and active in our communities. Our love was evidence that complementary personalities and opposite upbringings could work forever. We proved that life together was all we needed.

You may or may not be surprised to hear that I was a Christian. Or you may wonder how a consuming struggle with same-sex attraction began. To say this caught me off guard would be an understatement. Looking back, I had a sincere faith and modeled what most would consider a disciplined Christian life, even during my first three years of college. I genuinely knew and loved Jesus Christ. I prayed constantly, studied and memorized Scripture, maintained community, and kept a careful eye on the situations I placed myself in. Yet for all of my attempts at holiness and managing temptation I unknowingly left the door open to sin I never expected. A perfect storm loomed that I never saw coming.

Our marriage was finally right around the corner, just a continuation of the life we had and always wanted, but now we'd be fully *out*. It was time to go all in. Everyone in our lives would know our secret. People could either celebrate us or move on. Everything was exactly as it should be. Except for one thing. The haunting of the Holy Spirit. My ultimate *but God*.

INTRODUCTION

Beware. You are about to read a book that was rejected by a lot of publishers.

Most said a book on the topic of female same-sex attraction would only appeal to a niche audience and wouldn't meet sales targets. Many questioned if this was really an issue among women inside the church. A few said the topic would be divisive among their readership or their authors. Others said it had already been done. None of them could figure out if it was a memoir or a self-help book and wanted me to pick just one genre. They all told me to wait a few years until I built a following and a platform.

MY WHY

My reformed rebel heart heard all this and knew I had to get my book out anyway. And God provided a way for me to self-publish. But the overwhelming motivation, more than any of the pushback I received, was that the Lord was entreating me to join Him in more. I wrote *Getting Out* because I had to. I have to proclaim the wonders that God has done in my life.

I have to give testimony that *getting out* of the lesbian lifestyle is not only possible—it is worth it!

I also desperately want to make available another resource for women who struggle with sexual and relational brokenness, one specifically written by a woman who recently *got out*. Not many biblically faithful and trustworthy Christian resources existed when I really needed them. In the beginning and middle of my confusion, I wanted to know if other Christian women had a similar experience. *What did they do? What did God do?* And so here in these pages, I add my testimony to the countless Christian women who found themselves dealing with relational idolatry and have been set free all while proclaiming, "How great Thou art!"

Ultimately, I wrote *Getting Out* because I want Christian women to have hope. Not hope in a specific outcome, but hope in the one true God who holds us and holds all outcomes.

MY TARGET AUDIENCE

In this book, I am specifically writing to women who are Christians seeking to confront their same-sex attraction and emotional dependency. This book is written for you. I believe that the Lord has something special for you in these pages. Maybe you hate God and gave up on Him a long time ago. Or maybe you love God and are desperately pleading for Him to intervene. Even if you are happily engaged in a same-sex relationship, this book is for you. I was all of these things at the same time. I was a Christian who felt surprised by a sudden experience of same-sex attraction to a close friend, got involved, loved it, became stuck, and then owned it. I chose to live how I wanted. But the Holy Spirit kept interfering with my happiness, whispering enticements of more.

If you are a family member or friend of a believer who experiences female same-sex attraction and you are seeking to know how better to understand and pray for her freedom, you will also benefit from reading *Getting Out*. All of you are welcome to enter into my story and see Satan's classic deceptions and the choices I made to embrace them. You will also get a glimpse into my tension. That is, the conflict of being a believer in Jesus Christ who struggles with sin—including an unexpected struggle with female same-sex attraction. I pray that you, being rooted in truth and love, will be able to pray boldly and speak the words of God. And that you, too, will be encouraged.

MY GOAL

That said, I know our stories will be very different. Many factors have led us to this point. So much brokenness exists that has manifested itself in countless ways. But that doesn't mean God is unable to create something beautiful and specific for you. Despite our vastly different situations, timelines, and reasons our remedy is the same. Our God is exactly the same yesterday, today, and forever. Even though my story is not your story, and vice versa, our God is our God. His Word is powerful. His Spirit is relentless. The Father reaches each of us uniquely wherever we are and tells us of the same hope.

In reading my story, you may be able to recognize a lot of similar sentiments, even if you can't quite articulate them yet yourself. Perhaps these words can help you to express your groanings to our God who hears. Perhaps you will be able to recognize similar underlying belief systems, thinking patterns, or responses to the tensions you face. Regardless, I am confident that Jesus Christ will meet you here. He knows you best. His promised Holy Spirit is in you to sanctify you. I pray the Father uses these chapters and the word of my testimony to spark in you a renewed hope in the Son. And that it will foster a movement in you to risk believing again that God is up to something beautiful in your life.

While we may not understand why we do what we do or love what we love, God is not surprised, repulsed, or forced to opt for a backup plan because of us. Our brokenness is neither unforgiveable nor unchangeable. God is in authority and He providentially governs over all things. Our God understands our age-long plight and has given us all we need to fight and overcome. You are never too far *in* or so far away that His arm cannot reach you. He knows that there is an epic battle for our hearts between two loves calling out. In His compassion, the Lord is always saving and graciously leading His people out.

By the end of *Getting Out*, you will have accomplished my goal for you if you emerge with revived hope in Jesus Christ as your always-rescuing Savior. May you grow to know more of His loving kindness, pursue ongoing sanctification, and be set free from the power of brokenness.

BOOK FORMAT

This book is both a memoir and a resource. The chapters alternate between telling my story and sharing with you what I have since learned. I did this to try and put some pieces together for us and see how our experience with same-sex attraction and emotional dependency fit within the framework of God's kingdom and His teaching. As I weave in and out of the narrative, I recommend that you read slowly. Do not rush through reading this book. It's not a race. I know it's lengthier than the classic format and perhaps more complex, but I believe we can handle more and want more, especially if it includes contextualized content. I simply wrote the book that I wish I could have read then. So use *Getting Out* as a guide of sorts. Take your time in the teaching sections and the story. Mark the pages. Check the boxes. Consider. Listen. Underline. Cross out. Circle. Inquire. Wrestle. Groan. Pray.

One of the unique features of this book is that you will find that I capitalize a number of nouns and pronouns in a way that may make your inner-editor cringe. But it's all to demonstrate a key point. As the object of my greatest affection changes, you will notice my subtle and not-so-subtle choices in ascribing my allegiance and honor. I highlight my shifts in worship through capitalizing the name of my god of choice. Whether proper or improper.

I've also included a few reflection questions at the end of each chapter for you to answer. Use these pauses to create a space where you can be free to process, learn, rage, pray, lament, be honest, and feel known. No one will read it. These responses are for you and the Lord.

I've also included endnotes that you will find located at the back of this book. The citations are a mix of Scripture references and content for further study. As you will soon see in my story, I didn't always quote or understand Scripture correctly in its context. So some of the citations are direct quotes and some explain how I got it wrong and what is right.

At the end of *Getting Out* you will find some additional resources. There are a number of great books that I recommend written by women on the topic of female same-sex attraction. There are also some wonderful Christian ministries that can offer support to individuals, families, friends, parents, and spouses of those who are seeking spiritual and relational restoration though Jesus Christ. They provide confidential one-on-one care, online support groups, in-person support groups, counseling, and content that you and the global Church can greatly benefit from. Please take advantage of the wealth of trustworthy biblical resources available to you.

THEOLOGICAL POSTION

First of all, I'd like to be very clear. I am not a Bible scholar. I am not on staff at my church. I'm not a professional writer or licensed counselor. I don't have or want a platform or following. You won't find me on a speaking tour or social media. I'm not married. I'm just a normal person. I put my flip-flops on one foot at a time, just like everybody else.

But I also want to be very clear about what you can expect regarding my theological position. I wrote this book as a Christian with a Christian viewpoint. Therefore, my beliefs about topics like creation, the *imago Dei*, the Fall, Jesus Christ's incarnation, atonement, resurrection, and ascension, and the Godhead are historically Christian orthodox. So are my views on marriage and homosexuality.

- I believe that there is only one God. I believe that God eternally exists as one essence in three distinct persons— God the Father, God the Son, and God the Holy Spirit, each of whom is fully God, yet there is one God. God is perfectly triune, overflowing in love, identical in attributes, distinct in persons, united in one will, and interwoven in all divine behavior.[1]

- I believe that the triune God has revealed Himself to all His creation and continues to reveal Himself to all of humanity. God is evident through His image bearers and all created things. The creativity in humankind, the beauty of the natural world, and the expanse of the universe declare His invisible attributes and His common grace. I believe all knowledge of God is a revealed knowledge and that God Himself is the sole and proper witness to Himself.[2]

- I believe God also continues to reveal Himself to humanity. The two forms of His gracious self-disclosure are the incarnation of the Son and Scripture. Both Jesus Christ and the Holy Bible are believed and understood by the power of the Holy Spirit. Special revelation is salvific in nature and declares God's specific grace.[3]

- I believe that the Bible is the Word breathed out by God and written by human authors by the power of the Holy Spirit to declare the love of God. I believe the entirety of the Bible is true, inerrant, inspired, authoritative, sufficient, and clear. It's God's book about God. Scripture is the only infallible rule of Christian faith and practice.[4]

- I believe that Jesus Christ is the eternally existent and eternally begotten Son of God. I believe Jesus Christ is both fully God and fully human. He is the image of the invisible God, the exact imprint of the Father, equal with the Father and the Holy Spirit in essence. As the God-man, Jesus Christ came to represent God on earth, live in perfect covenantal obedience to the law of God, provide a model for redeemed humanity, and also bear the covenantal curse on behalf of disobedient humanity as the only perfect sacrifice. Jesus Christ rose from the dead, ascended to heaven, and sits at the right hand of the Father. By grace through faith, everyone who believes in the name of Jesus Christ as Lord will receive eternal life.[5]

- I believe the Holy Spirit is eternally sent by the Father and the Son, is of their exact same essence, and applies salvation. The Holy Spirit accomplishes the work of faith, repentance, adoption, regeneration, illumination, sanctification, perseverance, and empowers believers for Christian living. The Holy Spirit does nothing on His own and is entirely self-deferential for He only magnifies the Son, who always points to the Father. The Spirit of God only speaks and teaches according to the Word of Jesus Christ.[6]

- I believe in God the Father almighty, maker of Heaven and earth. I believe that the Father has no origin and yet He is the origin of all things. The Father initiates salvation and is the source of all divine behavior. There is order and unity of will and action in the Godhead as the Father sends the Son and the Holy Spirit to humanity. All things are from the Father, through the Son, by the Holy Spirit.[7]

- I believe that God created humankind in His image to glorify Him forever and to rule and reign over creation. I believe that God created Adam and that it was not good that he was alone, so God created Eve to become one with him and that the union was very good. I believe God designed men and women to flourish together. I believe

God designed sex to be enjoyed only between one man and one woman only in the context of marriage. I believe that homosexuality and same-sex attraction are conditions of the Fall, distortions of God's image, a hindrance to communion with God, and do not glorify God.[8]

DEFINITIONS

Before we get started, I also want to briefly define a couple key terms. You will also find more detail around these descriptions in Chapter Two.

GOD'S DESIGN

Both same-sex attraction and emotional dependency subvert God's design for human relationships and sexuality. When God created humanity, He made a man and a woman who were both naked and unashamed. Their union is the archetype for both sexuality and marriage—one man and one woman in a lifelong covenant. This ethic echoes from the opening pages of the Old Testament to the very end of the New Testament. Sex and marriage go hand in hand. God created marriage as the context for sexual expression, as a stable means for procreation, and as a reflection of Christ's love for His Church. The Bible considers all forms of sexual expression sinful outside of the context of marriage between one man and one woman.

That's why the stakes are so high when it comes to sex. The act itself is one meant to tether us to another, to become one flesh in a way that reflects our triune God. And when we fail to follow God's design, we harm ourselves in addition to muddying the gospel to others.

EMOTIONAL DEPENDENCY

Emotional dependency is at the heart of female same-sex attraction, and it finds its home in the futile attempt to draw worth and security from a relationship. The hallmark of emotional dependency is trying to get all our emotional needs met in one relationship. Continued and constant connection is needed to feel content with yourself and to face each day. Emotional connection often escalates into physical connection that is severe, euphoric, complex, and addictive.

The intensity typically leads to sexualized thoughts and sexualized behaviors. Emotional dependency can morph into same-sex affection, attraction, and arousal. The connection grows deep with roots stronger than those formed by sex which makes them even harder to dismantle. It prompts people to act in all kinds of unhealthy ways in order to preserve the relationship at any cost. Emotional dependency is not the same as love. It is inherently selfish and toxic. It is also sinful. The beliefs and behaviors associated with emotional dependency come from a compulsive need for another person to provide security and worth, something only God can ultimately provide.

FEMALE SAME-SEX ATTRACTION

Same-sex attraction describes the kinds of affections that attract us to someone of the same gender. Same-sex attraction is comprised of relational and emotional desire and it is almost exclusively sexual in nature, which distinguishes it from healthy same-sex affection in friendship. Same-sex attraction along with all other forms of sexual brokenness is a result of the Fall, which has affected all aspects of the human condition, biology, and experience.

In females, sexuality is more fluid than male sexuality and often shifts over time with changes in emotional attachments. Attractions are based on feelings, which can reorient women psychologically, physically, emotionally, relationally, and sexually toward someone of their own sex. Many times same-sex attraction begins when legitimate needs for affirmation, attention, and affection are met in unhealthy ways. Female same-sex attraction is fed by a desperate desire to be known and cared for by another woman and leads to all sorts of behaviors that are absent from healthy female friendships. Once sexual expression is introduced, the female embodiment and connection grows stronger with use. By engaging the heart, mind, and behavior, same-sex attraction moves from natural brokenness in Adam to unnatural brokenness for which each woman is responsible. Same-sex relationships seek to meet legitimate needs in illegitimate and sinful ways.

OUR HOPE

Getting Out is my story, but it's really God's story. It is evidence that God is doing the same work He has always been doing among His people. Our hope in God is secure. Within the context of this memoir, I am eager to proclaim to you the greatest story of how God is establishing His kingdom around us, in us, and through us. That He is reordering all our loves, transforming our hearts, and restoring all things.

I also want to encourage you that this struggle with sexual and relational brokenness is not your only story, just like it is not mine. Some days it may feel like it, but I assure you there is so much more going on than what we can see or feel. God is working even now as you pick up this book. May God be near and grant you peace. The Lord is accomplishing many new works in you and through you, and soon you will be able to recount innumerable stories of His specific faithfulness to you.

Sister, I pray that you find truth, comfort, and hope in *Getting Out*. I pray you will rediscover the love and power of the Author of our salvation. May you, your friends, churches, and the people of God be educated and bolstered in confidence in our Lord Jesus Christ. I pray that you will be set free from the power of Satan, sin, and death! And infinitely more than our human plight, may the name of Jesus Christ be glorified.

Carly Hope

PART 1

GETTING IN

MY BEST FRIEND

My story is perhaps that of the unexpected same-sex attracted female. The one from a solid, biblically based upbringing. As a born-again Christian rooted in Christian community, I was always a strong independent woman who had her life together, mostly. I earned straight A's throughout school and became a fitness fanatic as well as a leader in my sorority during college. After graduating, I landed a dream job that afforded me a trendy loft, which I considered a necessity for nailing singledom. Only, I wasn't actually single. I was in a relationship with my best friend. I had a hidden life on the side that I managed well. I had the power and capacity to do exactly what I wanted, which hit every category of personal success in my mind. Yet for all of my happiness, I knew something was missing. *What's going on with me?* I had everything I wanted, plus an amazing woman by my side, and I still was grasping for more.

Beginning at the age of five, I sincerely followed Christ. I professed Him as my Savior, got baptized, and the Holy Spirit sealed the deal. For the next sixteen years, I walked closely with God growing in my relationship with Him. I craved His Word and loved both His people and His church. Throughout my time in grade school and college, I shared the gospel with everyone around me—my friends, teachers, teammates, and classmates. I also sought accountability and discipleship with various women in my church, and mentored students from my school and youth group. Early on, my walk with Christ was never shallow. It was raw, deep, and personal. But that time in my life also required me to walk through numerous valleys of pain and loss, which began to take their toll.

I never knew life above the poverty line. My parents lost jobs, my dad's health suffered, and we were forced to move to a new city on multiple occasions. Our lives were full of turmoil and heartache. During those years, I learned to pray big prayers hoping that they might change God's mind. I thought my persistence could convince Him to let up, lighten our load, and give us the answers we asked for. The Bible taught me that God is good, but our situation did little to confirm that for me. Witnessing my family's suffering contributed its own emotional pain. When you see someone you love crying out to God with no apparent change, it can be your undoing. It seemed like a simple request that God provide for my family, but I only heard deafening silence in response to my family's prayers.

In eighteen years of growing up, nothing about our situation changed from my vantage point. In fact, it seemed to grow worse, which caused me to become angry. I felt hurt and disappointed by the God I loved. Believing He had abandoned us was heartbreaking. *Don't faithful Christ followers deserve better? Is this what my obedience and faith would amount to? Suffering? Silence from my God in my times of need?* It all seemed categorically unfair. I couldn't understand His ways, and in my impatience I took control. I tried to ease the tension between what I knew to be true about God and what I was experiencing. The disparity just made me pray and work harder.

As the eldest child, I took on the parent role by necessity as much as self-election. When God failed to be who I expected

Him to be, I attempted to fill in the gaps. I shielded my siblings from suffering, earned money to pay the family bills, bought things in case we ran out, strove for perfection so my parents didn't have to worry about me, and tried to be the best friend my parents didn't have. I taught myself by repetition that if you want something done, you've got to do it yourself. *I alone can be trusted.* In doing so, I became my own savior. And I was good at it. My success in making things happen propagated this mindset to all my other relationships and situations too. I could save, I could help, I could rescue, I was enough. *No one else can be trusted.* My authority was best. Self-rule was better. I'd still pray, but invest less hope. It was easier that way. Coping how I wanted didn't require me to feel anything. My faith and reasoning became pragmatic and I created answers to my own prayers. My mode of operation and my truth felt more reliable. Later, this way of life would lead to plenty of trouble because it simply wasn't true.

I entered college with a sincere faith, excited about all God would do in my life. I grew tremendously in my walk with the Lord, albeit at a less manic pace. I had never loved God more.[1] Going to college in the south east along the ocean was so much fun and I made many new friends, all the while serving my community and maintaining a perfect GPA. I also led a Bible study in my dorm and counseled women struggling with food issues, addictions, and guys because I struggled with many of the same problems. Adding on all of these responsibilities to my school load, sports, and club leadership required a ton of work, but it was worth the effort. I felt that I was doing my part on the front lines, engaging darkness and pursing freedom for myself and others. I knew I needed wisdom to keep me from discouragement. So I sought out older women in my church for accountability and discipleship and built a strong network of male and female friendships and Christian community.

Still, I continued feeling like I needed more. First, I longed for romance. Despite many male friendships, none of them developed into anything serious which sucked. My plan had been to marry in my early twenties, travel the world, and begin having children a few years later. It seemed like a reasonable timeline for God to deliver on. *And shouldn't He want to?* So I prayed fervently for a godly man, like all my other friends had. Second, I felt alone. I wanted a really good friend in my life. Even with all of my friendships and leadership positions, I felt unknown. I looked around and saw other girls with a best friend. They seemed fulfilled by a close friendship and I wanted one—a best friend who could know everything about me and still love me. I prayed fervently that God would give me a close female friend, just like all the other women had. *That's what I'm lacking. A best friend is what I need.*

Coupled with each of these longings was my unhappiness with my appearance. I did not feel beautiful. Physically, I fell short of my own standards of beauty and fitness, standards I could never seem to attain no matter how much I trained, dieted, or denied myself. I felt different, I felt like I looked different. These feelings caused my physical body to become my enemy. So I hid myself in clothes that covered my imperfections and worked on my personality and spiritual life. If I couldn't have the body I wanted, at least I could offer people different reasons to love me. Here, I felt that I could regain a sense of control. Personal development became my work-around for an area of life that I could not manage due to uncooperative genes or calorie control. I worked at crafting and strengthening enviable traits, like kindness, love, advice-giving, prayerfulness, understanding, independence, confidence, humor—*anything* that would set me apart as unique.

I never considered women as anything more than friends, but I watched them closely, comparing myself to their bodies and personalities. When I felt I didn't measure up, I would either try to copy whatever trait of theirs I admired or diminish the value I placed on it. I judged other women, either envying them or despising them in my heart. Constant comparison fed my desire for a different version of myself. I wanted others to admire my outward appearance as well as my inward. But my body seemed to betray me. It behaved in a way that was incongruent with who I thought I was. To quiet my shame, I tried to separate body and soul through compartmentalization of the physical, spiritual, and relational. I stuffed down my feelings of inadequacy, writing them off as silly and childish. Instead, I pursued friendships with those I admired and sought applause for my achievements and admiration for my character. All of it was an effort to create many ways for people to love me more. If they did, maybe I'd like myself a little more and forget about the ways that I felt "less than."

I convinced myself that once I was godly, disciplined, patient, and skinny enough God would reward me with the desires of my heart.[2] So I worked for God's appreciation so He'd know I was worthy of being granted these particular good gifts. Unfortunately, the Lord did not follow my timeline or seem to respect my wishes and eventually I grew tired. I was tired of the pursuit of holiness. I was tired of serving others who got what they wanted. I was tired of God's silence. I was tired of feeling alone. I was tired of not feeling pretty. I was tired of being ruled by addictive behaviors that God never seemed to solve entirely. I was tired of trying. My self-denial was not yielding any joy and my growing list of expectations for happiness inevitably created disillusionment with God. *You are withholding from me, God. I need more from you.* What was the point of remaining a virgin, pursuing Christian men, and standing up for my beliefs if God refused to reward my obedience? Or answer simple prayers? Why continue to share the gospel if I still end up wanting? *Why would I try to compel anyone to this Christian life?* Here, more than anywhere else, I began to isolate emotionally and hedge my faith in God. I'd try to make deals with God. My prayers digressed into demands. Yet I still could not move the hand of God. Perhaps, someday He would provide me with what I desired—money for my parents, romantic love, and the feeling of being truly known. A place where all would be right in the world, but

GETTING IN

GETTING STUCK

GETTING OUT

apparently it was not "His time" yet. *Guess I have to be lonely and unfulfilled until He's ready.*

My constant husband prospecting made me keenly aware of the ongoing failures among men. *All males are emotionally and relationally shallow. They're just boys.* None of them measured up to my standards so I grew bitter toward the displays of ego, sexual deviance, and passivity that I saw in so many. *Guys suck.* Before I knew it, my distaste for men became repulsion for the male gender. It felt like a cruel joke that God had set us up to partner with men. Men and women were too different. Submission seemed completely ridiculous. Why should a man rule over a woman if the woman was better at everything? Women were smarter and more in-tune with life and me than any guy I'd ever met. *I would rather be single, independent, and successful than depend on a man. That way I will be safe from being seduced, rejected, or powerless.* If I were going to depend on people, it would be my female friends.

As I thrived in college, my frustrations with God increased. Back home, depression began stealing my father. My whole life, I had watched him beg the Lord for help providing for his family, only to be met with silence. It broke my heart to watch. My mom stood by his side, but their joy faded as they fought to keep from drowning in the waves. Forget thriving, they

A lifetime of faith and obedience became less and less compelling.

were barely surviving. I felt like they were victims of God's absence. And I couldn't rescue them. How could God be good or kind and still ignore the prayers of my faithful parents? *Is this how this Father responds to His children?* A lifetime of faith and obedience became less and less compelling. Instead, I yelled at God. Tested God. Accused God. *You have crushed us! You broke your promise!*[3]

Looking back, I believe this is where my frustrations began, laying the subtle groundwork for seduction. I didn't understand what God was doing. My family's experiences fell short of my expectations. They suffered despite their godliness. I thought fervent prayers and right motives convinced God to grant our requests for good things. At the very least, basic human needs like food, water, and shelter seemed like minimal requirements for life and a default expectation of God. *God is denying us life!* My parents weren't asking for riches, but they were still left wanting. Feeling abandoned by God led me to distrust Him. I wanted physical presence and physical provision. It was in scarcity and silence that the roots of my bitterness toward God matured, watered by Scripture I thought I understood, promises that weren't for me, desires that weren't from Him, and my growing narcissism.

I never spoke about or displayed my bitterness visibly, but my heart filled to the brim with wishes and demands rather than prayer. Desires became needs, then expectations. I estimated I'd experience some suffering and pain, but not *only* suffering and pain. I fully expected there to be seasons of trials and tribulations, but a *lifetime* of them? I thought that after we suffered "a little while" that God would fix it.[4] *Well, if I am not going to get the promises or pleasures from God that I anticipated, then I can get them from the world and myself.* My lack of trust in Jesus's sufficiency made me fiercely independent, and my success at self-management emboldened my belief that God was weak and I could overcome Him through sheer determination. If He refused to ease my pain or provide me with companionship, then I'd turn to my own plans. *If He won't provide for us, I will.* Slowly, the presence of God was no longer the comfort I desired. Instead, I wanted Him and something more in order to be happy. And until I figured out exactly what that "something" was in my new equation, I just needed to do me.

I spent the majority of the fall semester of my senior year managing social activity and preparing to transition into the real world. I networked to secure a job that would grant me the security I was lacking. Before long, I would start a new life in a new place. Throughout that final year of college, I faced the sadness of separating from my friends who already graduated, the disappointment of my singleness, and jealousy over my engaged friends. The anxiety of eventually moving away, schoolwork demands, the heartache of watching my parents' less-than-thriving marriage, and my dad's catatonic state made me feel out of control. My life was primed for the relief of a rescuer. And that's when I met Her.*

She and I both attended an event at my apartment complex where we played sand volleyball alongside one another. The first thing I noticed when we met were her eyes. She looked at me as though She could see directly into my soul, though I had never seen Her before that day. As we exchanged small talk, I found out that She was a student athlete that just transferred to my university and didn't know anyone yet. I offered to help Her get settled and navigate a new campus. Right away, we hit it off. In a matter of days, we had moved from acquaintances to Best Friends. The magnetism of our connection surprised me, but we also enjoyed a great level of mutual respect and admiration as we shared our life stories. Since we lived in the same apartment complex, we began to spend every moment together. I honestly thought all true friendships were supposed to feel like this. *Like Soulmates.* Always desperate to hang out again. She and I were so different, but had so much in common. Even more, She is a Christian! I had found the best, Best Friend ever. We trusted one another completely and I found a level of comfort and emotional honesty with Her beyond anything I had known prior. She was everything I had been looking for. She was my Person. She was street smart, I was book smart. She was physically strong, I was emotionally strong. We grew up totally different, but somehow ended up exactly the same in all the best ways! We physically looked like opposites, and still everything about Her was ideal. *We are the same!* I thought that the Lord had finally given me a life line. *This is it! She is*

---

*Refer to the "Book Format" section of the Introduction for the purpose of the ongoing capitalization of certain pronouns and nouns and other important notes.

what I need! God has given me what I asked for!

Thanks to our mutual faith and love for fitness, we studied the Bible and prayed together in addition to playing sports and going on beach trips. Before I met Her, I embraced my roles as rescuer and mentor to many, which forced me to be "on" all the time. With Her, I could let my hair down and be the real me. There was no expectation for performance. We simply cared for each other. For once, I could be honest about who I was while feeling safe and known in the process. I trusted Her. I trusted *us*. I finally felt at home. We had people who wanted to be our friends, but in the end She only wanted to hang out with me. I loved that about our friendship. Now, I knew that I could face the world because it would be *us* against it. Before long, we began to isolate ourselves from other friendships becoming completely absorbed with one another. It was awesome.

Little did I know that my behavior and belief in the supreme fulfillment of a soulmate laid the groundwork for our progression from friends to lovers. That process felt intoxicatingly slow, though it occurred over the course of only about two months. Early on, I welcomed Her into my schedule. She became a part of my decisions, quiet times, shopping trips, grooming routines, and family life. She had access to my whole world.

> *There were no secrets. Nothing was off-limits.*

There were no secrets. Nothing was off-limits. Before Her, I was not a very touchy-feely person, but in our time together She awakened physical affection in me. I hugged Her often and held Her in my arms. We would play with one another's hair while watching a movie and nap together on the couch. At first, such close physical proximity to a female felt weird, but it also felt natural. I had seen other women display similar affection with their friends without a problem. *Why can't I?* I reasoned that this is what true friendship must be like. *Love, comfort, touch, trust!* We'd constantly express our love and loyalty, affirming each other in ways only Soulmates could. Life became brilliant with a Best Friend. Her presence made me feel more alive than ever before.

Yet in my euphoria and bliss, I became deaf to wisdom. It didn't even cross my mind that I had begun pursuing something dangerous. Quite the opposite, I was certain this Relationship was my long-awaited blessing. Our growing affection and dependency were idyllic. We became inseparable. Life was so much fun! We'd stay up late talking to the point that we started staying at the other's apartment and even sleeping in the same bed. What began as innocent proximity moved to constant touch, progressed to cuddling, hand holding, escalated to petting, and soon became romantic. Neither of us intended for it to happen, but it did. And it wrecked me.

The first time we kissed I cried out to God horrified and completely destroyed. *What the hell?! What have I done?!* I was overwhelmed by shame and shock. I hadn't been sucked in through rebellion or defiance. I hadn't fantasized about Her. I just wanted to be close to my Best Friend. Other friends seemed to enjoy this level of comfort with their friends and never slip in the same way. The whole situation caught me completely off guard. We committed to never let it happen again, but it did, and it escalated quickly despite our attempts at restraint. *Our love is just too strong.* Kissing continued and soon it became sexual. After our "stumble," I was really convicted of my sin and faced a spiritual conflict: The Relationship that first seemed like a gift from God suddenly felt like a cruel trick. I begged God through tears to take away the sexual part of my friendship with

The Relationship that first seemed like a gift from God suddenly felt like a cruel trick.

Her and fix whatever was going on with me. I pleaded with Him way more than three times. I wanted God to solve my romantic and sexual inclinations for Her, and Hers for me, while maintaining the Relationship that She and I had formed. I thought this answered prayer would further strengthen our commitment to God and each other. *Surely, He will want to heal Us.*

I never knew that becoming sexually involved with your Best Friend could happen. She and I discussed plans for how we'd stop, but we could not figure out how. Our shame kept us silent. Instead, we continued to engage in sexual intimacy. This tug-of-war toward and against each other also kept the ties tight. Because of our

Even worse, my sin ceased to horrify me. It became my precious secret, one that I both hated and loved.

spiritual and sexual-angst dynamic, it afforded us even more opportunities for deep conversations, praying together, and a constant exchanging of our hearts' longings for one another and the goodness of our friendship. *We are in this together. We can figure this out on our own.*

But sexual and relational intimacy kept happening and kept growing. It was addictive. And soon, I felt hopeless about expecting any kind of change. Plus, I was falling hopelessly in love. I didn't cry out to God as often anymore. Even worse, my sin ceased to horrify me. It became my precious secret, one that I both hated and loved. Somehow it seemed that our romance solved my body issues because I no longer felt insecure or ashamed about my body. *What a beneficial swap!* For the first time ever, I felt fully known and fully loved. We had a strong, committed relationship and maintaining its secrecy fueled the excitement and intensity. With Her, I felt emotionally and relationally connected and physically fulfilled. We were hooked on one another.

OPENING THE DOOR

GETTING IN

So far in my story you've read about how my life-consuming struggle with same-sex attraction began. To say this caught me off guard would be an understatement. Looking back, I had a sincere faith and modeled what most would consider a disciplined Christian life, even during my first three years of college. I genuinely knew and loved Jesus Christ. I prayed constantly, studied and memorized Scripture, maintained community, and kept a careful eye on the situations I placed myself in. Yet for all of my attempts at holiness and managing temptation I unknowingly left the door open to sin I never expected. A perfect storm loomed that I never saw coming.

Like many young teenagers who have grown up in church, I recognized early on the deceit in my heart. I was taught it wasn't "safe" to be alone or vulnerable with guys because of everyone's raging hormones. So I had to guard my heart, protect my body, and manage my behaviors, especially because I wanted to be pure enough to earn God's favor to someday be loved exclusively by a godly man. Basically, I had adopted high boundaries with men and none with women.

The desire for marriage is good. On their own, there's

GETTING STUCK

GETTING OUT

nothing wrong with desires for love and intimacy, but I allowed them to drive me. Unchecked passion created a lustful thought life and fueled desires to act outside of God's boundaries to experience what I craved. Quick to self-regulate, I began to treat not only my specific desires, but also all romantic feelings as untamable and birthed from evil. Rather than processing them in a healthy way, I decided the safer route would be to not feel them at all. So I locked them away while simultaneously banking all my trust that one day God would give me a man who could unlock all the love and affection that I was restraining for marriage. I believe this is part of what cracked open the door to seduction. I covered my emotions in shame and put all of my hope in a future person who would be the payoff for my self-denial. I also reprimanded myself for letting a desire for intimacy become more powerful than my aspirations for personal growth. One I couldn't control and the other I could. I condemned my heart for being awake. *What successful and strong woman allows something as silly as a crush or a desire to be in a relationship to get in the way of accomplishing her goals? Only weak girls get sidetracked by love.*

During high school, I also started masturbating frequently, which provided me with a level of comfort and sexual exploration, but also birthed its own shame in my personal life. Masturbation brought temporary satisfaction, but it always led to deeper loneliness. In my gut, I knew it was sinful, but I rationalized my actions by believing I was entitled to erotic pleasure. *And besides, I'm not doing it with an actual guy so who cares?* One of the inevitable effects of experimenting sexually in secret was that my sin became less horrifying. It also increased my desire for sex. Engaging in empty sexual intimacy made me believe that I could satisfy myself without implication and that monogamous sex in marriage would someday provide ultimate satisfaction. I banked on love and intimacy as the rewards for a godly life. All widening that crack in the door.

When it came to my social life, I was an extrovert; the more the merrier. I had a ton of solid, fantastic, long-term friendships with males and females. I was a peacemaker and can't think of one relationship that I ruined. Always priding myself on being a strong judge of character, I stayed discerning and kept a wide circle of acquaintances and a small group of closest friends. However, over time, I had developed a baseline distrust of men, but not because of daddy issues or any kind of abuse. I simply could not find anything valuable that they offered. Some of my female friends surrendered their ambitions and identities to men who were beneath them. Some males felt above women and dismissed their worth. Plus, I was rarely the target of male pursuit like my pretty friends.

Over time, that perceived lack of male value and over-realized female esteem morphed into what I later realized was a common belief among same-sex attracted women: We are better than men. Or we feel like we are better at acting like men than men. Even more so, I tended to gravitate to my own gender because I found them less complicated and I enjoyed the familiar company of women. It's an easy thing to do. Women have a shared language and the generally familiar experience of being female. We can articulate feelings or sense things without words being spoken. We tend to enjoy many of the same activities, have high levels of emotional intelligence, and feel safe enough with one another to be open and honest. We love quality time. These are all beautiful attributes for healthy, same-sex friendships, but not when I treated them as solutions to broken thinking or a method of escape. Or an alternative to God's design.

The problem with making my own judgments about men and women is that they warped the way I saw everything. The result of trying to ignore my true feelings and harboring lust is that they did not go away—they just started to grow unhindered.

By the time I entered college I had both a strong Christian faith and a strong paradigm to protect myself.

GETTING IN

GETTING STUCK

GETTING OUT

Plus, a collection of unmet expectations that I blamed God for: He had not eased up on my family. He had not given me the blessings I believed I had earned by my sincere obedience and wholehearted devotion to the Lord. He had not solved my personal sin issues. *Where is this "help" I was promised?* My understanding of God was that He would answer all my prayers. So when things were unresolved and I remained in bondage to repetitive sin issues, my theology had no answer. I was frustrated. I was also ashamed to keep returning to the same throne with the same questions and the same sins.[1]

DEFINITIONS

SAME-SEX ATTRACTION

What did that perfect storm produce in my life, you might ask? One of its fruits is obvious—same-sex attraction. Before going any further, however, I want to offer a brief definition of what I mean by that term, though it may seem self-evident. "Same-sex attraction" describes the kinds of affections that attract us to someone of the same sex. Same-sex attraction is comprised of relational and emotional desire and it is almost exclusively sexual in nature, which distinguishes it from healthy same-sex affection in friendship. Same-sex attraction along with all other forms of sexual brokenness is a result of the Fall, which has affected all aspects of the human condition, biology, and experience.

Attractions are based on feelings, which can reorient people psychologically, bodily, emotionally, relationally, and sexually toward someone of their own sex. More than anything else, female same-sex attraction is fed by a desperate desire to be known and cared for by another woman and leads to all sorts of behaviors that are absent from healthy friendships. In my situation, I found myself attracted to the "person" attributes first and not the gender. I admired Her character qualities and personality to which I compared myself and lusted after. Some of Her attributes seemed more masculine and some more feminine, but all of them seemed perfectly personified by a female. And once we became intimately acquainted, that embodiment became all that I desired. Same-sex attraction moved from natural brokenness in Adam to unnatural brokenness by my own behavior. Basically, the feelings of same-sex attraction expanded from being a condition of the Fall to sin once I engaged my flesh in its unholy desires.

EMOTIONAL DEPENDENCY

In addition to same-sex attraction, that perfect storm surfaced another form of brokenness I never knew as problematic—emotional dependency. To me, emotional dependency was part of what it meant to be in love. It was loyalty to one person, open communication, honesty, safety, and true friendship. *What's wrong with that?* As it turns out, emotional dependency is at the heart of female same-sex attraction, and it finds its home in the futile attempt to draw worth and security from a relationship. The hallmark of emotional dependency is trying to get all our emotional needs met in one relationship. Continued connection with them is needed to feel okay about yourself. Emotional dependency feeds on insecurity that appears as love and care. On the surface, it seems innocent enough, but underneath there is a desperate need to connect with this other person in order to face each day.

The most complicated part of same-sex attraction, especially with females, is this emotional part. The emotional connection is extremely messy and confusing. It is also euphoric, which is why it is easier to give ourselves over than to challenge it. The intensity typically leads to sexualized thoughts about the other person and often leads to sexualized behaviors. Basically, emotional dependency can soon morph into affection, attraction, and arousal. Finally, it becomes addiction. And once sex is introduced, that intimacy becomes all the more severe and complex. When we are in an emotionally-dependent relationship, we believe no one else is worthy of our trust and that we are most capable of loving her in the best ways possible. Our hearts become utterly tied to this person. I always heard that sex could have this kind of effect, but so can emotional dependency. The connection grows deep with roots stronger than those formed by sex and even harder to dismantle. It merges our lives with our partner's. Her dreams become ours along with Her brokenness. Emotional dependency promises forever and it also makes you feel stuck. That was certainly true for me. I only needed Her. I gloried in Her love. She was my highest good. I never recognized how emotional dependency fused me to Her for the next eleven years of my life. I just thought the loyal, till-death-do-us-part devotion was a natural byproduct of our love and the best part of lesbianism.

However, emotional dependency is a captor that holds its victims in a cell of bondage. It prompts us to act in all kinds of unhealthy ways in order to preserve the relationship at any cost. Or, if the relationship proves unsatisfactory, we're required to find a new one that promises to meet our needs with a partner whose role in our lives cannot change. Or end. Ever. This form of dependency is not the same as love. Though it may look praiseworthy, it is toxic to healthy and godly relationships. Even a truly Christ-honoring relationship and heterosexual marriage cannot include emotional dependency because all believers are called to point others, even our lovers, to dependency on Jesus Christ. Not to enslave them to a deeper reliance on our self. Whatever we call it, this kind of behavior is unhealthy and comes from a compulsive need for another person to provide us security, something only God can ultimately deliver.

GOD'S DESIGN

Both same-sex attraction and emotional dependency subvert God's design for human relationships and sexuality. When God created humanity, He made a man and a woman who were both naked and unashamed.[2] They were made to depend on God and glorify Him as the author of life. Adam and Eve were instructed to partner together to rule over the created order. They were granted governance to take care of the Garden and subdue it to reflect the love and authority of their Creator. Together they enjoyed intimate fellowship with God.

The Lord invited Adam and Eve to fill the earth and flourish in the Garden. The union of Adam and Eve is the archetype for both sexuality and marriage—one man and one woman in a lifelong covenant. This ethic echoes from the opening pages of the Old Testament to the very end of the New Testament.[3] Sex and marriage go hand in hand. God created marriage as the context for sexual expression, as a stable means for procreation, and as a reflection of Christ's love for His church.[4] The Bible considers all forms of sexual expression sinful outside of the context of marriage between a man and a woman.[5]

That's why the stakes are so high when it comes to sex. The act itself is one meant to tether us to another, to become one flesh in a way that reflects our triune God. To mirror a love that unifies and multiplies. And when we fail to follow God's design, we harm ourselves in addition to muddying the gospel for others. It's the Creator's love and authority over all His creation that make God's design a very good and right requirement. And it's our love and dependence on our Creator that makes obeying God's design a very good and right response.

GETTING IN

GETTING STUCK

GETTING OUT

PRIMERS & TRIGGERS

Every day while I lived in this place of utter confusion about God's purposes in my same-sex attraction, I had no idea if I would die in this sin or if God would rescue me. If it was for my eventual good, it felt like the worst risk for sanctification that God could make. *How about a struggle with alcohol or anorexia instead?* But this was apparently it. My sin of preference. A sin that was not preferable. Over the years, it didn't feel like Jesus was teaching me anything because sin seemed to be winning. It no longer felt like God had purpose or a plan for my struggle, it just felt like He forgot and was silent. It seemed as if God gave me up, or gave me over, or I gave myself over—I had no idea.[6] I didn't know that when I opened the door to the sin of a same-sex relationship that it would last for so long or that my core sin issues would prop it open.

Clearly, certain lifestyle factors opened the door to emotional dependency and same-sex attraction, but what specifically drew me to those ends? While that's a question I'll never be able to fully answer, through my interactions with other Christian women who have similar struggles I've found that there are a number of common primers that make us vulnerable to seeking relief in a female same-sex relationship. Here are six precursors that I experienced and found most common:

1. Wrong thinking patterns
2. Comparison
3. Lust
4. Pain avoidance
5. Entitlement
6. Distrust of God

WRONG THINKING PATTERNS

No one lies to us more than ourselves. I wove an intricate tale of fiction in which God was deaf to my prayers and any kind of success in life depended entirely on me. Rather than talking with others about my thought life, I locked away these patterns of interpretation in my mind, which gave them a life of their own. My wrong thinking patterns infiltrated my theology and I failed to recognize the harm they produced. It's true that what we believe determines how we live. When we replay these false recordings in our heads and keep these fiction reels hidden, we begin to believe all the self-talk. It is easy to turn up the volume of life to keep from having to deal with God who insists we give up wrong thinking.

COMPARISON

Comparison is the thief of joy and it makes an idol out of inadequacy. All of my friends were engaged or married and I wanted that same experience of falling in love, being in love, and making love. I desperately wanted to be in a committed relationship. Despite the fact that I had accomplished more than my peers, I desperately coveted their relationships. *When will it be my turn?* I also wanted to be skinny and physically desirable. *Just like them.* I felt like my life would have meaning, and I would have greater worth if I looked like all the other women and had a significant other or spouse who loved me. Someone to spend my life with. Then I would be satisfied. Envying the lives of other women was an accusation against God's goodness, not just that He made me wonderfully and gives good gifts, but that He is wonderful and good Himself.[7]

LUST

Lust is a desire untethered from the sanctifying work of Christ. It can start as an attraction or a craving for what someone else has, like an easier life or an intimate same-sex friendship. Or it can grow from a natural desire left unattended, like the desire for sexual intimacy. My lust grew as I dreamed of romance and looked for it everywhere, and it surfaced and seized opportunity within the context of my same-sex relationship. The beauty and strength I desired and found in Her became the objects of my lust. *I see it, I want it, I take it.*[8] Sexual lust in particular grows and leads to disordered thoughts and it creates a desire to consume another person relationally, emotionally, or sexually. Lust is never satisfied. Above all, lust is rebellion against God because we believe that our unhindered desires are better than His desires.

PAIN AVOIDANCE

Coping methods work for a while, but pain invades numbness and calls us to attention. Severe hurt inspires a response revealing what we depend on for safety and security. I wanted to avoid pain at all costs. The problem was that it appeared everywhere I looked—in headlines, my family, and my heart. I felt deep pity for those who were undeservingly hurting and blamed Jesus for being inactive. God didn't seem to shield me or His people from the pain and that "injustice" angered me. I used my hurt to build my case against His goodness and numbed myself with activity. The busyness distracted me enough to begin entertaining dangerous thoughts: *God is not actually real. He is not good. He doesn't care. He is not like a father protecting his children.* It's a myth that the Christian life is one meant to be free of pain. What changes for the believer is that Christ becomes our enduring hope in the midst of suffering.[9] Avoidance of pain can lead us to reject God, which opens us up to anything else we determine to be a suitable savior.

ENTITLEMENT

By the time I entered college, I had given God all I knew how to give, but I rarely experienced joy in my obedience. I shared my faith, led small groups, pursued accountability, kept my family afloat, and remained celibate. I served my community and was kind to the outcast. I believed these were marks of a true love for Jesus, but they were shortsighted. I believed I deserved specific outcomes to all sorts of sincere prayers. *Otherwise what is the point of prayer?* I believed my family deserved better. I believed that I deserved romantic love now. I thought that what I wanted was best. When God did not answer, my victim mentality and martyr complex convinced me that He was withholding. I felt He had *sorta* held us up His end of the bargain for yesterday and today, but I was uncertain about tomorrow. I no longer wanted provision for just today, I wanted guarantees for every day following. And what He'd given me so far was not what I desired for my tomorrows. I wanted more. The truth is we are never at a place to bargain with God or inform Him no matter how exceptional our obedience and know-how. Entitlement is a sign that something is amiss in our view of God and needs resolution.

DISTRUST OF GOD

Perhaps the strongest primer encouraging my same-sex sin was my unwillingness to see God as trustworthy. It seemed safer to set up my world the way I wanted and take what was mine. Rather than look to all that was promised to me through a relationship with God, I sought a different rescuer, friend, helper, and lover. Simply put, it was easier to distrust God than to accept His unknown plans. It was also less painful than hoping and praying for a resolution that may never arrive. I reasoned that if I began with no hope and experienced disappointment, then I would feel nothing. Being numb was better than being heartbroken. Except eventually I felt complete hopelessness, which is way worse. It was a fatalistic and self-fulfilling prophecy. I did not trust that God would be faithful today or in the future, so I chose to depend only on what I could see and what I could control.

Each of these primers prepared me for seduction and emerged as byproducts of my sinful desire to do things my own way. I was no passive party. Rather, I challenged God all the time with acts of rebellion. And all the while, He remained silent, which I took for weakness and continued chasing my narrative. *If you are God, why don't you say or do something?*[10] If we're honest, it is easier to look elsewhere for what God promises to give. It doesn't take long to find alternatives providing the things we desire. They can all open the door to being surprised by seduction.

In addition, I found many other situations common among my lesbian circles. Many of these create a perfect scenario for being seduced by Satan into a same-sex relationship. There are plenty of primers to contend with. Check those that apply.

PRIMERS

- ☐ Wrong Thinking Patterns
- ☐ Comparison
- ☐ Lust
- ☐ Pain Avoidance
- ☐ Entitlement
- ☐ Distrust of God
- ☐ Unchecked affections/Dislike for the characteristics of women
- ☐ Unchecked affections/Dislike of the characteristics of men
- ☐ Bitterness or conflict with the church or having a parent in ministry/missions
- ☐ Confusing relational or sexual experiences with males or females

☐ Needs for affirmation, attention, or affection were not met in healthy ways

☐ Trauma or sexual abuse

☐ Death of a parent or close friend

☐ Rejection by someone you love

☐ Failure of your heterosexual relationship/marriage

☐ Strained/Co-dependent relationship with a parent

☐ Unappealing relationship between your parents (divorce, unstable marriage, abuse, etc.)

☐ Co-dependent relationship with someone with addiction

☐ Responsible for the care of an individual with an illness or disability

Once the door is opened to same-sex attraction, it is easier to return to what is comfortable when life gets uncomfortable. Any number of scenarios may prove tempting to help us cope or can spark a desire for lesbian love. And once those primers are in place, certain triggers can prompt the act of pursuing homosexual connection. Note that a trigger to an outcome is correlation, not causation, but the connections only grow stronger with use. Triggers vary with each person, but one thing is the same—we tend to cope relationally, emotionally, physically, and sexually to get relief. Here are a few common triggers that come knocking at the door:

TRIGGERS

☐ Stress/Anxiety

☐ Rejection/Break-ups

cont'd

☐ Energy/Excitement

☐ Loneliness/Isolation

☐ Sexual arousal/Masturbation

☐ Transition/Change

☐ Our periods/Hormones

☐ Crisis/Trauma

☐ Illness/Death

☐ Holidays/Vacation

☐ Boredom/Depression

☐ Comfort/Safety

☐ Knownness/Validation

Satan uses primers and triggers to lay a groundwork for seduction in order to revoke our clear-mindedness. To be clear, if any of these exist in your life it doesn't mean you are destined to battle same-sex attraction. They are simply pre-existing characteristics or experiences that can compel us to find comfort in something other than Jesus Christ. When our primers and triggers are revealed we have to bring them to the Father so that He can lead us in the right response. He asks us to trust that there is a better way to live and respond to suffering and life's challenges than turning to emotional dependency and homosexual connection. Trusting Him in the middle of life's ups and downs is difficult to do, but it's crucial to our sanctification and life with God.

THE PULL

Our primers and triggers influence our attractions, which are unique to every individual who struggles with

GETTING IN

same-sex affections. In healthy relationships, we can admire what we find beautiful in someone else without it becoming sinful. Where it goes wrong is when that beauty becomes the god we chase. What I've found common among many women who struggle with homosexuality is that we're drawn by physical attraction to be sure, but we're also pulled in by mutual desires. It's not just a certain "type" of woman, it's much deeper. It's mutual brokenness. In my situation, I found that we wanted the same things, and we believed in the right to get them on our own authority. I also saw some of my own baggage in Her. I sensed Her needs and knew I could meet them. And likewise. We believed our romance would mend every wound. Our Relationship would meet every desire. The pull was overwhelming. The familiarity invited me in and the longer I allowed that door of intrigue to stay open, the more rooted my attraction became.

While appeal can start with a focus on personal attributes, like physique, honesty, kindness, and loyalty, what drew me to Her fundamentally was the entitlement that grew from my distrust of God. I believed I deserved Her and did not think God would ever give me what I needed in terms of my desires for romance and intimacy. Or

Drawn to one another by complementary bents and disenchantment with holiness.

GETTING STUCK

if He did, I believed it would be less than what I wanted. She seemed so overwhelmingly perfect and I felt so overwhelmingly ready to give myself over. It's no surprise that two broken and deceived women would end up drawn to one another by complementary bents and disenchantment with holiness.

Same-sex attraction is powerful. It has the potential to unravel entire groups of people. I've seen it ravage collegiate teams, sororities, accountability partners, dorms, friend groups, and even families. Many times, a woman shares her

GETTING OUT

struggle with a friend and the friend wants to help. The secret information leads to intense loyalty and co-dependency. The needy one becomes needier, and the nurturer needs to be needed so the relationship escalates. Once healthy friendships became strewn with complications. Emotional and sexual. In many scenarios I witnessed, same-sex attraction seemed contagious. One person fell and took another down with her like a track of dominoes.

The secret of a same-sex relationship is especially powerful between believers because of what it requires us to give up for one another. We have to set aside the Bible, Christian theology, and our Savior, Jesus Christ. That relinquishing of faith creates an intense loyalty, a sworn oath to a new god: *Her*. For me, it was a calculated tradeoff, as She became my new eternity. Connecting homosexually claimed to be a lifetime of salvation and I decided my affection for Her was worth giving up the health of not only my soul, but Hers as well. Lesbianism is inherently selfish. Each person satisfying themselves at great cost to the other. The deposits feel worth it, but the withdrawals are lethal.

Lesbianism is an enticing path to follow, as a community of fellow sinners feels safe. Rather than simply telling others of the forbidden tree, we share its fruit.[11] We tell others of its sweetness. *We see it, we want it, we take it, we share it.* It feels like home with other women and in Her arms, but the warmth is temporary. While it's comforting, it's a heavy blanket cloaking a Christian. The weight plunders the soul creating bondage, depression, and isolation. We think we can get out whenever we want, but dependency takes over before we know it and we are stuck. This downward spiral can steal so much of life, like it did for me. I failed to recognize that

> *The secret of a same-sex relationship is especially powerful between believers.*

lesbianism is a thief that trades in the darkness. Jesus Christ continued to offer me the way to take back what the enemy had stolen, but I fell in love with the plunder.

GUILT & SHAME

What began first as conviction over engaging in a same-sex relationship quickly began to feel like oppression, and the shame that resulted fueled my flight from God. For the Christian, one of the defining indicators of a relationship with Jesus Christ is where we turn with the weight of our sin. Do we flee from the Savior who already knows every dark corner of our hearts? Or do we run to Him? Our response tells us exactly what we believe about God. Shame results from focusing on self, on the mess. It causes us to feel as though we are too dirty to enter into the presence of God, which is one of Satan's favorite lies. But what we see in Scripture is God reaches down to His chosen.[12] He heals those burdened by the weight of their shame. He draws near to murderers, rebels, and adulterers with the promise of freedom. As His people move toward Jesus Christ, He forgives them and grants victory over Satan's oppression, even as they stumble in obedience. Jesus Christ looks in their eyes and removes their shame. And He calls them faithful.

The better remorse over our inability to measure up is guilt. Guilt can keep us running to God while shame keeps us running away. It is a healthy feeling of conviction that acknowledges our breaking of God's Law. Unlike shame, consciousness of our *Grace doesn't eradicate guilt in us. Instead grace gives us a place to take it.* errors is a tool God uses to awaken us to our shortcomings. What we do with that responsibility will either lead to shame or compel us to our Savior, Jesus Christ. We can experience conviction any time we fail to meet God's standard, like usurping His design for sexuality. There is only one source of mercy for the weight of sin and that is the blood of Jesus Christ. This grace given by God does not mean that we were never guilty to begin with because sin is always blameworthy. Grace doesn't eradicate guilt in us. Instead grace gives us a place to take it. Grace is God doing for us what we could never do ourselves. We all sin and no one escapes the responsibility for their sin, but grace abounds in our Savior whose righteousness is counted as our own by faith when we come to Him for rescue.[13] Basically, when we are wrong we can always repent and point to the Cross. Christians should never hide from culpability. Rather, we ought to take account of it as the Holy Spirit testifies to where we have fallen short. Guilt is not a death sentence for believers. Most times, it is evidence of true belief because it means that we know and believe God's Word is true and that we desperately need Him. Guilt is God's grace to us.

If no conviction exists, it is most likely an indication of a hardening heart. Choosing the wrong responses to the Holy Spirit's conviction moves our love away from Him. Over time, denial of our offenses against Jesus Christ are evidence of calcification. But we are not left to die. Christ is faithful to keep pursuing us. He is faithful to remind us of Himself and who we are in Him. Christ is faithful to cover all our shame and guilt and exchange it with His right-standing before God. Sin demands blood, but we have a great High Priest who took on our penalty and became the sacrifice to cleanse us and pronounce us free to sin no more.

WE HAVE A CHOICE

I spent years trying to close the door on my same-sex attraction and caved to sin every time. Its allure enticed me to keep the entrance propped open, even just a little bit. I grew weary trying to get out, but that fault did not lie with God. I failed because I sought to do it my own way: I would only get out if I could take Her with me.

Perhaps you find yourself in a similar situation. If so, hear this: Through Jesus Christ and by His Spirit, you are empowered for holiness. Though certain primers and triggers exist, you have a choice to slam the door in Satan's face. The simple fact that you are still breathing means that there is hope! Do not live under the heavy cloak of shame. God sent His Son to clothe you in righteousness and He has given you the Holy Spirit to strengthen you against the allure of sin. Keep running to the Lord when you fail to meet His standard remembering that He will never grow tired of your attempts to walk with Him. God knows every thought and desire that has ever darkened your heart and every remnant of faith. And our God remains eager to save no matter how far or the direction you have run. Open your hands, sister. And close the door.

GETTING IN

GETTING STUCK

GETTING OUT

QUESTIONS

1   What do you believe makes someone a Christian? Do you consider yourself a Christian? Why or why not?

2   Have you experienced or are you currently experiencing emotional dependency and/or female same-sex attraction? Circle **Yes** or **No**

3   Based on the definitions found in the Introduction and in this chapter, write a brief definition of each of the following terms:

Emotional Dependency

Female Same-Sex Attraction

God's Design

4   Which of the Primers and Triggers have you experienced in your struggle with emotional dependency and/or female same-sex attraction?

PRIMERS	TRIGGERS

5   How might the guilt produced by your sexual or relational brokenness be a means of grace for you to enter into the presence of God? How does Jesus Christ respond to your sin?

MY INCONGRUENCE

Compared to my other relationships, this secret life was so superior that I disengaged from my Christian friends in order to fully commit. Still, I carried plenty of shame and guilt. I was well aware of what God's Word had to say about same-sex relationships, but She had become too much of a treasure to me.[1] I wasn't even convinced this was a lesbian relationship, it was just a deep friendship that got a little complicated. We isolated ourselves because we only wanted ourselves. Our retreat into the shadows was one of the ways we could protect what we had started to build together. Aloneness was a safeguard from the potential of any outside interference from people or God. Yet the Lord kept reminding me that I was sinning.

Eventually, we reached a point where we stopped talking about convictions or battling sexual temptation altogether. It seemed unloving to continue doing so. If I felt guilt, I'd look again at the treasure that I had in my Best Friend and strengthen my resolve. *I just love Her. It isn't my fault that my perfect match is a female.* I worshiped Her. I worshiped Us. I convinced myself that this same-sex relationship looked enough like what God had in mind for me—love, monogamy, and commitment. I assigned to Her and our Relationship god-like qualities wrapped in human form. *We know all. We can withstand all.* I would protect to the death this golden Relationship that I'd fashioned.

I often wondered whether any of my friends noticed a change. If they did, they never made a point to talk to me about it, which I used to justify my isolation. *Can they tell that my life has changed? Do I seem different? Happier? Guilty?* But no one said anything. No one asked, or maybe none of my friends knew what to ask. They probably just thought I found a new cool friend who made me happy. Little did they know that I judged them for their absent reaction. Their lack of awareness to my subtle shifts in worship was my test and everyone failed. If they didn't care enough to ask me about Her, why should I care enough to be vulnerable with them? Clearly, they were too busy with their own lives to notice me or that I was deep in sin. So I wrote them off. But I also took note of how well I seemed to be evasive in my double-life.

> *No one asked, or maybe none of my friends knew what to ask.*

Following graduation, my Girlfriend and I uprooted and headed north where we purchased new homes and began our careers in the city. Right away, we filled our social calendars with adventures and new friends as well as a small community of women who identified as lesbians. She and I checked items off my bucket list by traveling around the world and trying new things, which was way more fun than thinking deeply or feeling sad about who and what I had left behind. Instead, we had each other for advice, to talk about our day, and for passion and comfort. We laughed and loved often. This is what I had always wanted. It just so happened that my dream came to fruition in the form of a woman instead of a man. But that part was God's fault. *It's because of the woman you gave me.* For the first time, we felt free to be a same-sex couple in a minor public way, all the while surrounded by love and security. We lived as a quiet same-sex couple. No picketing, social media ranting, or family drama—just us. Traveling, cooking, playing sports, and pursing our dreams. Even better, we hoped our example would encourage this lesbian community to enjoy monogamy with their own "The One" in similar ways. Serving newfound purposes and celebrating our sameness took on a greater importance than attending to our nagging souls.

Still, I did not have rest in my relationship with Christ. I did not abandon Him, but I had to reconcile the tension somehow while I waited for God to give me peace. So I chose to operate out of the morality I had learned through previous years of walking with Him. For appearance's sake, I made sure that my behaviors did not betray my secret lifestyle to my Christian friends or my family. I liked the benefits of being ethical and fruitful, what it avoided and what it afforded. Like defenses against scrutiny through being ever-giving, but never hurting. Plus, I believed that being virtuous would help me be a better person, partner, and family member which appeased my conscience. Good character also had social benefits in the lesbian community. My moral compass caused me to stand out among my gay friends, some of whom suffered from the consequences of bad choices. I thought my good behavior and Relationship with Her could give them something to aspire to and maybe I could even provide a link to God they did not have before and may never have again. I rationalized that I should stay close to my gay community so God could use me. *If they had just a little bit of God in their life, they could be better people, and have it all. Just like Us!* God for salvation, and a girlfriend for happiness—this was my new calling. To make peace with God and my sin, by introducing God to them with no mention of sin.

On the outside, I wanted to be the nicest, most successful same-sex attracted female people would ever meet to challenge their convictions and preconceived notions about my lifestyle.

GETTING IN

GETTING STUCK

GETTING OUT

Plus, everyone loves being around lesbians. I wanted people to be perplexed. That way if any Christians found out, they could not allege that sin was damaging my life. I wanted people to know that *I* was the one who was faithful, loving, kind, and trustworthy. Enviable attributes of a good rescuer. Then I could prove that I could love God *and* my Girlfriend equally without consequence.

Sometimes I'd feel the Spirit's conviction and would try to pray or read my Bible, but I no longer trusted God or His Word. So I began to substitute Scripture for mantra. My new motto became, "Eat, drink and be merry for tomorrow we die."[2] *After all, it's in the Bible. Somewhere.* I'd pick and choose which Scriptures to believe and when to be obedient. I'd use rhetoric and reasoning to reinterpret verses to justify my behavior or cast judgments about God. I also embraced, "Sorry, not sorry" and "Nobody's perfect." And my favorite mantra of all—"It is what it is." *I am who I am.* I excused myself, becoming the reconciler of myself to myself. I blatantly traded out many things in attempts to try and piss off God. Maybe then He would leave me alone.

Rather than wave a rainbow flag demanding the allegiances of those around me, I purposefully kept quiet about my Relationship to ensure no one could accuse me of allowing it to drive my identity. I also knew that "coming out" and gaining the approval of others would be insufficient to solve any issues. At best, it may offer only a temporary reprieve. Thus, maintaining the secret was a path I believed would lead to more freedom, power over God, and peace in my sin. But building the storyline was exhausting. Somehow being hyper-good was not enough. Strategizing was not restful. Whitewashing a life is a lot of work.

In my early twenties, I was happier and healthier than I had ever been. She made life better. Yet, no matter the level of perfection I enjoyed in my Relationship, a certain disquiet always remained within me that needed resolving. *Is this really what I want my life to be? What happened to me?* In rare moments of reflection, I contended with how to live out my commitments: Should I "come out" publicly or "get out" of the mess I had created? Should I return to my God who continually called to me? I desperately tried to love Him more and asked Jesus to change my heart toward Her. But since my attractions had changed, I didn't know if they could ever change back—if I would ever be the same. I could no longer see God as more beautiful or more worthwhile than Her. I did what I could to diminish my affection for Us, but I could not gain traction.

I was caught between two competing loves that vied for my soul. My attempts to exile the Holy Spirit made me miserable and the Lord would not relent. No matter how hard I persisted in my sin, He would interfere with my happiness and haunt me with His presence. The farther I ran, the closer He came. No matter how loud I turned up the volume, His whisper could still be heard. His words telling me to come to Him. His Holy Spirit was haunting me. I was angry. I couldn't be fully happy in my sin, and I couldn't be fully happy in my obedience. I was stuck. *What the hell does He want from me?!* Somehow I had to kill this Jesus who wanted me for Himself. But until then, I was having too much fun making up for lost time. The time I'd wasted waiting on Him. The time I'd invested in belief.

TAMING TIGERS

GETTING IN

GETTING STUCK

Let's be honest: sin can be a lot more fun than obedience. It's enticing and offers some form of benefit otherwise it would never fool us. Sin looks attractive and tastes sweet, always seeming to hold new promise. It beckons us to come and enjoy what it has to offer. Often, the allure of same-sex attraction feels stronger than God's allure. Somewhere along the way, we convince ourselves that if we drink from its well then it will satisfy us more than before. Instead the water is stale. We end up with a mouth full of gravel. What was sweet turns bitter. It's a cycle of insanity that feels both familiar and exhilarating. But eventually, it makes us sick.

One of the best illustrations I've found for the nature of sin came straight out of the headlines a number of years ago.[1] A taxicab driver living in New York City purchased a tiger cub and decided to raise it in his apartment. Knowing it was illegal, he kept everyone in the dark, even his neighbors. The cub purred and squeaked when he played with her, responding well to his commands. She was endearing. While the tiger was easy to train, her diet required specialty foods and cleaning up after her became increasingly time consuming—and expensive—the more she grew. But he loved the animal and

GETTING OUT

continued to protect his secret.

She lived with him for more than three years, growing fully mature and learning an impressive array of tricks along the way. When his neighbors inquired about the smell and loud noises coming from his apartment, the man managed to explain them away. He protected his lie because it was his hidden happiness and the tiger was a covert association that gave him a sense of comfort and purpose. As the tiger grew, she required more space and more attention, but he didn't mind. She became powerful, which made his control over the animal exhilarating. Proximity to something so beautiful and strong was an extraordinary experience, addictive even.

His fondness toward the animal blinded him to its DNA. He convinced himself that he could tame the beast, that she would never hurt him intentionally. Over time, the risk seemed slight compared to the value he derived from her companionship. He trusted the tiger. When he purchased the cub, he never considered what it would become until the day he checked himself into the ER bleeding severely from gashes on his arms and face. True to its nature as a predator, the tiger betrayed his trust nearly killing him in the process. Despite his attempts at controlling the beast, she had grown into an animal he could no longer bridle. Fortunately, the doctors recognized his wounds as far more severe than the dog bites he claimed they were and alerted the authorities who met the man at his apartment following his release from the hospital. His wounds exposed his secret, not for lack of training, but because the nature of the traumatic injuries indicated there was another story going on.

Few of us are self-deluded enough to purchase and raise a tiger cub on our own, but we are all guilty of treating our sin like this man did his pet. We invite it in believing that we can keep it under control and tame it. *Surely something so small would never hurt me. Entertaining same-sex attraction is no big deal.* We love our sin and it can be fun, all benefits that blind us to its ploy. But day after day it grows stronger, more dangerous, and begins to exhibit behavior beyond our control. Our connection and emotional attachment grow with it though it no longer obeys or respect our boundaries. Personal discipline is insufficient to manage the increasing requirements of our sin. Instead, it preys, waiting for its chance to attack.

Sin's nature is rooted in destruction.[2] It seeks to consume and feed and while it may start out small, it will grow into something beyond our control. Like a tiger, sin cannot be domesticated. It will always act in accordance with its nature. And the nature of sin drives it to systematically ruin everything. Don't believe the lie. Sin will never be your friendly pet. Female same-sex relationships are sinful alliances that Satan uses to deceive and wound us. Sin is ravenous seeking whomever it can devour. Eventually, the very hand that feeds it.

> *Sin cannot be domesticated. It will always act in accordance with its nature.*

ORIGINAL SIN

How did all this brokenness begin? Why do we have desires that are contrary to the way God designed us? God created a good world without sin.[3] He placed the first man and woman in a lush garden filled with abundant fruits and wildlife. All of creation was healthy and whole. Adam and Eve were free to flourish and free to not sin: But they did. Sin entered into creation when Adam and Eve believed the lies of the devil rather than trusting God's command, one He meant for their good.[4] That moment echoes throughout human history affecting everything and everyone and is called original sin. This fracture changed our nature. Since the Fall, we are born sinners with a broken nature that loves darkness and hates the light, which is a clever way of saying that we would rather rebel against our Creator than serve Him.[5]

GETTING IN

GETTING STUCK

GETTING OUT

Original sin explains the genesis of our condition. All of our desires, dispositions, and tendencies, like same-sex attraction, trace back to it. But our nature is not a passive one. It's easy to look back at the story of Adam and Eve and convince ourselves we would have acted differently and that we were unfairly implicated in their rebellion, but our lives prove otherwise. Every day, we do many good things, but we also conduct ourselves in ways that show we prefer autonomy to kingship and creation to our Creator, which makes us all blameworthy. No one taught us how to sin. As children we bit and screamed at others, took what wasn't ours, and lied to our parents. We wanted our own way. Then we grew up and became more creative with our selfish inclinations, hiding envy in our hearts, and omitting certain portions of the truth for our own benefit. Making our own way.

It was in the Garden where our nature was changed and that brokenness can only be solved by the new nature we receive through faith in Jesus Christ. It was at the Cross where our old, fallen nature was transformed into a new nature for those who receive new hearts through salvation.[6] And once this redeemed nature is imparted to believers, it can never be broken again. The Christian's will is free to choose Jesus Christ every day. The Christian life comes with the power to be obedient and love God more than anything.

When it comes to our struggle with any sin, there are three primary sources that fuel the fire:

1. The devil

2. The world

3. The flesh

All of it began with Satan. He is the apex predator of this story. He initiated the fall of humanity and his deception forms a strategy that has worked for thousands of years. When Adam and Eve ate from the tree God had forbidden, they aligned themselves with the devil inviting his destructive appetite where it was previously prohibited. Because of that fact, we now live in a broken world. It does not function according to God's original design. Simply reading a few of today's headlines will confirm that truth. Wars rage, hunger remains, people die, and every inch of creation groans for reprieve. Our enemy uses the brokenness of our world as a seduction for sin, but he also encourages our flesh, another casualty of original sin. When the Bible refers to "the flesh," it's describing the desires we have that run contrary to God. Sin has infected humanity's very nature. Our loves became

Our loves became disordered.

disordered so that we elevate wrong things over right things. Whereas in the beginning God created humanity without sin to dwell with Him forever, our rebellion invited in a DNA-level sickness that craves many things that can never actually heal us.

Satan loves to use the demonic, earth's fractures, and the flesh for his own destructive purposes, especially when it comes to Christians. Our new identity in Christ alone incites the wrath of Satan. Salvation places a target on our backs as the enemy works to keep us from intimacy with God. He calls us out of relationship with the Father, promising no guilt and no consequences when we choose our own way. He beckons us with a harem of darkness that looks like light and whispers lies that sound like truth.[7] But don't overlook Satan's limitations. While he is sharp and cunning, he is finite. He is limited in ability and scope. He does not know the future and lacks agency over creation or our flesh. Rather, the devil is a studious observer of humanity. He knows our weaknesses and seeks to capitalize on them. He is dangerous and compelling, but a puny foe compared to the triune God. One created and cursed, a belly crawler the Lord has promised to do away with altogether one day soon.[8]

Until then, Satan and his minions will continue laying subtle death traps for all people, which is why Scripture tells us to remain on guard, to test the spirits, and to examine our hearts daily to see if they entertain any evil desires.[9] All of these spaces are Satan's playground for seduction. We must be relentless about opening up our lives for holy evaluation. What is true about homosexuality is true about all sin—it is a seduction born out of the false hopes supplied by our enemy. And from desires that remain from our old natures. God did not design us for sin and He does not tempt us toward it. Our sinful longings have a different source, that of the serpent patiently awaiting his chance to strike.

MISCONCEPTIONS & MANIFESTATIONS

During the time I spent living in a same-sex relationship, I thought I knew my sin. I thought I knew my enemy. But I was self-deceived. He waltzed right in and I invited him to stay a while. I didn't know that same-sex romance, which appeared so beautiful to me could cause so much hurt. Sin promises to provide happiness outside of Christ, but only to destroy its victims. That lack of understanding on my part about the comprehensive aim of sin fueled much of the behavior that followed. While knowing the truth about sin cannot save us from it, that knowledge can alert us and drive us to the One who can save. My misconceptions about sin fell into three main categories:

1. Its nature
2. Its consequence
3. Its impact on my faith

For the longest time, I distinguished between what I thought were two different types of sin—that which happened in the mind and that which played out in actions. I was guilty of them both, but more importantly I was guilty of an oversimplified view concerning the nature of sin. The definition of sin is preferring anything—or anyone—over God.

It's a broader and more accurate definition than I preferred. Jesus Christ is the only one deserving of our worship, yet we substitute His place for minor saviors, like money, reputation, or in my case, a same-sex relationship. *Her.* More importantly, sin is not static. Like a tiger cub, it continues to grow and eventually grows beyond control. When that happens, it will always resort back to its natural pull to try to rob God of His kingship and destroy whatever might cause us to turn to Him.

In a similar way, I underestimated the consequence of my sin. *After all, every sin is equal in the eyes of God, right?* The answer is a little more complicated than that. All sin is equal in the sense that it separates us from God. But where it is not the same is in its consequence. For example, Scripture clearly labels deception a sin, but choosing to steal candy does not have the same consequence as killing another human being. Additionally, a one-time trespass has different consequences than indwelling sin. The same is true for ongoing, same-sex behavior. It's implications were comprehensive. Its far-reaching effects in my life made me wish for a "simpler" sin, something less taboo like a shopping addiction or former sins like eating disorders. So while all sin is equal in terms of separating us from God, the levels of consequence, injury, and wreckage vary in degree to the sin.

Misunderstanding sin's nature and consequence led me to underestimate its impact on my faith. All along, I knew salvation was sealed and secure for those who believed in Jesus Christ. I could point to Bible verses promising that nothing could separate me from God's love given through His Son, which meant I had found a loophole to continue in my sin.[10]

Salvation is not a loophole.

Because I had believed in Christ, God had to forgive me if I asked. He had to let me into Heaven. *It's just a small sin.* But once again, the truth was not so convenient. While our salvation is sealed and secure through faith in Jesus Christ, our faith does not place God in our debt. Even more, the fruit of genuine faith is a life that perseveres in warring against everything God declares deadly, like all sins. Salvation is not a loophole. Treating it with such license may in fact indicate a hard heart, a faulty understanding of what being a Christian requires, or a lack of salvation altogether. God warns believers to not presume upon Him and to persevere in faith until the end, but engaging in a female same-sex relationship made that really hard. God saves not so we can live the lives we want, but so that we can live the life He wants. This was a stumbling block for me even though He promised it would always result in joy and love that lasts.

Somewhere along the way in my life, I bought into the lie that God had a duty to remove every sin that owned me as a result of my salvation. I thought the absence of temptation was the freedom God promised. Over time, that lie disillusioned me because not only did my sin remain, but temptations also multiplied. When I could not reconcile my expectations of God with my experience of the Christian life, it became easier to engage my defenses and rely on my misconceptions about sin. That lack of biblical understanding created some major gaps in my ability to tell the difference between the light and the darkness. My faith became flimsy because it was based on loving a God I no longer really knew. And I unwittingly used the Scripture I did know to create both a god and religion that could not care less about my sin and cared most about my tranquility and pleasure.

Sisters, it's crucial that we examine our lives constantly to see if we are housing any secret sin, engaging in willful sin, or allowing indwelling sin to stay unaddressed. Sin is seductive and can arise from seemingly nowhere to baffle us. Sometimes it feels like a trick or a trap because we would have tried to address it had we known its hiding place. Though sin surprises us, it does not surprise God. Nonetheless, its presence makes us blameworthy because it found a welcoming home somewhere in our desires. This is the deceitfulness of sin. It steals away life by depositing just enough gratification to keep us preoccupied with its pleasures. Many women resonate with this experience because in the beginning they believe the lie that embracing same-sex attraction will never harm them when in reality it will always grow if left unchecked. And the homosexual lifestyle has a way of consuming everything.

But the Lord is kind to call us out. Our hidden faults are only hidden once and we must not keep our sin a secret once the Lord brings it to light. Once sin is exposed, ongoing compliance is rebellion. There is an awareness of conscious disobedience in willful sin. We know it's wrong and we do it anyway. Ongoing sinful behaviors are not things that we are forced to do against our will, they are our objective will. Whether active or passive, our eyes are open even if we plug our ears. The repetitive silencing of the Holy Spirit is where habits are formed and soon you will not be able to hear Him. We must not be ignorant of the growing and escalating nature of the trespass. All sin is an indictment against God. Sin finds its root in the preference of anything or anyone to God so we must always examine what we want and what we love. Our heart is the seed of our will, and God desires to transform it to be like His.

TAMING THE BEAST

While Satan is powerful, he cannot cause us to sin. Neither can the world. Neither can our bodies. Neither can our lover. They are simply influencers enticing the desires already present in our lives.[11] One of the universal similarities between all human beings is that we feed what we want to grow. When we comply with our desires, their appetites increase. Our sinful nature is never satisfied. Feeding our flesh incites a craving for finer foods and more frequent satisfaction. Greater pleasures are needed to feel the same level of fullness. But God gives us another option. Scripture repeatedly instructs us to starve the flesh and its never-ending appetite.[12] We must starve what we want to kill. Otherwise, our sinful proclivities will grow and eventually consume us.

In ongoing compliance with the pull of same-sex attraction and emotional dependency, we tend to make provisions for sin much like the taxi driver did with the tiger cub. We create space for it in both our schedules and our theology. Investing in the pleasures of sin requires work. It's easy to commit sin, but requires effort to maintain. Hardening the heart to remain in sin requires long-term intentionality:

> I look again. I approach Her. We go out. I return to the gay club. I stay on the team. I move in with my Girlfriend. We vacation together. We buy assets. We get married. I make provisions to sustain my love. I promise forever.

Feeding the flesh begins with morsels. Before long, we learn its diet and gather specialty foods, all the while our desires continue to grow less submissive to instruction. And we get more and more attached. We'll look specifically at the progressive Cycle of Sin in a later chapter, but until then know this: you cannot tame the beast on your own. Apart from Jesus Christ, it will mature into a predator that will inevitably kill you. Though you may smile at the tiger now, Satan has your grave in mind. In these days, the enemy roams around seeking those he can devour, but one day, Jesus Christ will return and destroy the accuser. There will be an end to brokenness for those who belong to Him. But you cannot wait until that day to flee—it will be too late. By the power of God, burn the provisions you have put false hope in. Discipline your flesh and starve what longs to destroy you, even if you still find it beautiful.

And while sin may seem small, it is never inactive. emotional dependency and homosexual activity will expand beyond control and invade spaces you never thought possible. Sin always ends up taking more than it gives. Worse, it will threaten those you love, even those you sought to protect. Sin escalates and with it comes potentially fatal injuries. Yet, you always have the choice to tell God the truth: the sin you housed has now taken ownership. If you repent and ask Him for the strength to fight sin out of your life, He will be faithful to intervene. Ask Christ to take over the control you granted your flesh.

A tiger will always mature according to its nature. It is destined to devour. Sin bears all the marks of a predator. It is ravenous, but it can only feed on what it's provided. Don't believe the lie—sin cannot be managed. It will manage you.

GETTING IN

GETTING STUCK

GETTING OUT

QUESTIONS

1 What is the nature of sin and what does it do? In what ways have you invited sin into your life and cared for it as the man did his tiger?

2 What characteristics of God's divine character make Him more powerful than Satan, the world, and our flesh?

3 What resources have you gathered and what provisions have you made to help sustain the ongoing sexual and relational sins in your life? What resources has the Lord already provided that you can receive in order to help you no longer be ruled by the power of sin?

MY CASTLE

GETTING IN

GETTING STUCK

GETTING OUT

Contrary to popular belief, my life did not begin falling apart as I lived in a same-sex partnership. Even after four years, my Girlfriend and I thrived in our affection for one another. I swore that She would be the only one that I would ever love like this and the feeling was mutual. If by some act of God we didn't end up getting married, we swore to each other that we would never have a romantic relationship with another woman because what we had was too perfect. Still we made allowances for the possibility of God's intervention. If He convinced us to stop, we planned to date men, marry them, and start families, all the while reconciling our sexual attraction in order to remain friends forever. Then She would stand beside me at my wedding and we could be roommates again in old age once our husbands passed away. *We would always be Best Friends.* I could choose who and when and how I loved, and God, being all-powerful, could either keep our friendship intact by resolving the sexual sin between us or allow it to continue. Either way, we would always be together. That was the only outcome we'd allow. *There will never be anyone better than Her. And our story will be a beautiful testimony to His power!*

For years, everything worked according to plan. I never called myself gay or bisexual because I only found myself attracted to Her. I loved Her and that love did not deserve a label. *I am not like other lesbians and homosexuals. I am different.* I believed I had the power to change and choose my affections and thus, my Relationship didn't define me or Us. *I'm a Christian first, and this is just part of who I am now. I just love who I love.* Why define or draw negative attention— or any attention at all—to something so good?

At the time, I could not have verbalized it, but I had begun an ongoing building project in my mind. It was my perfect "Castle" filled with many levels and rooms that supported our dreams and Relationship. Here I was creating what life would be like for Us. I built proportionately: God had His quarters, but so did my goals and the desire to live happily ever after. I left space for an exchange of philosophies and self-actualization, but no place for the Holy Spirit. I also labored in a way to model unconditional same-sex love to those on the outside. *Wouldn't it be a beautiful new testament to the world if we helped build a tower of unity to help others rise up?* They could be with God if they wanted, or not. This was my attempt to construct a progressive paradigm on a contemporary foundation that would inspire me to persevere. My Castle was a palace and a fortress. It felt safe and I believed it would stand forever because I was building something new in a way that had never been done.[1] If I could just demonstrate that life outside of God's design could remain pretty and assembled with no wreckage, I was certain my guilt and shame would cease and my perfect fairy tale would endure.

Behind closed doors, She and I actually had some issues within our Castle. A constant pendulum swung between who possessed the most control in the Relationship. Nuanced wording and subtle manipulations helped us feel like we had managed the power struggle we faced. We dealt with jealousy, unrealistic expectations of each other, competitiveness, and unhealthy parental co-dependencies. We were jealous for ultimate affection. We also mutually sabotaged things, disrupting time we would rather have spent at the gym or with family. And it was always under the guise of needing *more* time together, heightening our commitment to *Us*. We continued communicating about everything all the time, but were careful to avoid potentially contentious topics—like what God's Word said about our Relationship or why we had stopped praying together.[2] We couldn't really hold each other to any particular standard or practice because in our hearts we knew that each of us had already disregarded most of the foundational ones. *Maybe that's why I'm seeing some cracks in the walls?*

Additionally, questions about our future festered. *When are we going to tell everyone our secret?* The secret that we were going to get married someday. *Where are we going to live after we exchange vows? Who gets to bear our kids? Whose parents will accept Us more? Which friends will we have to cut off?* As a more acceptable form of passive aggressive behavior, we yielded to the other constantly. But underneath it all, each of us vied for control, doing whatever it took to keep tension at bay and peace primary. And each of us, eternally bound to Us.

Because we were in love, it was easy for me to sincerely offer Her affirmation, but praise became hard to receive. Even though I recognized a few issues between Us, I purposefully kept my list of qualms short. I'd excuse my frustrations with a longer list of things that I adored about Her. *So holy of me.* During the times I felt like the doormat of our Relationship, I'd justify myself as the bigger person, the one more willing to forgive. Dismissing any injustice or hurt feelings, because I was generous, in love, and selfless. But I refused to be a doormat for God when He came knocking.

A few times when we felt convicted about our "perfect" lesbian relationship, we'd push one another toward mediocre guys who we thought could solve the issue of Us. I mean, we were kind of attracted to men too. We'd try to date guys at the

GETTING IN

GETTING STUCK

GETTING OUT

same time that we dated each other just in case one of Us could find more acceptable happiness. *Maybe a great guy can get me out.* This attempt at "fixing" our situation was the catalyst for our greatest fights, tears, accusations, and make-up sex. It wasn't so much a game that we'd play as believing Satan's lie that we could overcome temptation on our own by trying to replace Us with men. We thought that a transfer of the object of our affections would result in the self-discipline and control necessary to overcome our passion for one another. *If I can find someone I love more than Her, then God is with me.* Then we could marry men. We wrongly believed that the right guy or strategy would uncoil the death grip and deep love we had for one another. *If I can just find a godly guy, a compelling Bible verse, a flaw in Her, or a worthwhile benefit of God then we can separate sexually and still be Best Friends forever. No one would ever have to know that there even was an Us!*

It was an emotional roller coaster. We'd let the other go for the "last" time, always find the men lacking, and again be launched back into even deeper emotional dependency. More intensity. More promises. More love in our Relationship. At the end of each tumultuous attempt, we'd find solace and comfort in each other, always reclaiming that we already had what was best—*We* are what is best. Quickly, we decided that dating men was not what we wanted. *Men are too different. Why keep trying to stir my affections for what tastes bitter?*

This was the repeating cycle of my twenties. My frustrations with my situation grew and I was all over the place spiritually. Some days, I looked around at what had become of my life and longed for Jesus to untangle me from the mess I had made. But most days, I loved the Castle I created and couldn't conceive of anything better. I had never felt happier and was determined to move toward peace of mind despite the fact that I had no peace of soul. I was deeply confused by this God I had loved and whom I thought loved me. *Isn't Jesus supposed to stop me if I'm headed the wrong way? Or help me out? Or change my feelings if I ask? If I can't figure out what I actually want, how can I pray? How can God even help?*

In my well-crafted life of duplicity, I had multiple circles of friends that I kept from intersecting. I maintained friendships with godly people from my past who I kept up with when I wasn't with Her. She supported these friendships because She knew they had contributed to who I had become, but She always avoided getting to know them. At the time, I thought I understood why. She was just giving me my time like I did for Her. We'd always love each other more than our friends, which made spending time with others no threat at all, even though I desperately wanted to share Her with everyone I knew. But my godly friends were intuitive and discerning, which made me paranoid that they would question Her presence with me. If they were suspicious, they never addressed me about it. I figured I was too cunning for them. Everything I truly loved and wanted, I protected with a shroud of secrecy because when two worlds intersect, it gets complicated. Dangerous, even. There could be fallout.

None of my Christian friendships fulfilled me like She did, but keeping Her a secret created a distance. My secret life kept me feeling like an outsider because it barricaded me from true intimacy. Concealing my true loves created a huge chasm in my relationships, especially among my Christian female friends. I couldn't accept their friendship as authentic because they didn't know the real me. If they did, they would surely disapprove of my commitments and either walk away or make me choose between them

I knew it would never be the same if my friends knew, so I never told.

and Her. *And they won't win.* I knew it would never be the same if my friends knew, so I never told. Whether or not they noticed my duplicity, I always felt suspicious and separate, and projected the blame on them. I questioned their loyalty and began regarding them with caution. *What are their motives?*

Do they know? Would they still be my friend if they found out the truth?

Soon those relationships started to wane in depth and lose importance. It's obvious to me now why I lacked intimacy with others. I only gave them access to certain rooms in my life, but I forbade them from entering the restricted wing of my Castle which contained my greatest treasures, the ones I would protect to my death. I knew that if they found them, they loved me enough to address me. I couldn't survive a confrontation, and our friendship couldn't either. Even if my Christian friends refused to leave, I would. I would reject them because I didn't want tension, conflict, or pain. I didn't want a friend extending sympathy that I didn't need. Or to tell me about a Savior I didn't trust. Or to feel convicted about a life I loved. I knew I'd lose lifelong friendships over my secrets. In fact, I grew angry at the mere thought of them challenging me to submit to an authority I no longer recognized. If they knew the truth, it would mean they saw me for who I was—a rebellious daughter who desperately needed to return to her Father. But He's not who I wanted.

When I could no longer stand the discomfort of my dual life, I turned to other friends, like those among the lesbian community or the ones who simply didn't care about my sexual preference. They were just like me and we enjoyed the same things. We would work out together, attend sporting events, play ultimate frisbee, cook barbeque, raise money for charities, and have late night sleepovers. It was great to feel part of the club. We'd talk about everything and nothing all at the same time. It was an escape from thinking deeply in exchange for loving widely.

In this friend group my choices and desires could be

known and applauded. Our same-sex relationships and exploits were always a source of conversation and entertainment, so I could share freely about my Relationship and get a response that mirrored my own excitement. After six years together, my Girlfriend and I were still crazy about each other, a fact my gay community loved. Their admiration and acceptance was one of the distractions that kept me from remembering God, that still small voice whispering about the emptiness I pursued. The one who was always calling me out.

These were our "safe" friends. Our family. Our group cared for one another in everything from each other's kids to broken marriages and former abuse. We all had a set of keys to one another's lives. The women were sensitive and kind. Generous. Smart. It was also honest, despite the fact that everyone had really big secrets. Some slept around on each other and others had really dark lives with shifting loyalties. But we were all too experienced in the lifestyle to be shocked or judge. Many of us participated in the same things at some point, so we didn't say much. We were tolerant and accepting of whatever each woman believed was best for her. It seemed unloving to address or question the way we all coped with our own life experiences. We let no one out and no one in our friend group without the proper credentials and proofs. Our love was supreme and had to be protected.

It would be a lie to say that these "safe" friends were enough. They had access to the vast majority of my life and knew what occupied the secret corners of my Castle, but they couldn't even begin to understand the God I tried to keep locked in the basement or the Spirit that coursed throughout my dwelling. I didn't want them to

I didn't want them to know the extent to which He haunted me.

know the extent to which He haunted me. Even if someone talked about God, what I heard was usually untrue and I knew it, but my heart was too heavy to disagree. Living like I had no Jesus created a gap in certain conversations because we couldn't communicate on core spiritual matters in any way that was meaningful or helpful to resolve my faith and my same-sex attraction. *They don't really understand me either.*

Looking back, I realize that I was looking for someone in this group who was discerning enough to notice the restricted wing of my world—the part of my Castle that housed Jesus—and ask to see inside. Someone other than Her. But no one asked. They seemed content with the access I offered, assuming they even knew another wing existed. If they saw windows to unknown spaces of my life, perhaps they knew enough to let it alone. Those rooms could be a threat to what we loved. Just like me, my friends that identified with lesbianism had tons of restricted places. Old faith. Old lovers. Old hopes. Doors to remain locked forever, never to be opened again. But they affirmed my choices and that was enough. My lesbian friends didn't care if my foundation was cracked so long as I still loved my house and that it was big enough to fit all of them.

Hoping for peace, I buried any brokenness where I thought I could forget about Jesus and my former faith. That's how the mirage works. If it is beautiful, no one asks. If it's hidden, no one seeks. If the walls are high, no one knocks or comes in. If you reframe history, maybe your past never happened. In my Castle, I created a theology that justified my hidden faults, one where sexual immorality wouldn't have to stay in the shadows. My love could be on display, all in hopes of finding lasting peace.

FINDING IDENTITY

Depending on where you look, you'll find any number of explanations for the origin of personal identity. People tell us to search deep within to find who we are. Psychology tends to argue that we are born with our truest identity. Culture claims that we can create our identities. Personal experience suggests that we are always evolving, searching for our "best self" along an elusive continuum. Most often, what we see today is the belief that we possess the right to choose our identities and can change our minds at any time. All of these sources try to inform us of the truth about God, the world, and us. With so many voices, it's no wonder we face such an epidemic of confusion about the idea of identity.

In a matter of just a few years, my life had changed drastically. I had progressed, too, along with how I viewed myself. For me to persist in my gay lifestyle and same-sex relationship, I had to shift my thinking by ignoring the faith of my youth and pursuing beliefs based on experience. My emotions became primary. I let my feelings dictate who I was and what was most true. My unstoppable love story became the interpretive force of my functional theology, which is a fancy way of saying what I actually believed about God was evidenced through how I lived and what I loved, not by what I said I believed. I claimed a different authority, altered God's requirements for sexuality and marriage, and swapped out His Word for mine. Basically, I projected my worldview over God's and interpreted identity and sexual ethics through my lens of experience. How I lived and what I believed about God varied vastly from God's words about Himself and how God instructs us to operate in His world. But I didn't care. All of this change was necessary to forget Jesus and silence the haunting of the Spirit. It felt easy, but it was not simple.

Along the way, I listened to every voice considering what each had to offer and what sweet morsels I could add to my evolving definition of identity. At a foundational level, I continued to embrace my being made in the image of God, but I no longer wanted the rights and responsibilities of being a new creation. I didn't want to be His daughter. I did not find Christ as desirable as what I could make with my own two hands. Stone by stone, I began to deconstruct what I knew and build a new structure out of materials that perpetuated falsehoods. My way felt more trustworthy. *My Castle will be worth it.* My life was beholden to no one, which meant that rather than pursuing a godly life, I could chase a happy one, all the while pretending my old self and new self were not waging a desperate war within my body and soul. I wanted a world where I could be someone of my own making. *Why should I continue to suffer as a child of God and from unfulfilled desire when a place of freedom and harmony awaits?*

SEARCHING FOR PLACE

Maybe you've experienced a similar sentiment. I was not content living the adventure of being under the authority of God's kingdom, so I sought a new "place" to settle that was not my own. Some of us may not understand our God-given identities in Christ and believe that we are "other than." We long for a place with others who feel the same way so we can build something new together. When we deny our permanent place in God's household, we begin to search for a new home in a land that promises highs without the lows. No more suffering. No more pain. No more tension. We can begin to believe that a redefined identity or the layering on of a false self will be more fulfilling and more like our natural state. We want to go back to how it was before we were brought in to His household. We want to be outside wearing fig leaves.

I searched for a new home because God's call to be a wanderer in a land not my own seemed ridiculous.[1] Especially, when my hands were capable of building something permanent anywhere. So I planted myself in the middle. I concluded that eating the spoils of love and settling on neutral plains was safe.[2] It didn't take long for me to find that I could tolerate life outside of Christ, and accept those who teach other gospels. Double-mindedness afforded me the luxury of living on the fence. My Girlfriend was a secret and I wasn't fully out, yet could still go and be a part of the gay community when I wanted. Participating always fed my desire to make a home there. Every day, I looked toward that life and longed for the freedom that place promised. Proximity and practice were perilous to my soul. And sabotaged any of my attempts at getting out.

But I also maintained my place on this middle ground to run to God on the days when I needed Him. He, too promised freedom, but He also told me of the costs. When they got too high, I could retreat to the fence where my Girlfriend waited

I loved my life. It had not yet betrayed me.

patiently with arms open wide. For the Christian wanderer that professes a faith in God and their sin, the paths are well travelled *both* ways. Between rebellion and home. I truly thought I could make peace with God and my lifestyle by identifying with both. *He should be happy that I'm still around at all.* If I ever decided to return to God, I knew there was no condemnation or ultimate penalty for my years spending my birthright.[3] In my heart, I knew for certain the Father would welcome His prodigal daughter home with celebration if I ever decided to return, but I loved my life. It had not yet betrayed me.

STRIVING FOR SELF-IDENTIFICATION

As is often the case, personal sin affects others. We cannot reject our God-given identities without impacting those around us. I knew my choices impacted many people, but the person most affected—other than me—was my Girlfriend, who I dragged along in my quest for a justified life. I didn't necessarily consider the harm to the image of God or Her soul. Some of us think we are doing our partners and families a favor by leading them along the easy way, denying that it leads to death. Thinking our love and approval grants them eternal peace. Or reinforcing the notion that romantic love is what makes life worthwhile. Despite what the Word of God says about who we are, we refuse to believe it is enough and agree that lesbian love will help us find our truest selves. We help shroud other people's God-given identity with the comforts of darkness. In doing so, we reject that claiming a false identity separates souls from their Maker. And I think God has special wrath for those of us who help others to deny Him by proclaiming a different gospel—either by our words or by our loves.

I thought the source of our true love was selfless, but the nature of our partnership was self-indulgent and God defying. At times, I even convinced myself of the narrative that God was unaffected by my chosen lifestyle, which expanded my view that both God and I were concepts I could shape. I never considered my sexual identity ultimate, but it was the lens through which I saw and received life. Any time I met someone new, I had two immediate thoughts: "Are they gay?" followed by, "Are they with or against us?" So I guess it was my functional identity since it is how I sorted whom I would

GETTING IN

GETTING STUCK

GETTING OUT

accept as true, even if I did not outwardly identify as a lesbian.

Among my same-sex attracted friends we found commonality celebrating our individual sexual desires, whatever they were that day. Our highest value was not our true identity—being made in the image of God—but the right to autonomous self-expression. We got our value from within ourselves. What gave us worth was our emotive self and what we thought. Or from those we chose to love and be intimate with because they were an extension of us. Sexual expression was paramount within this community, as it empowered us to form a united front against those we considered oppressive. Which was everyone who did not agree with *us*.

Among those of us who experience same-sex attraction, homosexual behaviors can be the unifying tie that provides us with identity, a sense of place, and companionship. Group identity in the lesbian community is powerful and complex because we feel like both the minority and the majority. Both the victims and the victors. The ones who are free and the ones who are bound. Plus, we loved being different. But we also loved sameness with others who were also separate. Those who feel "other than" are our people, the ones who get the "real" us. It was hard to live in opposition to societal and religious norms while simultaneously creating our identity with less support. So when we overcame any internal or external obstacle, it built an increasing commitment to people and our way. Over time, I became more confident in my strength and God's powerlessness over this particular sin. Those who endorsed it seemed to be winning. I thought *I* was winning.

But elevating the value of old distinctions, romance, and sexual intimacy causes a crisis of self when anything starts to change. And things always change. Then disruption threatens identity. If the situation changes, there is fear. If the object of my attraction changes, there is core conflict. If my affections shift, there is chaos. If pain results, there is despair. So rather than questioning the integrity of my lesbian paradigm, I pushed even harder to make it always true. My highest attractions had to be pursued in order for me to feel in control and fulfilled. I could not figure out who I was or where I was even though I was trying really hard to appear steadfast.

As the redeemed, we reject the notion that romantic love and sexual expression are life's prize. We do not pursue them at any cost. Our feelings are fluid, they are prone to change so we cannot build our identities on them. Romance is not ultimate or supremely satisfying. Defining ourselves by how we feel is unwise.

USING "I AM" STATEMENTS

It's good to know ourselves. It's helpful to take the measure of our frame by describing who we are. Everyone has at least one "I am" statement. They help us better understand ourselves and contribute to an image for others. Foundationally, there's nothing wrong with them—if they are true. In fact, they can be a beautiful melody for our lives. Today, I would characterize myself with true statements like:

> I am a runner. I am a sister. I am a daughter. I am empathetic. I am compassionate. I am disciplined. I am independent. I am free.

These are a few of the characterizations that describe me, but other "I am" statements are deceptions that can't ever be true about us. For example, here are a few additional claims I believed that helped me maintain a false identity:

> I am indestructible. I am the expert. I am my own authority. I am a good person. I am enough. I am in control. I am unlimited.

Obviously, some of them are more insidious than others, but twisted self-talk contributed to my belief that I could continue pursuing self-identification and a life of sin free of consequence. I felt that if I claimed who I was on my own merits, it would make me stronger and more resilient.

OTHERS & "I AM"

It's also possible define ourselves by crafting "I am" statements that require another person for comparison. However, there is danger in defining ourselves based on other people. For me to claim, "I am good," I usually have someone in mind who I think is worse. There's nothing healthy about that approach. It's not the way in which we are judged by God nor is it how we ought to judge others. We can't dismiss our own sin because we perceive someone else's to be greater. In this same vein, it's especially dangerous for women who struggle with same-sex attraction to define themselves constantly in relation to other women:

> I am not as beautiful as her. I am stronger than her. I am not as confident as her. I am more damaged than her. I am better than her. I am bigger than her. I am not as tough as her. I am nothing like them. I am just like them.

Comparisons cause us to fluctuate between overvaluing distinction and overvaluing sameness as either an indictment or validation of ourselves. Either way, the claims make us feel better for a moment.

Sometimes we also look to align ourselves with other women. We believe the association itself gives us a stronger sense of worth and identity.

> I am Hers. I am with Her. I am friends with them. They know who I am. I am one of them.

There is danger in believing people are essential to our identity. It's then that claims can take on an idolatrous influence. The pride that fuels our pursuit of defining ourselves in relation to others only temporarily stabilizes an identity clamoring for a place of security. Comparison to other women—and men—leads to chaos. We can't look to others to help form our identity. Or give us theirs. Stability can only be found in the unchanging identity we receive from Jesus Christ, our unchanging Savior.

LIES OF "I AM"

Lastly, "I am" statements can also emerge as one of two kinds of lies. On the one hand, there are the negative lies that take the form of subtle deceptions that make us feel powerless:

> I am unlovable. I am unable to change. I am invisible. I am worthless. I am beyond God's reach.

None of these are true, but given enough time *negative* "I am" statements can become so ingrained in our minds that we absolve ourselves of any hope for redemption and rescue. This makes us to feel justified in giving up on Jesus Christ. Negative lies hurt, but we come back to them like a crappy chorus because despite the pain, they make us feel safe from the unknown as we wallow in unworthiness. And when we feel unworthy, we often do things that reinforce this false belief.

On the other hand, there are positive lies that take the form of subtle deceptions that make us feel powerful. They sound like healthy forms of self-awareness while offering us confidence in what is positively false:

> I am autonomous. I am deserving. I am good. I am a rescuer. I am in control.

Aside from their falsehood, what makes *positive* "I am" statements particularly dangerous is that they are rarely alarming. Worse, they are often admired and when encouraged they strengthen the conviction that we have no need of Jesus Christ. Positive lies hurt too, since they are like a really arrogant pep-talk that never works long-term.

"I am" statements can help us find our place in the world and offer characterizations about how creatively God made us. None of that is intrinsically bad, but we have to be wary of the dangers that accompany such statements so we can give them proper place and weight or deny them altogether if they claim something that can never be true about humankind. You've got your own list of statements, hopefully with a higher dose of truth than mine. True "I am" statements invite us into flourishing, while false ones steal our very life. Lies of identity are really hard to undo which is why so many women get stuck here. False beliefs about our nature lead to many different sin patterns.

CLAIMING "WE ARE" STATEMENTS

Humans were created for relationship with God and with one another, but in female same-sex relationships, we don't just want to be in tandem with someone, we want to be fused with them. We seek to define ourselves with another person as *one* person, which creates deep levels of co-dependency and enmeshment.

> We are the same. I am Her. She is me. We are one. We are better together.

This shared identity of "Us" is another hallmark of female same-sex relationships. This dual identity is common and is built upon "We are" statements. I leaned on these statements even more than my excuses or self-promoting "I am" claims. "We are" statements appeared loving, humble, and even holy. They were my crowning glory. When I secretly found myself lacking or felt the disparity of living in the duality of my sin, my "We are" statements came to my rescue:

- When I am unloved, We are loving.
- When I am different, We are the same
- When I am worthless, We are worthy.
- When I am complex, We are simple.
- When I am low, We are high.
- When others are hurting, We are healers.
- When others are closed-minded, We are open-minded.
- When others are lonely, We are together.

- When others are weak, We are strong.

- When God is inactive, We are initiators.

- When God is powerless, We are powerful.

- When God is wrathful, We are merciful.

"We are" statements provided me with comfort when I felt insignificant because together She and I could be significant. They allowed me to be honest about my weaknesses by embellishing the strength of "Us." If I felt unfulfilled alone, I knew we could be fulfilled by one another. It felt like selfless deference to place Her and Us first. But it was not. It is now so clear that all along I was simply humming on repeat, "Me, me, me, me, me. . ." It's dangerous to align our sense of self with people we deem essential to our identity. My claims were evidence of my own relational idolatry. Still, I hopelessly bound my identity, worth, and hope to Her. Losing Her would mean losing myself. Separation would lead to certain death. So we worked harder at investing in our Relationship by reinforcing the claims of our "We are" statements. In the name of love, we were trying to balance a double yoke on our shoulders. It was pretty and yet so very heavy. What felt like freedom was, in fact, bondage.

I'm not sure why so many of us feel such a strong need to constantly define and redefine our identity outside of Christ. All I know is that when I thought often and deeply about me, I found a way to not think often and deeply about Jesus Christ. Despite all our methods of self-identification, we are not sufficient on our own to create a lasting identity. Attempting to do so is exhausting and completely unnecessary.

RECEIVING HIS IDENTITY

Christianity teaches that identity is received, not self-determined. It comes from above us, not from inside of us or with another person. At salvation, God grants us a new identity.[4] We become His. We are forever adopted as sons and daughters of the King.[5] It's in our relationship with the Father that we find the ultimate acceptance and fulfillment we desire, not in our created self or sexual expression. We were created by Him and for Him, and when Jesus Christ takes up residence in us, it fulfills what we were designed for—unity with Christ. Your identity in Christ will always be the truest thing about you.

> I am made in the image of God. I am a Christian. I am His.
> I am Beloved.

Our identity received from Jesus Christ is the most secure reality. When I know what He did on the cross, I can really know who I am. For women confronting same-sex attractions, one of the issues we often face is doubt about the security of our identity or our salvation because of the ongoing reality of sin. Thoughts begin to cascade causing us to question whether or not we're still saved. Or still loved. This was a huge question for me. I was afraid that God had not just given me over, but that He had let me go. Fear and doubt made me unable to rest in any kind of assurance.

I am His.

The only hope for these kinds of doubts is a constant return to the truth of the gospel. If you have put your faith in Jesus Christ and believe that He is the Son of God, you are sealed with the Holy Spirit as a guarantee of your salvation.[6] You are kept. You cannot forfeit your salvation because you were not responsible for it. A calloused heart cannot revoke your adoption because you do not hold it. Doubt can't decrease reality. The One who holds you has promised to never let you fall from His hand. God opened your eyes to believe and He will be the one who keeps you.

If you are a Christian, you can never lose your new identity or terminate your union with Christ.[7] Even if our affections for Him change, our shifts in loyalty will never have implications on the completed work of Jesus Christ. It is finished. And it is ongoing. Our receipt of a new identity in Christ is never impacted by our false claims of "I am." Interior change in emotion or thinking doesn't revoke our adoption. Our new name never changes. We cannot die again. This is because Jesus Christ's is unchanging and unwavering in His comprehensive love for us. He does not change His mind. His affections for us never change, which secures our identity in Him for eternity.

A temptation for many Christians who struggle with same-sex attraction is to believe our new identities in Christ are not enough to overcome ourselves. We want to be obedient, but we cannot seem to be able to do so. Having received a new nature, we have the ability to not sin, but we still do. It's a frustrating life, one that can grow tiresome, which makes it easy to blame God for the loneliness and heartbreak and the sin itself. *If only He would have protected me. If only He would take these attractions away.* To resolve that tension, we look for new sources of fulfillment outside of God's design for marriage, friendship, and sexuality. We think by layering on another experience it will connect us to our purpose or give us fulfillment. I did not chase my gay Relationship to rebel, but because I was discontent living out my place in His story. I didn't like living according to His will. Rather than pursuing the Lord, I sought a new home in response to my suffering and pain, a desire echoed by many like me. I just wanted to love and be loved how I thought best. I wanted to resolve the tension somehow. Often, we don't even consider the harm caused by such a decision because it's automatic. We simply want what we want.

All human beings are made in the image of God, which makes us all worthy of value. Being an image bearer is fundamental to our identity. And it is very good.[8] Satan's deception in the Garden of Eden was encouraging Eve that she could be an image bearer and also be the image herself. She thought she could identify as human and god to gain what she lacked, which was nothing other than what was God's alone. She did not believe what God had created and given to her to steward was enough. This deception caused sin to enter the world, which is why we are no longer sinless, but slaves to a shitty master. From conception, we are sinners separated from God by our sinful natures. But God, knowing our natural state, sent His Son, Jesus Christ, to re-Edenize the world.[9] He is the one who opens our eyes to recognize that we are in need of a Savior. And with the righteousness we receive through Jesus Christ we gain a new identity, and the Holy Spirit is faithful to always remind us of it. And together our God continues to transform whatever sin remains.

Being an image bearer is fundamental to our identity.

Living contrary to God's kingdom and His design is no passive act. It's active rebellion. I responded to these crises of self by attempting to redefine myself again and again, continuing to declare a persuasive lie. The fantasy of self-identification distracts us from what is real. And that deception is always growing to ever-increasing spaces in our lives that result in a divide of self. If you have not yet experienced this gap, don't assume it's because God accepts your way of life or definitions. While one Christian may experience this divide of self, another may experience a seared conscience. Yet in all, He will call you to attention.[10] He will tell you about your new name. His ways of reminding us of our true identity in Christ are consistent, but unique to each of our scenarios. By His loving kindness, He brings us to another crisis of belief where He provides an opportunity to rediscover our new identity, surrender remnants of the old, and reclaim the power to choose righteousness.

That's where most of us are today—somewhere between healing and home—but the gift of being a new creation does not change, which means we have a choice: We can either fight our purpose as image bearers, or we can embrace the identity offered to us in Christ. Trusting God is work, yes, but so is striving against Him. And rebellion will not end well. The new nature afforded to His daughters by our adoption gives us vision and strength to believe that our identity in Christ is most sacred. When I know who I truly am, I can see God for who He truly is. The good news is that our new identity in Christ also comes with benefits. Unlimited power. Unimaginable freedom. Incomparable joy. And unlimited access to the place where His glory dwells.

QUESTIONS

1 How do you tend to identify yourself? What is your truest identity?

2 What might be some reasons you tend to use "I am" or "We are" statements when identifying yourself in relation to others? What dangers might arise from viewing your identity in these ways?

3 Knowing that your identity is received and not self-determined, how then should you live?

CHAPTER SEVEN STORY

MY STRIVING

GETTING IN

GETTING STUCK

GETTING OUT

One of my favorite parts about my gay crew was our shared affinity for sports. We organized teams for flag football, basketball, softball, soccer, and kickball. It didn't take long before I started spending time around the best athletes on each team. I admired their strength, confidence, and athletic abilities. I wanted the physical challenge and felt affirmed by their acceptance. Even with non-sexualized friendships, I felt I could assume their appeal by proximity, especially when it came to the captain of my flag football team. Dark, beautiful, and untouchable, she was by far the best athlete on our team. Before long, I started finding excuses to be around Her, which is when I realized I was venturing into dangerous territory. So I begged my Girlfriend to join my team because I wouldn't admire this other woman with Her around. But my Girlfriend wasn't interested and Her schedule wouldn't allow it. So, I played on deciding there was no sin or danger in proximity.[1] *A little bit of fascination never hurt anyone.*

To no one's surprise but my own, I became deeply attracted to the Captain. For the first time, my same-sex affections began to expand beyond my Girlfriend, which horrified me. My heart betrayed the story I created to justify my lifestyle. All these years, I had touted the fact that I found no other women attractive—I only loved my Girlfriend—but now my storyline was betraying me. I could not keep myself from fantasizing about the Captain, craving Her attention, and longing to be with Her too. My expanding attractions scared me far more than my same-sex Relationship ever did. I could not control my feelings. My sin was growing!

> *My expanding attractions scared me far more than my same-sex Relationship ever did.*

Over time, my affection continued to morph and escalate to the point that I became regularly attracted to even other women who fit my type—gay or not. I conjured conversations with them reasoning that my compassionate character drew me to them, not my growing emotional dependency and same-sex attractions. *I just want to make sure they have friends so they won't be alone like I was.*

If they seemed emotionally closed off, my goal was to soften them. If they were weak, my goal was to loan them my backbone. I determined to show them they were loved, understood, and accepted. If they were experiencing trials or self-doubt, I believed that it was my kindness that would lead them to reconcile with themselves.[2] I could rescue them from their current situation too. And most women dream of an unwavering rescuer. My sin began to embolden me in ways I'd never felt before. I took more risks spending time with other same-sex attracted women, hanging out with their friends, and dancing at clubs with them. I even fantasized about straight women. They were a challenge that I felt up to taking. *I mean, I was straight once.* It wasn't simply a certain look I chased, but a vibe. I could tell if someone carried a kind of brokenness that matched mine. I knew if they were gay. *Or would be.* I could recognize need and opportunity. If I could make them desire my closeness, maybe then I would feel like enough.

Strategically, I picked off my prey, not always for romance, but for stability and worth. I offered myself out of what I thought was compassion, empathy, and love only to end up once again in the realm of fantasy. I imagined that if the relationships "accidentally" turned romantic, I could have what I want—validation—along with the power to dismiss her and return to my Girlfriend. *See? I'm still in control. I will only ever make love with Her.* I also began to envy the lives of lesbians in power or with superstar status. I wanted to meet them, emulate them, or follow them because it seemed like they were perfectly whole. *Maybe I will feel at home if we become friends?* These experiences would always leave me wanting and heighten my commitment to my Relationship with Her. Clearly, my attractions were escalating beyond the boundaries I had built. And even if I never followed through with all my fantasies, I knew I could. Worse still, I wanted to. It scared me that my lusts had shifted so far from my First Love.[3]

It scared me that my lusts had shifted so far from my First Love.

The only way I found to curb these desires was to plummet deeper with Her at home in our Castle. We began to talk about characteristics of other women we knew to the point that our lustful conversation lost its natural shame. We started watching porn together too. All of it rekindled my excitement and connected me to Her further through the ties of our shared secrets and inside jokes. I only acted on my sexual impulses with my Girlfriend, or with myself, but I was fueled by new lusts and ideas that quickly became normalized. The gay community that threatened to draw me out of my monogamy soon lost its allure. Allegiance to them was not as pleasurable as monogamous relational intimacy with Her. We believed ourselves to be the only ones unchanging. She was most real. She was the inexhaustible well to which I would always gladly return. *See? Our love is better than anything.*

GETTING IN

GETTING STUCK

GETTING OUT

Even as my Relationship deepened, my parents remained a constant. Throughout my life, they have spoken openly with me about Jesus Christ. Our conversations have always been raw, deep, and fruitful. But as the years wore on, my tongue felt heavy and my words grew sparse about the Lord. When I spoke with my parents, I longed for them to tell me something about God that I did not yet know, something that would help me believe again so my faith would survive my pain or change my life. I hated the strength of their faith. It seemed too heavy for me to bear and to watch them carry. I felt like we were pawns in a cosmic dispute for which hope in God felt pointless. So I began to press them by asking questions I knew they could not answer and challenge prayer's effect on any given situation. I was building my case, baiting them to follow me. The truth is their faith also threatened my highest allegiance. *Me.* All of my efforts were an attempt to poison them against God, to inspire them to question Him like I did because I knew a day was coming when I would have to tell them that I hated God, was in love with my Best Friend, and renounce my faith publicly.

Everywhere I went, I carried with me a collection of evidence that proved I was an abandoned daughter of the King. It was a heavy box that I'd been filling for decades and I believed my faltering faith demonstrated the weight of my point. I wanted answers and railed against God when He did not meet my expectations. He appeared inactive and passive in His love for me. Cruel for giving me something He hates. My faithful parents interpreted my anger as a reaction to the Lord's lack of provision for our family, or a lack of good godly men in the world, which I gladly allowed. But I knew my pervasive angst was due to my ongoing sin. Yet no matter how hard I tried to pry my parents from God with my well-crafted spiritual negotiations, they would respond with a simple question and answer: "To whom would we turn? Jesus has the words of eternal life."[4]

A day was coming when I knew I would have to tell my

family about Her. My hope was that by the time it arrived they would understand that She was in fact good for me and love Her and Us as a result. Maybe they would eventually realize that I had never been happier and more secure than I was with Her. The story of my life only made sense with Her. I banked on my parents' love for me as their daughter as the factor that would silence any of their attempts at confronting my lifestyle. And if it didn't, I'd make them choose between holiness and harmony. Relationship or rejection. They would end up being the ones feeling guilty. If my family experienced heartbreak, that was on them. After all, I was happy.

Unfortunately for me, happiness could not outweigh the unrest in my soul. None of my reasoning, efforts, or strategies proved sustainable. I was angry and exhausted. No matter where I turned, my sin demanded a decision. The Spirit of God would not relent His haunting of my Castle. I felt no peace with Jesus because of my Relationship, and faced constant turmoil in my Relationship because of Jesus. I was stuck.

> *I felt no peace with Jesus because of my Relationship, and faced constant turmoil in my Relationship because of Jesus.*

BUILDING BABEL

Early on in the book of Genesis, there's a story about the tower of Babel. The events surrounding it happened pretty quickly after creation. Humans forget fast. Adam and Eve were driven out of the Garden and the generations born after them were filled with evil.[5] They rejected God, as He patiently endured humanity's wickedness for hundreds of years until He willed to wipe out all of creation with the flood as a sign of judgment. Except for one remnant of belief. God chose Noah and his family as the means by which He would begin again.[6] Even still, the story of Babel appears only a few chapters after that of the flood revealing something that remains true about humanity today—we are prone to cycle back to what makes the most sense to us. We elevate the created. We build according to our plans. We worship idols and other false gods.

The story of Babel appears in Genesis 11, and although it is short, it's a clear example of how humans tend to self-elevate. The tower began with a bunch of people trying to build a structure that would rise up to the heavens, not so they could be with the one true God, but to make a name for themselves. Rather than disperse over the face of the earth as God commanded, they gathered together like-minded people and built a city where they could all dwell, act like gods, prostitute their bodies, and rise above any flood. *Come, let us build together!*

Making a home is not a bad thing, but for this people making a home was ultimately a façade for making much of themselves. So they stacked brick upon brick and raised stair over stair, until the tower loomed over every other structure. Then comes my favorite part. The passage says that God "came down" to observe the tower they were building.[7] *Come, let us go down.*[8] He had to step down to this group of people who had convinced themselves they could reach into the heavens and escape God's wrath. All of their hard work amounted to little more than an anthill of self-elevation compared to God's infinite transcendence.

His mandate for them and all humankind would continue by God's mercy. Even against their will.

Like all created things, the tower and its purpose would eventually fail and God knew that its completion would only propagate further wickedness that the people had planned in their hearts. God would have been just in killing them. Yet in

His kindness, the Lord came near and addressed their sin in their lifetimes by confusing their language, which caused them to disperse—the very action He had commanded in the first place.[9] It was their mouths that multiplied their sin, so He restrained further evils by communicating to them by confusing their speech. His mandate for them and all humankind would continue by God's mercy. Even against their will.

The sin in this historic tale is no ancient relic. It's the same lie we believe today, an echo of Eve's deception.[10] *You can be like God. And then you won't need Him anymore.* When I compare it to my own story of building my identity on lesbianism, the parallels are obvious:

- I was discontent with all that God had given me. I wanted a place of my own so I created one where I thought I could rule and elevate what seemed best to me.

- I heard God's command about homosexuality but I gathered people to be on my side.

- I thought if I built something strong and lasting, it would be the barrier that would keep God out so I could be unhindered.

- I resisted God's design believing I had the power to choose the kind of life I would have without interference from the One who made me.

In my labor, I gathered my Girlfriend and a handful of self-identified lesbians, and together we started to build what we thought was beautiful and necessary. We created storylines, mantras, and value systems. We invested in giving, sacrifice, and service. Even though some of us identified as Christians, we set aside the Bible and set up doctrine around the benefits of worshiping love, monogamy, morality, and a kind ethos. We cherished our favorite verses like, "God is love."[11] We manufactured idols like they were going out of business because they were fun and profitable. My roots grew stronger and I held my head higher. *It's good to create a place where we can live in peace and share the comforts with all of*

GETTING IN

GETTING STUCK

GETTING OUT

our people. Despite God's commands and the consequences of my sexual sin, I chose me. I created a lifestyle where freedom reigned and I could rise up to be king. In my Castle, I could express my sexual preferences in whatever way I wanted and elevate what I desired. My tower was an overt middle finger to God who Himself raises the dead.

I really didn't think that God could get out of the basement or live within my walls. Or reach me in my lofty tower. I was hardened beyond His reach, too messy to deal with. I thought that He had to politely knock on the door of my heart and I had the choice to let Him in. But when God moves to establish His glory and protect His children, He doesn't have to ask permission. He comes down and moves in power.

REPEATING CYCLES

GETTING IN

GETTING STUCK

GETTING OUT

Hopefully by now my story has assured you of a piece of good news: you are not the only one. Struggling with sin is common to humankind. Even better, none of your desires are new to God. People may invent more creative expressions, but the sin itself has not changed. There is nothing new under the sun.[1] God sees everything without surprise or alarm. Shame and pride will tempt us to believe that we are too far gone, but God is greater than both. He has made His own provision for sin and is willing and able to undo any mess because He is compassionate and kind. By sending His Son, Jesus Christ, into our world He has invited us into His grace, one that guarantees a future resurrection in which He will make all things new.[2] Nothing can stand in the way of His reconciling work.

Learning about the character of God is one of the ways we actively pursue healing as believers. Growing in a relationship with Jesus Christ requires knowing who He is, but it also requires an understanding of who we are. In Chapter Four, we introduced the story of humanity—God created man and woman, they disobeyed, and their disobedience invited sin into the world infecting every aspect of creation. It is part

THE SIN CYCLE

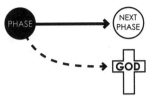

While in each phase of the Sin Cycle you have the choice to take the next step into deeper sin and entanglements or make the choice to turn to God.

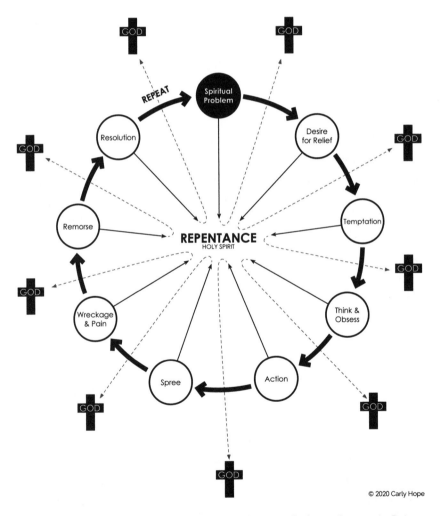

Each phase leads to the next in the cycle and eventually the cycle repeats. But there is always a choice to repent and turn toward Jesus Christ who gets you out. Repentance involves turning and ultimately a change of mind, heart, and behavior which is made possible by the power of the Holy Spirit.

of our condition. We are broken and in need of repair. But while the temptation to sin is beyond our control, it is not necessarily beyond our understanding. In fact, it follows a predictable pattern I like to call the "Sin Cycle," which dates all the way back to sin's origin.

The cycle began when Adam and Eve disobeyed God's command because they doubted His character. The same thing can be said for every human who has ever lived. No one's sin is unique. What began as misplaced trust morphed into a condition that threatens our well-being along with everyone we love. But the cycle also includes daily opportunities for repentance. God is familiar with sin, but He does not excuse it. Rather, He aims to break the cycle, which starts with turning from sin and clinging to the hope found through the cross of Jesus Christ. In this section, we'll take a look at the nine phases of the Sin Cycle and learn to recognize exit ramps God has placed along the way that lead us toward abundant life.

SPIRITUAL PROBLEM

The Sin Cycle begins with a spiritual problem common to all: we are born broken. We have a longing to be whole. Adam and Eve did more than simply eat a forbidden fruit. They rebelled against the God of the universe who had made them a home in His presence. This original sin fractured the world as we know it right down to our DNA. Even with the new nature we receive through faith in Jesus Christ, that brokenness provokes an internal tension between following God and doing what we think is right. It is a universal problem, one in which we are all complicit. We need to be back in His presence.

DESIRE FOR RELIEF

Because the world is broken we desire relief. It's perfectly natural to seek rest from the tension of life, as God created us to live in peace with Him. Where it goes awry is when our sinful nature calls the shots urging us to seek out other remedies for our longings, passions, and pain. We are bent toward preferring alternatives to God. This desire for relief quietly primes our hearts below the surface. In this stage, it's easy to dismiss red flags or diminish certain desires believing that they are not harmful, but human, as if that is cause for less concern. While the desire for relief from the brokenness of the world is not evil, it can lead to sinful desires, which is why we must care for the root system beginning to grow within us. Otherwise, it will grow beyond control.

TEMPTATION

As our desire for relief matures, temptation takes center stage. On its own, temptation is not sin. It is simply an invitation that can lead us to sin by stirring our affections for what God has forbidden. Here, lusts begin their assault promising to satisfy our craving for relief. They work to convince us of our need for something new to eliminate our groaning. And Satan knows how to grab our attention lobbing his most effective temptations our way. He plays to our natural desire for relief—one meant to lead us to the hope of Christ—with the aim of seducing and devouring his prey.

THINK AND OBSESS

Failing to close the door on temptation will lead us to think about and obsess over the satisfaction promised by temptation. We ruminate on its potential to ease our unsettledness, remove our pain, give us pleasure, and comfort our souls. Before long, our imaginations run wild planning and processing scenarios that prime our minds to respond. Sinful thinking may seem like a harmless fantasy, but the constant attention trains our minds to focus only on what we want and short-term outcomes. It also takes us out of reality. Rather than thinking eternally, our sights are set on our immediate felt needs. Our obsession is pleasurable and causes us to overestimate ourselves and underestimate Satan's intent to destroy.

ACTION

Eventually, obsession leads to action. It's human nature to satisfy what we value most. Without any restraint, our root desires began to entertain temptations that grew into obsession. Apart from surrendering to Jesus Christ, sinful behaviors will always follow in this stage. We want to act out according to our will and since there will always be opportunity to sin, it's only a small step to disobedience. The act always tastes sweet at the start. Our cravings increase as we eat in the dark—or out in the open—and suddenly what is wrong begins to feel right.

SPREE

Setting off on a spree is the natural next step. Our sin begins to own us, incestuously feeding and propagating further destructive behavior. We decide that more and more action will be more and more satisfying. During this stage, we experience all of the peaks and none of the valleys. . . at least not yet. We jump from one sinful opportunity to the next striving to feel everything and nothing. In our binge, we consume all that tastes sweet and we are able to hide our frenzy from others if we want. It is addictive and euphoric, but it never offers sustaining highs, which escalates our need for more.

WRECKAGE AND PAIN

As our sin escalates, it causes injury. The lows finally hit. We begin to feel the natural consequences of sin. There's no avoiding this stage. Impacts may not flash immediately, but they are coming. We cannot evade the consequences of sin no matter how hard we try. And there are typically unexpected consequences as well. But we attempt to blame them on something other than our brokenness. This stage reaps pain, ruins relationships, and can even result in physical death. But there is an even greater consequence than physical death—one the Bible describes as spiritual death for those who refuse to turn from their sin. Rather than a threat against His children, God means for this death to be a sober warning about the present and eternal consequences that exist for those who give themselves over to rebellion.

REMORSE

At some point, the cycle leads to remorse over the consequences of our actions or the fear of being found out. To some degree, this remorse is a sincere sadness over our behavior, but the losses may not outweigh what we feel we have gained along the way, which leads deeper into the cycle. Remorse itself lacks the power to make us change. It is simply regret for the consequences of sin, not necessarily for the sin or the deeper motivation behind our sin. The only cure for remorse is God transforming our hearts to see our sin as evil and God as good.

RESOLUTIONS

Once remorse sets in, it compounds the problem that started our cycle in sin and we seek to relieve the tension. What began as spiritual brokenness has grown in terms of its consequences as well as the shame we feel because of them. In response, we make resolutions to change. *I'll never do this again.* This stage of the cycle is full of ideas, strategies, commitments, and policies to avoid the destructive implications of our sinful behavior. It's often full of optimism about our ability to control our inner lives. But apart from Christ, our resolutions will always fail, which will eventually cause us to give up. To quit the fight. To go all in and become a slave to the cycle.

REPENT OR REPEAT THE SIN CYCLE

Though it may not seem so in the moment, no one is bound to repeating the cycle. Every step of the way, we have the option to turn to Christ by the power of the Holy Spirit or harden our hearts and ignore the Holy Spirit.[3] We are willful and complicit in both choices. Choosing the latter, is a sure-fire ticket to an unending ride on the Sin Cycle. Seeking illegitimate means of relief will always lead back to cyclical slavery, complete with expanding desires, greater risks, harder consequences and a growing sense of hopelessness. But there is a cure: repentance.

Repentance is more than confession. It is active change, a commitment to turning away from sin and clinging to freedom in Christ. It requires that we humble ourselves. Of course, it is a costly step because it means bringing sin to light, but God's way is infinitely kinder than the alternative. It leads to life. God invites us out of the cycle in every single stage. At every phase of the Sin Cycle He stands near to save. He does not stand at a distance judging our every decision. Rather, He constantly offers mercy to make us new if we will simply turn to Him. The Holy Spirit calls out to us and points us to Jesus Christ, and Jesus Christ shows us the Father, and the Father directs us back to His Son and His Spirit. God is wooing you to Himself. "Come to me, all you who are weary and burdened, and I will give you rest."[4]

God the Father knows the state of our problem. He hears our groans for relief and is aware of every situation that tempts us. He sees our actions and sprees. He is with us in the wreckage. Yet God has better and more satisfying things for His children. His invitations to repentance are constant opportunities for rescue and a way out. The Sin Cycle is a daily experience whether or not you contend with same-sex attraction. Don't be alarmed when sin comes out of hiding. Christian women struggle against the bondage of sin just like non-Christians. Remaining susceptible to the Sin Cycle does not mean that you are not being healed. Temptation will not cease on this side of glory, even when faced with our most holy efforts and sincere prayers. That's why God gives us grace upon grace. Grace to forgive and grace for the power to go and sin no more.[5] He is at work in the mess providing a way of escape in every stage of the cycle, thwarting sin's momentum. But it starts with actively opposing sin and trusting God to provide us with strength and change of heart as He leads us to freedom. Grace is not opposed to effort. Empowered by the Spirit, we raise our hands in faith. We move our feet. Healing happens in the mess and the Father rejoices in our return, though we stumble all the way home.

THE CYCLE OF FEMALE SAME-SEX ATTRACTION

While the Sin Cycle is common to all, it becomes personalized in our specific struggles. Female homosexuality follows its own pattern born out of the cycle of sin. It promises refuge and peace but delivers bondage and hopelessness. I first learned about this cycle from a trusted church leader who drew it on a whiteboard.[6] The pattern she laid out was shocking because it mirrored my story. Immediately, I became defensive. *No one charts my course! My love story is unique!* Embracing uniqueness was one of the ways I dismissed those trying to minister to me. Others might be able to find freedom, but not me. *I am different.* I was beyond hope and unable to change.

Having this cycle laid out in front of me popped the bubble of my perceived superiority. It was alarming and disarming. *I wish I would have known this before. . .* It showed me that my story was neither unique nor exempt from restoration. Apparently, many women have found themselves swept up in a pattern of same-sex bondage and still were able to escape the shithole by the grace of Jesus Christ. And surprisingly, I found comfort in their stories that I was not beyond hope.

Each of the nine phases of the Cycle of Female Same-Sex Attraction feels like the vibrant love we crave until it doesn't. Given enough time, the broken nature of lesbian love moves from phase to phase, sucking us in with shiny treasures, then

THE CYCLE OF FEMALE SAME-SEX ATTRACTION

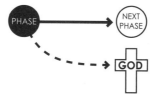

While in each phase of the Cycle of Female Same-Sex Attraction you have the choice to take the next step into deeper sin and entanglements or make the choice to turn to God.

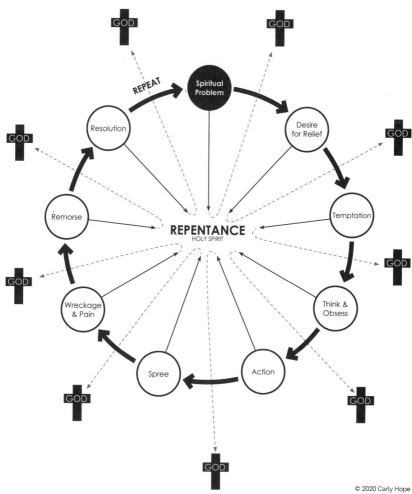

© 2020 Carly Hope

Each phase leads to the next in the cycle and eventually the cycle repeats. But there is always a choice to repent and turn toward Jesus Christ who gets you out. Repentance involves turning and ultimately a change of mind, heart, and behavior which is made possible by the power of the Holy Spirit.

pulling us down like gravity to hopelessness. But at every stage we have another opportunity to either escape through repentance or continue the downward spiral. And just like the Sin Cycle, there is hope in every moment. Let's take a look at each of these steps and see how same-sex attraction tends to play out among women.

SPIRITUAL PROBLEM

The Cycle of Female Same-Sex Attraction begins with a spiritual problem common to all: we are born broken. We have a longing to be whole. Adam and Eve did more than simply eat a forbidden fruit. They rebelled against the God of the universe who had made them a home in His presence. This original sin fractured the world as we know it right down to our DNA. Even with the new nature we receive through faith in Jesus Christ, that brokenness provokes an internal tension between following God and doing what we think is right. It is a universal problem, one in which we are all complicit. We need to be back in His presence.

THE DRAW

The Draw is a state of attraction where our affections ignite when opportunity walks through the door. *She's beautiful. She's my type. I can tell.* Same-sex desires assault our senses and attraction moves to temptation when it hits a nerve we want to feel again. So we look a second time or never break the stare at all to feel what we want and wait for her to recognize our attention. Often we are drawn to women with qualities we feel like we are lacking. The draw comes from a belief that our longings can be satisfied by this woman's affections. We may be surprised by our lust, but our hearts and minds and bodies were likely already primed to consider fulfillment outside of God so the pull of same-sex attraction can take hold.

COMPLEMENTARY BROKENNESS

Complementary Brokenness is when the temptation to connect becomes a reality and we recognize our sameness in one another. On the surface, it's clear that our interests and loves align, but what is really happening is that our deep sin fits with hers. It's a matching brokenness. We can recognize that our unmet needs match her unmet needs and it feels like we are known and accepted regardless. *I can help her. She can help me. We are different! We are the same!* One is needy and one needs to be needed. One feels insecure and the other appears secure. Complementary brokenness is cause for the speed by which same-sex attraction becomes entrapment. The sameness is comforting and creates a pull toward connecting emotionally and physically.

EMOTIONAL DEPENDENCY

Emotional Dependency quickly follows when we experience matching brokenness in same-sex attraction. We require our new companion to be all things for us and often detach from others. Unloading all of our baggage, we believe our lover is capable of carrying the weight and that her companionship will solve our deepest needs. *I'm addicted to you. I love you more than anything. There is nothing on earth I desire more than you.* The exclusivity of our reliance is foundational and aspirational for the same-sex attracted woman, but it is a captor. Emotional dependency is not the same as love, and yet it can keep us stuck even longer than love. Even when our minds reason that a same-sex relationship is unhealthy or should end, emotional dependency keeps us bound and entangled.

INTENSITY

The Intensity phase of female same-sex relationships is always growing. Affection and attraction rise off the charts and we want more. Expectations increase along with frequency of interaction. We express all our pent-up needs through constant praise, physicality, or proximity. *My heart longs for you. My body yearns to be with you. My insides ache without you.* Women in same-sex relationships exchange intimacy for intensity and begin to equate relational intimacy with sexual intimacy. We have a death grip on each other. In the jumbled mess, feelings are allowed to take power. Everything is emotionally charged. Passion ensues and it feels like selfless love, but it is really a lethal combination of fear and abandon.

FRIEND TO LOVER

Once the intensity of emotional dependency has taken hold, we develop romantic affection for our female friend. The relationship grows sexualized and we become lovers. Homosexual connection can happen earlier in the cycle, but in the phase of Friend to Lover the heart, mind, body, emotions, desires, and behaviors are all directed toward consuming the object of our affection. *When it's right, it's right. We can't keep our hands off of each other. Who knew that sex could be like this?* The desire to connect sexually comes from a brokenness that is seeking to find wholeness in another woman.

ABSORB AND ENMESH

The Absorb and Enmesh phase leads to full inclusion of all the things: activities, belongings, people, and children. But this phase is more than combining lives—it is an act of actually absorbing one another. We find our identity in another person and vice versa. We may never say it, but our worth and meaning are experienced from assuming their person into our own identity. It's complex bondage. We want to absorb her strengths and heal her weakness by cloaking her with our strengths as we try to diminish our differences. *We are one team. If we change, we change together. There is no loyalty or allegiance higher than ours.* We believe that lesbian unity and oneness will provide us power and protection as we operate in the world, and that someday we'll give an account as one single soul. We want a shared identity in addition to elevation of our own. Sameness feels like equality of partnership, but it's actually innately self-serving. It's mutual usury.

BREAKUP

The next phase of the female same-sex relationship cycle is Breakup. No matter the longevity of commitment or the depth of love, there will be a breakdown. It could last hours, days, or weeks, maybe forever. Regardless, the relationship will face wreckage eventually. *I can't fix what is broken.* Since the very nature of homosexual relationships is sinful, the relationship will always gravitate toward destruction. We cannot save it from its destined end. It is the nature of sexual and relational sin to constantly pull us to the grave. Even in lifelong commitments when there is no official breakup there are always brokenness and losses experienced in and around female same-sex relationships. Sinking soul costs. There is deep heartache and severe disorientation in breakups because not only do we lose her, but we feel like we've lost ourselves too.

ALONENESS

After separation, the next phase is Aloneness. We are so used to proximity and enmeshment that the space feels cavernous. We feel less than whole because we believed we found our true selves in her only to lose it all. Aloneness is our greatest fear realized. *Everything I trusted and built my life on is gone.* Because we have forsaken all others the closeness of other friendships feels far, and the nearness of God seems non-existent. Being alone is disorienting and we do not know what to do. When we are lonely, many of us attempt to numb and attempt to escape the tension. We tend to fill this space with all sorts of things that can be unhealthy for us, usually being tempted to resume contact with our old lovers. Being separate from what we have depended on for so long makes us feel vulnerable and exposed. However, when we are alone we may finally be able to hear God.

GO BACK

After a period of time, we forget the pain associated with our false worship and Go Back and repeat the cycle. To cure our angst we long for a rescuer. We know the quickest and easiest way to solve the tension and refuse to believe that sin caused our former breakup. *Being lonely sucks. Obeying God is too hard and He will not provide what I need.* When pain of separation is greater than the pain of staying together we go back to our old lover over and over and over again. She holds new promise that this time will be different. *Not like last time.* We think we are so far down the road of same-sex attraction that there is no hope for sexual and relational restoration. So again, we choose the good of *us* over the good for us and we go back to her. *We've invested too much. We are too far in. This is the best I will get.* Many times, a breakup causes us to believe the lie that we are ruined. Fixating on what sin took makes it hard to see what obedience can bring.

REPENT OR REPEAT THE CYCLE OF FEMALE SAME-SEX ATTRACTION

If we don't go back to our same lover, we simply find someone new. It is in this phase that we are tempted to believe another familiar lie: *there is still another woman out there that is perfect for me.* We repeat the cycle. The woman is different, but the intensity is familiar. And we return to the same old patterns of lesbian life. And the Cycle of Female Same-Sex Attraction repeats. Our taste buds are seasoned to believe that a new girlfriend will be sweet, not bitter like the last one. We've heard that Christ should be ultimate in our affections, but we pursue illegitimate solutions for our legit need for intimacy. We return to vomit. Our hearts and bodies have been trained to self-satisfy through illicit sexual and emotionally dependent relationships. So we cry out for the relief of a new rescuer and place our hopes and expectations again on a new lover. *This one will be worth it. She will solve the problem.*

There is a way to escape the cycle, my friends. Jesus Christ can solve the holy tension between two loves calling us out. We do not have to go back to who we were. By the Father's grace, we can repent of our addictions and homosexual behaviors and turn to God the Son. As we've said before, true repentance always involves turning away from sin and moving toward Jesus Christ by the power of the Holy Spirit. You do not have to hit rock bottom to see God. He is always with us and repentance clears our eyes. At every moment in the Cycle of Female Same-Sex Attraction God the Holy Spirit grants His people the ability to turn away from sin. You do not have to move to the next phase of enslavement. Only Jesus Christ can rescue us from the will and want to return to bondage of the cycle. If we humble ourselves, pray, seek His face, and repent, we can hear Him and He will forgive us. He will heal us from the inside out. He points us to our Father. We can cling to Him for rescue without fear, we cannot break Him. Even the highest forms of human emotional and relational connectedness cannot

We are not destined to be slaves to our sexual inclinations, nor are we unable to choose holiness.

plumb to the deepest groanings of our souls, but our God can and does. Depending on the Lord will never disappoint. We are created by Him, for Him, and we can find unmatched oneness and intimacy with Him. When we identify with God instead of Her we can experience the fulfillment of this love we crave so deeply. We can be in His presence.

As Christ followers we are not destined to be slaves to our sexual inclinations, nor are we unable to choose holiness. The Spirit enables us to walk in relational wholeness. He beckons

GETTING IN

GETTING STUCK

GETTING OUT

us to allow Him to fix all that is broken. Jesus Christ is the author and finisher of our faith.[7] Apart from Him, we can do nothing to untangle ourselves or others from homosexuality. Our best efforts at morality are as filthy rags because they are not the offerings God accepts. Broken and contrite hearts are the currency of worthy sacrifice.[8] Have faith that God can, and surrender that we can't. Humility of that posture invites repentance. Yes, our hearts can be deceitful and we have short memories, but God gave His Son to free us from the mess. He can dismantle and disconnect every tie that keeps us connected and bound to our loves that do not honor God. He can restore trustworthy affections. He can free us from the cycle of our same-sex attractions.

We must never call a friend who God calls an enemy.[9] Partnership with sin is evidence that we remain on friendly terms with unholy desires that enslave us to our old master who hates God. Jesus Christ offers us what is real and without harm. He is a true friend who is always seeking to restore and heal His broken children. He redeems us again and again. God is better than any sexual or relational pleasure and there is no escaping that truth try as we might. Jesus Christ can open our eyes and lead us to repentance. And He can lead us out of the cycle. It is for freedom that we have been set free.[10]

THE UNIQUE COMFORT OF GOD

God knows how temptations take aim at our hearts. God knows we are tempted from the broken desires that wage war within us.[11] God understands, so He stands ready to save. He is always sending His Spirit for our comfort, and He already sent His Son for our rescue. It's His pattern.

How great is our God that He sent His Son as our empathetic High Priest?[12] One who is fully God and fully human. Able to understand our human plight and able to save us from it. Jesus Christ was sent to be like us, but not exactly like us. On earth, even Jesus Christ was tempted, but not exactly like us either. Unlike you and me, the Son of God has no sin nature in Adam or broken desires within Himself for temptation to take hold. Jesus had no Spiritual Problem. Instead, Jesus Christ was tempted from outside assault when Satan asked Him exactly the same question that is at the root of all our temptations: "Will you obey God's will, or your own?"

In every respect, our temptation is the same. *Who will I choose to trust?* The temptation of Jesus in the wilderness and in the Garden of Gethsemane is a clear mirror of the temptation of Israel in the wilderness and Eve in the Garden.[13] Except unlike us, Jesus Christ was righteous in His response:

- He trusted God our Father to provide for His human needs.

- He didn't need to test God our Father to believe Him.

- He would only ever give glory to God our Father.

- He would always obey the will of God our Father.

The reason we can experience comfort from the temptation of Jesus is not because He is weak like us and can commiserate, but because He is perfect and yet compassionate. Jesus was able to endure by the power of the Holy Spirit, just as we are. Yet the events of the temptation of Jesus Christ offer us way more than sympathy or a model for how we should respond in the stages of temptation. It all points to a perfect Savior with a divine nature who can fulfill all of the righteousness we can't. This is why He can save us. Through the Word, Jesus Christ shows us that He is God and that His will is exactly the same as His Father's. That is why Satan's temptations would never work on Him. His humanity and divinity give us hope that He really is who He says He is.

Knowing more about Jesus Christ causes me to love the unique comfort He offers at all stages of my sin cycles. Jesus Christ did not have to embody our specific situation during His thirty-three years on earth to understand the depths of our

GETTING IN

GETTING STUCK

GETTING OUT

enticement. He doesn't have to have a sin nature or be tempted by sexual or relational sin in order to sympathize with us. He sympathizes because He is God and He knows all things. Jesus Christ is with us and His Spirit is in us. He knows our hearts. He knows our will. He knows our form. He knows our state. We are fully known. He knows how deeply rooted indwelling sin is in our flesh because He bore every detail of it in His own flesh on the Cross. I would contend that He actually understands our temptation more than we even do.

THE PATTERN OF DIVINE ACTION

There is a pattern that occurs outside of us and above us that can repeatedly bring us hope. Our triune God is a circle of love, unity, and order that has always existed, and the interaction of each person of the Godhead is often referred to as the dance. Love overflows from their communion and is always being sent to humanity to reveal the glory and goodness of God. It is a cycle unencumbered by us and our sin.

God the Father, God the Son, and God the Holy Spirit are united in one will and united in all divine action. Our God is one. God the Father and God the Son are always sending God the Spirit to us in our cyclical mess. The Spirit calls to us with the exact words of Jesus Christ. He bears no other message. The Holy Spirit always points us to the Son who is our only means of escape and full restoration. The Son shows us the Father because He is the exact imprint of the Father from whom He is sent.[14] All things are from the Father, through the Son, by the Holy Spirit.

The reason this pattern is important for me to understand is that it helps me see that all God's divine activity is meant to bring Him glory. In Himself, God is whole and complete, lacking nothing. Yet He chooses to invite humanity into His presence and pursues us as part of the dance. Trinitarian love helps me understand not only my worth as a daughter, but also His worthiness as Lord.

It began to make sense why constant whispers, intrusions, mercy, conviction, and opportunities to repent would not relent. The Father and the Son were sending the Holy Spirit into my insanity. When I realized that I could not escape God

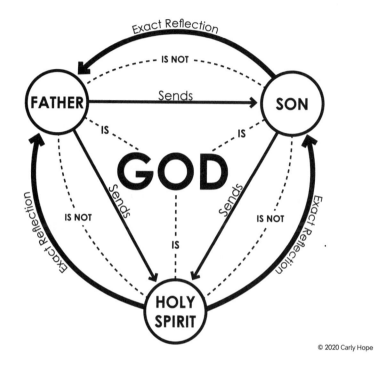

© 2020 Carly Hope

and that my rebellion did not cause havoc or a change in the Godhead, God helped me see my true position and recognize His true power. So now when I am stuck in sinful cycles, the pattern of how God loves me and reveals Himself gives me hope. He is consistently showing me the way out and a better way to live, a life that increasingly mirrors God. Together, our triune God is calling us out and into true freedom, and empowers believers to do so.

QUESTIONS

1   What is the Spiritual Problem we all face in both the Sin Cycle and the Cycle of Female Same-Sex Attraction? In every phase of the cycles we have the option of doing what two things?

2   Which phases of the Cycle of Female Same-Sex Attraction tend to be the most alluring for you? Which phases of this cycle tend to make you feel the most hopeless and why?

3   God the Father, God the Son, and God the Holy Spirit are always calling us out of the bondage of our sinful preferences. In what ways has God continued to offer you ways of escape? How can you pray for God to change your will to desire the freedom that Jesus Christ is offering you?

PART 2

GETTING STUCK

MY WAY

Running from God left me in a spiritual spin cycle. At times, I longed for His peace, but I wanted it at no cost to me. Life was hard enough already and She was the best part. I refused to give Her up. The problem was that I knew too much. I had seen God and nothing could change that. I knew His design for marriage and sex was not just a suggestion, and I figured true peace would still only come through a right relationship with Him. But if I had to choose, I would rather keep Her than have this ever-elusive God. I sat in this place of unrest for years, filling them with an ocean of tears, prayers, and groanings. All the time, I was pulled between two loves: Jesus Christ and my Girlfriend. I lacked the strength to choose one over the other entirely so I tried to remain neutral, though I harbored a secret hope that somehow, God would show up and pull me out.

To that end, I dabbled in "solutions." I tried many things to get out. I knew where a Christian ought to turn and had the experience to back it up. I started with the Bible, memorizing portions I thought would prove an effective sword against the enemy.[1] When that failed to meet my expectations, I turned to church. If reading God's Word didn't work, maybe hearing it would make the difference. I waited for the sermon that would tell me how to leave Her, the one that would give me the silver bullet I needed to put my love for Her to death. I even joined a small group and attended a recovery program through the church aimed at helping deal with issues that stand in the way of the life God intended. I sat selectively silent in these groups, baiting members to try and figure me out. But magic sermons never came and my secret life was not brought to light to my community, both of which were proof to me that I was too far gone to rescue. A few times, I tried taking Her with me on Sundays thinking that hearing the same message would help. It was awkward and never ended well. The gospel we heard threatened what we loved most. *Us.* Afterward, we had to recalibrate our loyalty. Applying what we could and easily dismissing convicting parts, we cited how our past experiences with church and God went awry.

We'd co-rescue each other from holy tension.

We'd co-rescue each other from holy tension and reasoned away each other's guilt. *You're not naked!* But we knew we were.

My search for answers emboldened me to seek out counseling, both biblical and secular. At first, those sessions were a comfort. They allowed me to speak openly about my Relationship, but they quickly grew expensive and I lacked the long-term commitment to stick with them. Plus, I didn't believe counselors could understand how great a lesbian relationship could be if they hadn't experienced one. Reading lots of books was next. I consumed self-help content and skimmed Christian content, always skipping over portions that had Scripture or platitudes. Or quotes from people I didn't know. I couldn't find much written by someone who understood my situation. I even committed to pray about it for the millionth time. But I was afraid of prayer, I thought it would invite God to do something that I didn't want. Make an outcome I didn't like. Just like everything else I had tried, the solution kept coming back to an action I would not take—break up with my Girlfriend. I was willing to do anything but *that*.

For the longest time, I felt helpless against the cycle of confusion until I finally realized it was because I never intended to follow through on what was required. I was never going to love Him more than Her. *I will never agree with God on this.* He could have the bits and pieces of my life that had already crumbled, but I would never let Him have Her. She was the best part of me and without Her I would surely die. *Doesn't He know that?* When God ignored the crumbs I offered as a sacrifice, I justified my unbelief. In an attempt to shut Him up entirely, I began to clothe myself in all sorts of lies. I had to in order to persist in my sin. One by one, I diminished and dismissed true things. I traded true things about God and me for my own version of the universe. It began in the hopes of forcing God's hand to write me off entirely. Then I could blame Him for being exactly who I expected Him to be. But somewhere along the way I got distracted and began to believe the lies, exchanging them for the pillars of my faith.

BELIEVING LIES

Satan loves to seduce and deceive Christians. We are his biggest target, because Jesus Christ is his biggest threat. Women who struggle with same-sex attraction and emotional dependency tend to have similar underlying belief systems. And they are faulty. Here are five popular lies we tend to believe:

1. This is who I am.
2. I can sin now, repent later.
3. I am worthless.
4. The right person will fulfill me.
5. God will not provide.

Embracing any of these lies is an attempt to shift responsibility away from ourselves. Believing lies about God or the power same-sex attraction holds in our lives excuses our need to feel bad about it. Once we've bought into these baseline deceptions, it becomes easy to flesh them out with more complex and devastating lies. Throughout the eleven years of my Relationship, I sought to undo the gospel with my brain and allow the reality of my experience to dictate what was true. Basically, I was lying to myself. And I loved it. Here is a list of some of the other common lies I crafted to keep me comfortable in my prison:

COMMON LIES

- ☐ This is who I am.
- ☐ I can sin now, repent later.
- ☐ I am worthless.
- ☐ The right person will fulfill me.
- ☐ God will not provide.
- ☐ Things will never change.
- ☐ God's highest goal for us is that we find love.
- ☐ God can't punish me if I don't think homosexuality is sin.
- ☐ Lesbian love is a pathway for me to heal from hurt done to me.
- ☐ I control my sin and its consequences.
- ☐ I can't change my same-sex attractions.
- ☐ God doesn't want me to be alone.
- ☐ Life without sex is impossible.
- ☐ Christians won't accept me.
- ☐ God does not love me.
- ☐ I can't change.
- ☐ My interests, hobbies, and body make me gay or straight.
- ☐ My temptation proves God has done nothing lasting in my life.

- ☐ I am my sexuality.
- ☐ No one can help me unless they have personally dealt with female same-sex attraction.
- ☐ No one can help me unless they have experienced as many years in my exact same situation.
- ☐ Hold out, sin gets better.
- ☐ God is okay with my choice.
- ☐ If God is sovereign, He should make me change.
- ☐ I will always want to be with women.
- ☐ Self-denial is oppressive.
- ☐ God cannot be trusted.
- ☐ God made me this way.
- ☐ Sexual fantasies are okay as long as I stay monogamous.
- ☐ Jesus wants me to be obedient and miserable.
- ☐ Christianity means being alone. Lesbianism means being known.
- ☐ Homosexual orientation is the one thing that Jesus can't fix.
- ☐ Sexual fulfillment is vital to human fulfillment.
- ☐ There are more pleasures in the world than there are in Christ.
- ☐ I'm too far in to get back out.
- ☐ Loving Her does not hinder my relationship with God.
- ☐ Men are bad. Women are good.
- ☐ Men are bad. Women are worse.
- ☐ Women are bad. I don't want to be a woman.
- ☐ Men are better. I want to be a man.

cont'd

GETTING IN

GETTING STUCK

GETTING OUT

> ☐ Women are weak and often victims. I don't want to be a woman.
>
> ☐ Men are powerful and don't get hurt. I want to be a man.
>
> ☐ Jesus is never coming back for me.

Even as I read this list today some of the lies sting. I can still see where Satan tempts me to return to what is familiar. But God in His mercy invites us into what is real by addressing our specific lies in specific ways. His approach to each of us is unique, but His methods and message are the same for all of His children. God acts consistently to confront us in different ways to address each of the subtle lies we believe. As this list shows, my deception grew into a tangled mess fueled by all kinds of influences. That is true for anyone who travels down the path I followed. While deception morphs, it tethers itself to claims of truth, our desire for self-elevation, and a flawed view of identity, all of which play crucial roles in perpetuating a false life based on false assumptions. .

CULTURAL LIES

As women who struggle with same-sex attraction and emotional dependency within a cultural context that celebrates our lifestyle, the approval of others offers a sense of reprieve and false security. Even some nominal Christian circles encourage the embrace of all attractions and homosexual behavior. Some Christians consider their acceptance of the homosexual ethic more important than God's rejection of it, often the result of confusing Christ's call to extend grace with granting permission to love what God hates.

Progressive lies appear new, but they are ancient, based on deceptions that recycle themselves every few decades. All of them aim to empower personal choice, diminish Scripture, and minimize our visibility from God. Authenticity is the name of the game. *As long as I'm being true to myself, then God is pleased and I am vindicated.* Here are some of the common cultural lies circulating today:

- ☐ God wants me to be happy no matter what.
- ☐ The Bible does not call monogamous homosexuality sin.
- ☐ Gay marriage can be holy.
- ☐ It's okay to be a gay Christian.
- ☐ My sexual ethics have no impact on my soul.

Each of these lies directly opposes the Word of God. Not only in blatant rejection of His commands, prohibitions, and warnings, but also in pious defamation of God's character. False claims about ourselves and God's words are all ultimately accusations against God that Christ and His way are wrong and our way is better. We think the love we offer is pure and wiser than God's. However the Bible is our direct record of who God says He is and how He has designed humankind to flourish. He created us and loves us so He tells us clearly what brings life and death. When we reject the way things really are and the goodness of God's design, we embrace the lie that says we can reinvent or redefine what will always be true.

SELF-ELEVATING LIES

Whereas cultural lies are external, self-elevating lies reside in the interior. They are much harder to spot because doing so requires honesty with our selves first and foremost, but also honesty with others. We were created with a need to elevate. Made in the image of God, we were meant to naturally elevate Him. But sin has so distorted that design that we lower our focus to elevate what is lesser, including ourselves. That's a sobering truth to admit because it requires owning the fact that we have committed to lies intended to make much of us. Here are a few self-elevating lies that wove their way into my story:

GETTING IN

GETTING STUCK

GETTING OUT

☐ Creation > God the Creator

☐ Human Love > God's Love

☐ Happiness > Obedience to God

☐ Romantic Love > Intimacy with God

☐ I am > God's Authority

As you can see, they are all focused on rearranging how God designed the world to function. No longer does He stand in priority, but He is reduced to our level and made to serve the whims of our hearts. Sin renders us vulnerable to pride and these kinds of lies feed on that weakness. They promise a rescue from the valley, access to whatever wisdom we desire, and the ability to divide right from wrong apart from God. But no matter how enticing they seem, they remain lies.

IDENTITY LIES

With culture bombarding us with truth claims and our pre-disposition for self-elevation, it's no wonder so many struggle with defining their identity today. It's one of the biggest struggles for women dealing with emotional dependency and same-sex attraction especially because we are trying to determine who we are on our own. We want to determine our own identity, choose our own gender, and redefine our roles, which can be easily done by twisting up our old identity with the new one we are given in Christ.

On one side of the spectrum, there are those who buy into what I call the "Old Identity Lie." They affirm that all of humanity is born into sin. By nature, we are objects of God's wrath. But whereas God's Word promises redemption, this lie removes any hope for change. *I am simply born broken and I stay that way.* The old identity lie says the old self is unchangeable.

However, the opposite view is no less dangerous. I refer to it as the "New Identity Lie." While it correctly affirms that we can change by the grace of God, it offers no assurance for the future. Rather than remaining steadfast in Jesus Christ, this lie prescribes a certain level of our own participation to guarantee the new identity God has given. *I am redeemed, but it may not last.* The new identity lie says our new identity in Christ is changeable. Thus, our level of faith, ability to resist temptation, certain experiences, and emotional state are all factors that may play into what is understood to be the state of our identity. And it's just as shaky a lie as its counterpart.

Some move beyond the "old" and "new" language altogether and simply identify themselves with their sin. *I am a lesbian. I am an adulterer. I am bisexual.* This is especially common among the gay community. *I am my sin.* But as Christians, sin is never our name. While it is true that we sin, we are not defined by our sin. That is what you were, but you were washed.[1] You are not resigned to live according to it. That's why I don't describe myself as "gay," "lesbian," or "homosexual." Not even a "gay Christian." Yes, you may still struggle with sins common to homosexuality, but don't claim lies of identity, it just makes you believe them more. You are not your sin. Our sin struggle is not our name. We are not even "sinners" any longer. You have been given a new name. We are Christians. We are Saints. We are *His.* We have been named "Righteous" by the One who imputed His righteousness to us, though we continue to sin. Sisters, we can no longer identify ourselves or others by names we choose.

> *But as Christians, sin is never our name.*

> *You have been given a new name. We are Christians. We are Saints. We are His.*

Those are the false names Satan hisses at us. Doing so means believing the name we inherited from Adam is more defining than the one name given to us by Jesus Christ. God does not label us by our propensities and we should follow suit.

For believers, the truth is that the old is gone and the new has come.[2] One of the great benefits of Jesus Christ claiming our souls is that Satan can never pluck us out of His hand.[3] Sonship can't be given up, taken away, or lessened in its effects. Our new identity is secure because Christ holds it, not us. God initiated it, not us. The Holy Spirit accomplished it, not us. Therefore, God names us, not us. Christian sisters, do not misrepresent your new identity in Christ by claiming personhoods that are not compatible with your new nature. A false identity will never solve the angst of our souls. How we identify ourselves and other believers reveals everything we believe about Jesus Christ. By repetition you learned to respond to the old name, and by divine intervention you will relearn your new name. And someday soon, when I am asked to give account, I want God to call me by my full and true name, the one I received from the Son.

THE TRUTH WE NEED

So what is true? God has a consistent pattern of coming down from Heaven and confronting our lies. He reveals Himself for who He is, and that is what transforms us. He counters the hollow lies of culture and weak spiritualism with His unchanging Word, humbles our pride with His grandeur, and renames us by the grace of His Son, Jesus Christ. We can only combat lies when we know the truth. And the Bible is full of truth. Consider this small sampling of vast realities:

- Jesus Christ grants righteousness to those who believe in Him.[4]

- God has made all humankind in His image.[5]

- His power is made perfect in my weakness.[6]

- Nothing is too hard for God.[7]

- God is good, even if I ask for good things and do not receive them.[8]

- His mercies are new every morning.[9]

- God glorifies Himself through me, despite me.[10]

- No one can snatch Christians from God's hand.[11]

There are thousands of truths like these found in the Bible that have implications and applications to all parts of our life that help us keep the faith. Thinking rightly does not just happen. We must teach ourselves what is true about God in order to learn what is accurate about us. Knowing and verbalizing Scripture is our sword and a shield against threats to our soul. Our hearts cannot change if our minds do not know what is true about God.[12] And we cannot love One whom we do not know.

Along the way, there will be times of doubt about who we truly are, but Jesus Christ never condemns those who doubt. Instead He moves toward doubters, especially those willing to ask Him for help with our unbelief.[13] The promises of our identity in Christ in the Word of God hold power and when we find ourselves confused, we should go to Him who wrote it and to God's people who uphold it to be encouraged in our faith. You and I cannot speak truth into being, but we are given the power to respond obediently to what the Spirit of God says is true. We are able to be transformed by the very words of God. This is what is true: *I am redeemed, and I stay that way.*

MORE THAN A TRADE-OFF

With sin, it's impossible to gain what we want for free. I felt enlightened by giving up God for pleasure, but that trade had farther reaching implications for my soul. My swaps ended up being way more than a series of trade-offs. Choosing sin created a life of unholy exchanges. Losses. For me, it boiled down to exchanging God's ultimate authority for my own autonomy and it led to more than a decade of striving to

GETTING IN

GETTING STUCK

GETTING OUT

keep in harmony my allegiances to both Jesus Christ and my Girlfriend. When God failed to alleviate my misery, I chose to dump Him and exchanged loving Him for loving His stuff, in this case, Her.

The thing about sin is that it is self-focused. We think we deserve "something more." When life becomes about fulfilling our desires, they soon turn into needs that grow into lots of expectations. Then we start to make demands that skew our worldview. When I reached that point, I would cry out to God, begging and negotiating in an attempt to coerce Him into providing what I expected from Him. Then when I received no response, I blamed God for not meeting my elevated wants in areas He never promised to provide. *Jesus is not giving me what He should!* I deceived myself into believing that God owed me lots of things, including romantic love. *He is withholding from me!* I also determined that my pain and problems should go away. *This isn't fair!* And those false beliefs led me to believe lies and make a variety of exchanges that dictated my life's path. Some of these exchanges happened consciously while others simply played out beneath the surface. Regardless, persisting in my same-sex Relationship while being His daughter required me to exchange truth for lies to get what I wanted to fulfill my own desires. Here are some ways that I did that:

> *Choosing sin created a life of unholy exchanges.*

- I exchanged: Intimacy for Intensity
- I exchanged: Soul for Sex
- I exchanged: Self for "Us"
- I exchanged: Inter-dependence for Co-dependence
- I exchanged: God for His Stuff
- I exchanged: Peace for "Prosperity"
- I exchanged: Difference for Sameness

- I exchanged: Self-Denial for License

- I exchanged: Healing for Shared Brokenness

- I exchanged: Eternity for a Lifetime

My heart issues made me prone to making exchanges. If I had the eyes to see what I got out of these trades, they would not have seemed like such a bounty. But a darkened mind sees nothing. Or sees them as worthwhile in the short-term and long-term. If pain ever resulted from my exchange, I wouldn't repent, I'd just blame God for more suffering. Accepting the hollow reality of my unholy exchanges was difficult because to me She felt the most real. My perception of reality distorted what I understood to be true.

Exchanging God's truth also means embracing counterfeits. Counterfeits look great and feel awesome, but they last about as long as the changing seasons. Or maybe a decade or two. Substitutes can't hold water. They leak hope. Counterfeit unions may be branded "good" by many, but they are not made by the true Creator and don't reflect His handiwork. The only way to spot counterfeits is to know the real thing. This is why it is so important to know the tangible character of God. To hold fast to the truth about His Son, Jesus Christ. To know how He interacts with His church. To know what He commands and why. We must know how He defines marriage and the boundaries for enjoying sexual itimacy. When we know God, we can accurately reflect His image. The more we know Him, the faster we will be able to recognize counterfeits. We cannot sin, lie, or trade our way to sustainable peace. And if we're really honest with ourselves, we would have to admit that the promises offered by lesbianism don't come to fruition. The lies and exchanges do not soothe our souls or silence the Spirit like we thought. Instead, they trick us into slavery.

God does not deceive. Since the beginning, He has warned us all of what will happen if we exchange His truth for lies. And He does not negotiate. He cannot be coerced, bullied, or

GETTING IN

GETTING STUCK

GETTING OUT

manipulated. He will not pander to our lies. He knows the most loving thing He can do is remind us of the truth. The God of the universe does not bend to our wills. Out of His love for us, He tells us the truth because only He is the way, the truth, and the life.[14] And only His truth can set us free.[15]

QUESTIONS

1 Looking back over the examples of lies that women believe who struggle with sexual and relational sin, list the lies that resonate most with your experience. What commonalities do you notice in the ones you marked for yourself?

2 Sometimes we know we are believing lies and sometimes we are deceived into trusting them. How have these popular lies infiltrated your thinking and led you to make tradeoffs in your faith? What might be at the core of what you are wanting to gain or lose in these dangerous exchanges?

3 What specific truths does God tell you in His Word are the hardest for you to believe right now? Are you willing to ask God to help your unbelief? Take a moment and ask God to speak the truth to you by the power of His Spirit through His words and to give you the ears to hear, the mind to believe, wisdom to discern, a heart to love the truth, and the will to be set free from Satan's deceptions.

GETTING IN

GETTING STUCK

GETTING OUT

MY TRUTH

After eight years of our Relationship, my hypocrisy was ripping me in half. She and I maintained an idyllic life on the outside, but my interior could not outrun the effects of living in sin like I had hoped. I had tried everything I could think of to silence the angst that was bothering me. The Holy Spirit made it hard to live a quiet and happy life. Before all this stuff, when I struggled with temptation, I'd tell a Christian sister and pursue accountability. *What if I told one friend, but kept it from my Partner? Would honesty and vulnerability lessen the Holy's Sprit's intensity?* Doing so would be a huge step that would test both my friendship and God.

The idea scared me to death. Sharing my story would mean letting go of a little bit of control. *What would a friend think of me if I told?* What if she told someone or offered up my secret to others under the guise of prayer? Then everyone would know—my friends, my Bible study, and my church. I'd be forced to break up with them all. Even worse, my family would find out. Despite all of these fears, I retained the slightest bit of hope and managed to find the courage needed to tell one of my godly friends. Her name was Stella and she was an old friend from college I trusted. She had also walked with the Lord through a lot of junk in her life, which freed her to talk about her sin openly. I loved her raw honesty about her ongoing struggles and how she saw God at work changing her from the inside. She had already shown that she could extend grace to others. *I guess that's a good sign. . .*

Still, I had plenty of fear to contend with. I worried I'd become a project or that it would change the dynamics of our friendship forever. I worried the nature of my sexual sin would disgust her, that she'd worry I would become attracted to her, and that she might walk away altogether. Was she someone I was willing to forfeit if the stakes got too high? *Shit.* As much as that question caused anxiety, the turmoil in my gut felt worse. I was scared to death, but I told Stella anyway. *My best friend is actually my Girlfriend.* I had never uttered that sentence to a Christian friend before and, to my surprise, Stella listened patiently to every word allowing me to share without judgment. In fact, she invited me to begin running with her on a weekly basis so that we could continue talking about what was going on with my Girlfriend and my heart. And so that she could point me back to the truth of the gospel.

When Stella spoke about Jesus Christ it was like waking from a dream. My memories of the Bible echoed in her words, but I remained confused because my experience with God was so different from her descriptions of Him. Her faith in what God said about Himself in Scripture was far more secure than the "truth" I had made up about Him. But inevitably, the moment I returned home from our runs, I forgot everything I had heard, quenching the voice of the Holy Spirit out of panic over the tension in my soul. When my Girlfriend got home, we often headed straight for the bedroom because sex was an effective way to quiet the Spirit's conviction. Everything about our life became devoted to that end—our conversations, values, and how we spent our time. All of the intimacy helped me avoid thinking deeply about the very thing I could not forget.

As this pattern continued, I grew comfortable sharing

with Stella to the point that any attempt at true repentance gave way to simply unburdening myself. I was transparent, but avoided vulnerability and would always sidestep serious details, like the conversations about marriage my Girlfriend and I had begun to entertain. Soon, my casual omissions matured into outright lies. I grew paranoid at the realization that I was not getting better and nothing had changed. *Isn't that the point of accountability?* My paranoia drove me to focus our conversations on her life and, if it could not be avoided, I'd steer her questions about my heart toward other issues rather than the one that was burning down my Castle.

One weekend, I invited Stella to a party with my lesbian intramural team. At the time, I was still dealing with my attraction to my team Captain and I reasoned that Stella's presence could be the silver bullet I needed to kill my escalating affections. Reluctantly, she went, but my motives were a mess. I thought exposing my darkness to her light would dissipate the strength of my desires and that she would see how much this community loved me.[1] I also thought she would extend to me greater levels of compassion, understanding, and tolerance because my gay friends were just so nice. But mostly I brought Stella to stop fantasizing about the Captain because it was interfering with my devotion to my Partner. And my attraction seemed beyond my control. But by the time we left the party, Stella did not find this group as compelling as I did. She wasn't impressed by our banter. She was not amazed by the Captain or the displays of physical affection that we all offered one another.

As time went on, my work schedule "somehow" increased, which thinned out time with Stella. All the while my sin continued to escalate. Sensing that I was pulling away, she suggested I talk with someone who had walked a similar path as me in regard to sexual sin. She had a mutual friend in mind that she assured me I could trust, even though I didn't know her well. I called this friend begrudgingly, more as an effort to people-please than to genuinely seek help. Her name was

Chelsea. At our first meeting, she told me her story of sexual sin and what God was doing to heal and restore her. Chelsea was strong-willed, articulate, and knowingly imperfect, which gave me hope for a real friendship. Above all, she understood my struggle and even had friends who returned to Christ after embracing a same-sex lifestyle. *Maybe this will work.*

My conversations with Chelsea emboldened me to share my secret with one other friend—Katelyn, a member of my former Bible study. For years, she had been one of my closest friends and training buddies. She was fiercely loyal. Katelyn had spent a lot of time with my Girlfriend and me without suspecting our Relationship or sensing my duality, but I knew she loved me and would listen and pray. Plus, Katelyn, Stella, and Chelsea were friends so I wanted to ensure Katelyn heard it all from me first in case the story leaked.

So I let them in. I told all three about my Girlfriend and about the Captain. While it was a big step, looking back it's clear that my main motive was to lessen my attraction to the Captain because it threatened my First Love. It was the first time my same-sex behavior refused to act in my favor. My interest in the Captain had become a big personal problem and telling them helped divert attention

My same-sex behavior refused to act in my favor.

away from inquiries about my Girlfriend. *Maybe the pressure of the Holy Spirit will lessen too?* Still, I had three women in my life that knew my secret, a trio of friends was warring for my soul. They knew my pain and were determined to do whatever it took to help me find my way out. I appreciated them tremendously and hated their involvement at the same time. They knew I was not okay, and they were not going to let me stay there. I was definitely uncomfortable. But I had some hope that they could help me find a way out.

These three women met me with compassion all the while persistently encouraging me to leave my Girlfriend and my gay friend group. I never let them take me to coffee or pray for me in person, but told them they could pray on their own time. During this season, I was already considering quitting my intramural league because I realized the friends I had made there were not my friends at all, nor were they as perfect as I pretended. Even my Girlfriend thought our athlete friends were unhealthy for us. They wore a façade of authenticity while shrouding parts of their lives in secrecy. There was internal strife and covert rendezvous among the women. Plus, many lies circling around this community that we were all too experienced to miss, but too guilty ourselves to point out. I had also begun to realize that my "moral" lifestyle did not inspire them to the degree I once thought. The truth is they didn't even care.

As all of this converged, the women on my intramural team began to distance themselves from me. *Me?! The one who embraced their melding of nominal faith and pleasure seeking?* Perhaps they sensed the tension I was feeling or felt compelled by something else to go another direction. Either way, I felt rejected by the community I had previously praised for inclusion. My gay friends were the only community that accepted the real me and endorsed the real Us. It upset me because relationships were one of my areas of strength and these were waning. But it also presented an opportunity. *If I left that crew, I could appease everyone.* It would satisfy my Christian friends, display obedience to God, and prioritize Her. *Whether false motives or true. . .*[2] So I found myself acting on the encouragement of my trio of friends and left behind my lesbian friendships and the Captain knowing it was a necessary part of starving what I needed to put to death. I knew they were probably right because their advice was what the Holy Spirit had been telling me all along. But it still made me angry.

Even worse, it made me feel alone. Like really alone. Suddenly, I only had four people left who knew the real me— my Girlfriend and my three accountability partners. And the latter would not let up just because I left behind my gay community and sports teams. Apparently, I had more work ahead, and I was not okay with that. *Haven't I done enough?* Their prodding only increased my tailspin. The pressure was mounting and my needs were elevating to the point that I felt like I was beginning to lose my mind.

WORSHIPING SOMETHING

Authority is tricky for me. I'm not good at yielding to it. Typically, I have a better way, a preferred method, a more creative idea—or at least I think I do. As a kid, bucking up against teachers and coaches gained me admiration and self-confidence. Pushing back on authority earned me titles like, "strong-willed" and "leader." It has never mattered if the authority is a man or woman. It is the fact that this person tries to control my way of doing things. I want to be the boss and do not want to feel weak. So I strive for power and self-rule because I want to live in a world of my own making. Unaffected. Unchecked.

Another word for this state of mind is *rebellion*. When people loved me enough to address my sinful same-sex behaviors, my insides twisted. Despite whatever demeanor I portrayed, I had no intention to concede. And soon my counselor, friend, or religion became my opposition, threatening what I believed about myself and what I thought best. My default response to all who tried to lovingly show me Jesus Christ's authority was to diminish and dismiss them on the outside and rage on the inside. Even when I outwardly yielded in word or deed, my heart would do whatever it took to defend my Castle from assault. The irony of it all is that my refusal to worship God through surrender was itself an act of worship—a rebellious and twisted form of worship.

WHAT SITS ON THE THRONE

Everyone worships something. We give power to whatever we love. And whatever we love most, we place on the throne of our lives. It doesn't have to be a person. It can be anything from a job title to a hobby or goal. And clearly, it can also be our sexual expression, a false identity, and ideas of romantic love. It can be Her. Or the possibility of Her. Whatever fills this place of honor sits high and exalted—untouchable. It holds promise for perpetual fulfillment, such that we will defend it at any cost. Think of what you value most. What do *you* love?

- ☐ Safety
- ☐ Family
- ☐ Experiences
- ☐ Stuff
- ☐ Applause
- ☐ Sex
- ☐ Alcohol
- ☐ Love
- ☐ Fitness
- ☐ Food

All of creation is designed to worship. We were created to ascribe greatest value and worth to our Creator—the only "something" that can satisfy our souls. We long to experience something larger than us, to be swept away in pleasures and caught up in something magnificent. We have this in Jesus Christ, but we often look for it elsewhere, like in lesbian romance. Satan's deceptions cause us to doubt that *only* God can give us lasting love. In Her, we think we have found a better free gift.

Removing Jesus Christ from His rightful place on the throne doesn't just poison the way we think about God—it ruins us. Unknowingly, what we consider an easier master always leads to slavery. Whatever we worship will eventually own us. We become like what we worship and I was becoming just like my idols. Hard. Cold. Dead. And I knew in my heart that I was harming myself through false worship. The freedom I exercised to pursue a same-sex relationship shackled me in chains. The truth is that placing any created thing, or ideology, above the Creator of all things always leads to bondage.

At birth, our natural state is self-rule. We are born believing the throne is ours. We are self-reliant, self-exalting, and selfish. On the outside, we learn to be kind, compassionate, and good, but inside we seek to operate independent of God and His commands. It is human nature to believe that we are in

> *Did God really say. . . ?*
>
> *—Satan*

control, but given enough time we are always confronted by our limitations. Self-rule is not sufficient for heart change or fulfillment, it leads to further brokenness and disordered lives.

Eve found this out the hard way. Satan pandered to her inner desire for self-rule in the Garden of Eden. Not surprisingly, he aimed to cast suspicion causing her to doubt the validity of God's instruction. Our inner dialogue echoes that of the serpent's original voice when we question God's rightful authority: "Did God really say. . . ?"[1] Eve believed the lie that she could sit on the throne, perhaps prevail as an even better ruler. She wanted to be all-knowing like God. Along with Adam's willing participation, they fractured the cosmos by their disobedience and were banished from the Garden. That's the reality we live in today—one marked by wayward worship.

GOD HURDLES

Why are we so easily led astray? I don't know about you, but I've never had an actual serpent speak audibly to me, but I hear his echoes every day. So what's at the core of our misaligned worship? Much like the first woman, it begins with

GETTING IN

GETTING STUCK

GETTING OUT

a desire and a question. For Eve, her desire was wisdom beyond the boundaries of what God had granted to humankind and to justify that desire she entertained the serpent's question: "Did God really say. . . ?" That is where it begins for us as well. We distrust God.

For years, I found myself wondering about His purpose in my same-sex attraction. My desire for freedom caused me to question His character to the point that I began to deny the truth about Him. My circumstances became what I call "God Hurdles." Everyone has them and if they are left unaddressed they will shape the way we view both God and our circumstances. As I look back on my God hurdles, it's clear that they stemmed from three distinct denials, which are common to many. I decided that He was not:

1. Good

2. Kind

3. Trustworthy

In response, I traded the truth for convenient lies. Since I no longer believed Him to be good, He became cruel. Rather than seeing His kindness, I interpreted His presence as evil. Instead of finding Him trustworthy, I became convinced He was a liar. But I kept all of this on the inside. Admitting it out loud seemed too un-Christian. I did not want a trite answer or reproof from friends who I categorized as "never having been through anything hard in their lives. " At the time, I'm not sure I even understood my issues well enough to share, but even if I did, what was the point of discussing God hurdles when I clearly wanted to move on from all things religious? So whenever people asked how I was doing, I'd deflect and offer up secondary frustrations in order to keep my real doubts to myself. The constant tension I faced was that of trusting what God said about Himself compared to my experience.

My God hurdles gave me an excuse to persist in my same-sex relationship. *Did God really say that being in love with a woman is bad? And if He did, He is bad.* I could never tell God what I felt about Him, despite His repeated invitations throughout Scripture to do so.[2] I was afraid He'd actually respond, possibly even expose my lies and set me on a path toward pursuing holiness. But that would mean self-denial. That would mean admitting I was wrong. That would mean losing my Relationship with Her. That would mean being alone with God who I denied many times. So if the battle remained inside my mind, if I never prayed or confessed, I thought it would keep Him out. I honestly believed my rejection of Him was more powerful than His reconciliation. I thought my love for Her was more powerful than His love for me. I really didn't understand the power of the cross or His ongoing reconciling grace. I didn't trust His character.

SOURCE IDOLS

False worship is idolatry. It is an act of trading life for what is lifeless. Most of the time, it begins with desires that are good, but when divorced from intimacy with God they become self-justifying guides to whatever kind of life we crave. These desires are considered "Source Idols."[3] They are deeply rooted, difficult to recognize, and manifest themselves in many different ways. More importantly, they are the reason why we seek what we seek, do what we do, and worship what we worship. They emerge as the need-behind-the-need. Among the stories I've heard of same-sex attraction and emotional dependency, there tend to be five main categories of source idols that make up the driving force of our Sin Cycles. These are at the core of what we worship:

1. Comfort
2. Approval
3. Control
4. Power
5. Intimacy

GETTING IN

GETTING STUCK

GETTING OUT

Each source idol has a goal and fear associated with it. There are consequences and lies with every single one. The game we play by serving our desires without regard for godliness causes disorder and chaos, even if we portray peace on the surface. Take some time to evaluate your story and struggles for holiness as you review these key source idols:

COMFORT SOURCE IDOL

WHAT
I have to have _____ to be happy.

GOAL
Comfort, freedom, privacy, and absence of stress

EXCHANGE
Productivity for ease

FEAR
Stress, demands, and people

KEY EMOTION
Boredom

IMPACT(S) ON OTHERS
Laziness causes collateral damage; effort is directed at creating environments that are enjoyable and away from deep relationships because they are too much work; people often feel unvalued by you.

PERSONAL WRECKAGE
No one knows you and you don't know yourself. You avoid conflict, tension, and confrontation, and live a shallow life. You are prone to repetitive behaviors.

MANTRA/LIE
God is not sufficient, I must satisfy myself.

APPROVAL SOURCE IDOL

WHAT
I have to be loved, accepted, and respected by _____ to feel valuable.

GOAL
Approval, affirmation, love, relationships, and applause

EXCHANGE
Inter-dependence for co-dependence

FEAR
Rejection

KEY EMOTION
Cowardice

IMPACT(S) ON OTHERS
People feel smothered by you or exhausted by your constant need for validation.

PERSONAL WRECKAGE
You never speak your mind for fear of losing approval or love. You often feel exhausted and find it hard to receive love. You cannot hold strong opinions. You are insecure in your relationship with God and honor people more than God.

MANTRA/LIE
God does not give me a valuable identity, I must make one myself.

CONTROL SOURCE IDOL

WHAT
I have to manage and be in charge of _____ to feel steady.

GOAL
Control, self-discipline, rules, safety, and certainty

EXCHANGE
Spontaneity for standards

cont'd

KEY EMOTION
Worry

FEAR
Uncertainty and change

IMPACT(S) ON OTHERS
People feel condemned, criticized, or micromanaged by you.
They can feel manipulated, trapped, dominated, or minimized.
Your worry spreads and causes anxiety in those around you.

PERSONAL WRECKAGE
Worry breeds anxiety and fear and when you realize you
cannot maintain control, it leads to more worry. Destructive
patterns may develop that lead to OCD, obsession, and
addictive behaviors. You experience no rest in your relationship
with God.

MANTRA/LIE
God cannot be trusted, I must do this myself.

POWER SOURCE IDOL

WHAT
I have to have power and influence over _____
in order to feel strong.

GOAL
Power, success, authority, influence, and autonomy

EXCHANGE
Integrity for victory

FEAR
Humiliation, loss, mediocrity, and weakness

EMOTION
Anger

IMPACT(S) ON OTHERS
People feel used and exploited by your efforts to increase
your influence, power, or success.

PERSONAL WRECKAGE
You root your identity in competition and comparison. Behavioral patterns include violence and addictions to games you can win. You require authority and you actively avoid situations where you may appear weak or have to be vulnerable. You fear being under God's authority.

MANTRA/LIE
God's sovereignty is weak, I must be strong.

INTIMACY SOURCE IDOL

WHAT
I have to feel known by _____ in order to feel secure.

GOAL
Intimacy, companionship, romance, affection, knownness, emotional connectedness, physical presence, and sex

EXCHANGE
All for one

FEAR
Aloneness, betrayal, loneliness, and celibacy

EMOTION
Insecurity and desperation

IMPACT(S) ON OTHERS
People feel as though you constantly require more from them, demanding increasing amounts of their time and effort. They feel drained, exhausted, and broken from the weight of your expectations.

PERSONAL WRECKAGE
You pursue emotional and relational dependency. Your attempts at privacy lead to isolation, which requires increasing levels of security that you look for in others. You feel rejected by those not sympathetic to your needs. You often feel betrayed and jealous of other relationships. You have low expectations on God and high requirements for people.

cont'd

GETTING IN

GETTING STUCK

GETTING OUT

MANTRA/LIE
God's indwelling presence is not adequate, I must have someone else.

The God-given desire for comfort, approval, control, power, or intimacy is not wrong. God created us to have desires so the answer here is not to absolve ourselves of feeling. But it is when we believe that life only has meaning, we only have worth, and we will only be happy if we have these things that God-given desires are elevated to idol status. We become idolaters. When we go outside God's design and commands to obtain them believing that they are more worthy of pursuit than God, they become ungodly worship.

Instead, we begin by acknowledging that sin's presence deceives us when it comes to what we believe is most pleasurable. God created us to find our fulfillment in Him and we must play an active role in that pursuit because it will not always feel pleasurable along the way. Apart from Christ, we will always chase after the wrong affections. And clearly, homosexuality is never a holy end or means to obtain life. It is not bad to desire intimacy in relationships or sex within biblical marriage, but these desires must never become our highest goal. It's not bad to desire affirmation or a position of influence, but they must never lead you to believe they are what bring life meaning and purpose. If they do, they cease to be good and become sinful idols that will own us. And sin never remains dormant. What begins as a root will always grow outward toward the surface.

SURFACE IDOLS

Once a source idol becomes rooted in us, sin begins to bloom and it extends itself in a visible manner. It grows into a "Surface Idol" that is more recognizable. Like we have seen before, it is possible to try and control the visibility of our idols through image management, but that does not make them any less present. We begin to seek certain things as the means to obtain the root of our idol. Here are a few possible surface idols:

☐ Money/Possessions

☐ Status/Influence

☐ Significant Other/Spouse

☐ Kids/Family

☐ Travel/Experiences

☐ Appearance/Image

While certain desires begin as source idols, they can multiply into surface idols that are more perceptible. These are the means by which we try to satisfy our longings. When we relentlessly find ourselves feeding these surface idols and never being satisfied, it may be an indication that there is a deeper source idol that needs to be laid down. Again, these items are not inherently bad, but when we elevate them to a status above God they derail us from our created purpose. Both surface and source motivations can be healthy if they remain in their proper lane and pursued in holy ways. When they become all we want or our means of coping we must address them.

When we cling intensely to worthless idols, we forsake God's grace and mercy. We become obsessed to the point of believing that without them we will surely die. *My life only has meaning, and I only have worth, and I will only be happy if I have this.* The best way to know whether or not the things we love have overtaken our love for God is to check them against Scripture. Are they true? Are they noble? Right, pure, lovely admirable, excellent? Praiseworthy?[4] Are these desires conforming me more to the image of Jesus Christ?[5] Are they hindering my worship of God?

Idols make shitty gods. They hold no power and they

GETTING IN

GETTING STUCK

GETTING OUT

are worthless. Anything that we hope in and elevate as more valuable than God is an idol. They don't always look like golden calves anymore. They have become prettier, more complex, more acceptable. Our desires are constantly producing them and our behaviors feed their appetites. We excuse them as core contributions to our identity. It is not hard at all for me to identify what was once my surface idol: I worshiped Her. She was everything to me. However, surface idols are usually symptom of something deeper that is going on. For me, there were three source idols underneath that fueled my pursuit of Her: control, comfort, and intimacy. These were the roots of my sinful preference.

Idols make shitty gods.

In Her, I found safety, confidence, and loyalty. She was a constant, whereas my experiences with God ebbed and flowed. For years, He seemed silent and undependable—characteristics that do not sit well with someone who craves control like me. I never knew what to expect from God. But She provided me with the comfort I desired. When God failed to give me what I wanted, I decided He was not sufficient and it was up to me to satisfy myself. I looked to Her for intimacy as well. Despite my many friendships, no one seemed to understand the real me. I needed someone to draw me out, someone who would know my heart, fears, sexuality, thoughts, and dreams. *Love me just the way I am.* God was not enough for me so I found Her instead.

To be sure, few of us only have one surface idol. We often have many idols with many sources, but once we can identify our source idols we can seek God's Word to inform and transform our deepest desires and motivations and the means by which we pursue them. It's not enough to try and fix them on our own. Our track records are not that great when it comes to saving ourselves. Chasing idols led me to get enslaved to cycles of sin. Divine heart transformation may or may not change the way your life looks or what you love, but it should sanctify the reasons, the ways, and the purposes of your pursuits. The goal of your desires will be reoriented. You will exchange wrong things for right things. The fears associated with faulty worship will disappear. And the damage to yourself and others can begin to heal.

Our endeavor of laying down our false idols should not be for the sake of healing alone, but for our joy and His glory. The reason God asks us to tear down our idols and drive them out completely is in order to replace them with Himself. You must exchange them for the right thing: Jesus Christ. The God of the universe has exclusive rights to our worship. And the worship of the triune God leads to ultimate meaning, purpose, and worth.

> *The God of the universe has exclusive rights to our worship.*

PRESUMING ON GOD

When personal experience becomes the lens through which we view life and godliness, it can lead us to some dangerous ends, like tweaking Scripture to make it palatable and presuming on God's kindness toward what He has called sin. We assume many things that are not true. We take verses out of context and make them heresy. We interpret Scripture to fit our presumptions about who God is. And what sin is. We accept whatever compels our intuitions. If we are happy and our lives look pretty and successful on the outside we believe our custom theology delivered. We expect God to agree with our beliefs, but defiance is rooted in presumption.

One of the more popular contemporary arguments for homosexuality's holiness is that monogamous same-sex relationships are a new category of love left unaddressed by the Bible. Monogamous homosexuality is not a type of relationship foreign to the Bible. It, too, falls under the category of sexual immorality and stems from wayward desires, which always prefers autonomy to the lordship of God.[6] It is not new.

GETTING IN

GETTING STUCK

GETTING OUT

Before anything else, homosexuality is an issue of the heart. That's what God is after—our hearts. And even as believers, our hearts often need reclaiming, as they are prone to wander. When we argue that the Creator of all history, the one who created relationships and marriage, did not anticipate a form of relationship that would emerge from the Fall, we create a pitiful vision of God. It is a lofty accusation that renders Him finite, lacking omniscience, and unloving.

God has made it clear in his Word what *is* holy and has clarified that His design for sexual behavior is to be enjoyed between one man and one woman in the context of marriage.[7] From beginning to end, Scripture treats homosexuality as sexual immorality wherever it appears not because God wants to restrain our joy, but because homosexuality keeps our hearts from Him. It ultimately hurts us. God tells us where we fall short to cleanse us, not to condemn us. Be careful that you do not mistake God's patience for acceptance of sin.[8] We are responsible now, and one day, we will all stand before His judgment seat and give an account for our lives.[9] God's Law is the standard. True belief leads to obedience and those of us who twist God's Word to justify our desires and same-sex attractions reveal how little we love and fear Him. Or believe His commands are for everyone's good.

> Do *not mistake* God's *patience* for *acceptance* of *sin.*

My most critical judgment of God had nothing to do with the fact that He defined my lifestyle as sinful and commanded me to leave my same-sex Relationship. Rather, it was that He was calling me to die to myself. And not just once, but on an ongoing basis. If I left Her, He would still ask for my obedience in other areas. And if I was obedient in other areas first, He would still ask me to deny my homosexual inclinations. And eventually leave Her. This is Christ's great call to sanctification, the life-long pursuit of holiness. I was most angered by this command because I believed God not only could, but *should* remove my same-sex longings forever in one mighty act. *Then I will want to obey.* But I was warned that He doesn't always do that. Sometimes He does, and sometimes He redeems us while allowing us to continue facing our weaknesses in order to train us in humility. Then we can war in His power and instate discipline in obedience even when it hurts. *For my whole life?! In all things?!*

I was confused because my desires to be rid of same-sex attraction seemed holy and deserving of divine participation. I could not figure out why I was still dealing with something I wanted to be free from when I had tried so hard. It maddened me to hear that I should lay it all at His feet, because not only could I never seem to do it very long, but apparently, I also had to keep trying and see myself fail. *I didn't sign up for this!* Dying to self included more than just letting Her go. It required tearing down my Castle brick by brick—a prospect that terrified me. That's a shit-ton of work to deconstruct all that I had built. And humiliating. And really painful. God was inviting me to participate in this obedience, which is the point I ignored.[10] I did not want to work for something I thought God owed me and that perspective became just another idol that expressed itself in my sinful Relationship with Her. Because I was enmeshed with Her, dying to self now meant trading in my self-identification too, not merely my moral behavior. Obedience required killing everything about Us. Everything about me.

CO-KINGSHIP IS AN ILLUSION

God will not share His throne with another.[11] We cannot worship God plus something else—whether source idols or surface idols or our beliefs about lesbianism. We can't find meaning and worth in Her and in God. Neither can we be on the throne and reign with Him. Co-kingship is an illusion.

We can't eradicate His lordship by our denial of His authority. If it ever feels as though we have overtaken Him, it is much more likely that He has given us over to be ruled by our object of worship. God never tolerates the hurdles that allow us to coddle our highest loves.

He will not share His glory with a Girlfriend.

What appears to be His inaction may be His wrath for our rebellion. He will not share His glory with a Girlfriend. Yet, mercy collides with our reality and we can be dethroned and changed. At salvation, you and I were transformed and transferred to Christ's kingdom. God opens our eyes to see and our minds to understand that Jesus Christ on the throne as Lord gives us rest for our souls in this life and the next. We find out that what He said *was* true. We look back at the lesser gods that we erected and can now see the carnage. They were never gods to begin with for there are truly no other gods but God. God's very Word proclaims that He is the best and only King.

When our wayward affections tempt us toward self-rule, we must plead with God for righteous affections. Jesus Christ can set us free. He can help us see that there are really shitty consequences to sin. Satan's deception coupled with human will encourages us to re-establish our natural, pre-salvation seat of self-rule. Even believers can find themselves tempted to resume this posture before God. But we fail to realize we were ruling from little more than a rickety highchair. It was never a real throne. Yet the god of self climbs back up toward the illusion certain that while it did not work before, *this time* will be different.

What can we do to change our affections? Look up, my friend. God remains seated on high. Jesus Christ alone is King. He has given you His Holy Spirit to transform your heart's desires and the broken ways that you pursue them. God can break your cycles of bondage and reorient your worship, but it starts with acknowledging the false idols that you seek. And *why*. May the King in His kindness give you eyes to see your golden calves as worthless. May you worship the Image and not the image bearer. May He grant you a mind that wills to tear down the high places where you spent your days serving and sacrificing to the wrong lord.

We become like what we love. Worshiping Jesus Christ makes us more like Him and only then do we find the satisfaction we long for. Good news: Jesus Christ remains on the throne. And you are made to be in His presence though you may stumble over some hurdles along the way. He is good, kind, and trustworthy. Bend your knees to the floor and worship the Lord for it is in Him alone that we find happiness.

GETTING IN

GETTING STUCK

GETTING OUT

QUESTIONS

1 List the five Source Idols discussed in this chapter and mark with a star the one(s) that you recognize might be at the root of some of your sexual or relational sin? How are you seeking to satisfy these desires through homosexual connection?

1

2

3

4

5

2 How should knowing that God is good, kind, trustworthy, and that He has all authority over your life help reorient your worship? What God hurdles do you face when seeking to love Him more than anything?

3 How can you test if the things you desire most have become an idolatrous pursuit? Mark the questions that you can ask yourself:

☐ Are these desires conforming me more to the image of Jesus Christ?

☐ Are these desires making me more like the idol I value most?

☐ Are these desires leading me to gratitude and peace?

☐ Are these desires hindering my worship of God?

☐ Am I seeking to find my ultimate value, worth, and happiness in God or in this other thing?

☐ How might disordered loves impact my relationship with God?

☐ Am I willing to pray that God will reorient my desires to be holy and pursued in a holy way?

MY LIFE

When I could, I snuck into church, unbeknownst to my Girlfriend and unnoticed by my friends. Just like old times, but completely alone. I'd slip in late and grab an aisle seat near the back, with a hat angled down over my face. During prayer, I stared detached at my pastor. I never sang in worship as I felt unmoved, but I was not unaware. Throughout the sermon, I locked on to my pastor, unblinking, eyebrows raised, focused. I was desperate, craving a truth I did not yet know that would crumble the wall surrounding my heart. *I want to believe, but my faith is shattered. I know that Jesus is my only hope, but He threatens everything I have built. I don't want to be exposed! I'm scared to death! But I want to know what is true! Tell me if there is a way I can have peace and keep Her close. I can't handle any more loss or pain.*

Each random week, as my pastor spoke I felt the Holy Spirit stir. Every sermon seemed crafted specifically for me, kindling the beginnings of a flame. But nothing was magic. He would plead with us to lay our mess before the Lord, but hadn't I tried that already? I begged God to rescue me from the mess I had made, but my bargaining was never met with holy participation. God had consistently asked me to believe that He was enough and I could not. Trusting the Lord meant sacrificing Her and surrendering control, which was too much to ask. *I have no reason to trust what I cannot see when I fully trust who I can see.* The problem was simple: I preferred my pleasure to Him. I demanded that I remain in charge of my life. I was asking Him to take my tears and replace them with peace on my terms. *You call this discipline, but it feels like abandonment, like you have given me up. Like you have given me over.* After all these years of seeking peace between Christ and my sin, I finally came to a breaking point. Faith and prayer had changed nothing. *Clearly, God has no interest in helping me so why should I reciprocate?* Nine years into my Relationship, I exited the doors of church with no plans to ever return.

But Stella, Chelsea, and Katelyn didn't get the memo. Even though I walked away, these women continued pursuing me for the next year, but they broke my rules. Two or three of them started praying together, which unleashed my paranoia. They kept calling me out of my Partnership. Their faithful fervor felt intrusive and unwelcome, something I could not control. And my Girlfriend didn't like it either. Along the way, She had remained patient with my attempts to reconcile my faith with my same-sex lifestyle, but enough was enough. Jesus was not coming back for *Didn't they know that if true heart change hadn't happened by now, it would never happen?* me and the constant intrusion of my accountability partners interfered with our intimacy. She needed me to sever ties with my church community and shut down these friendships for the good of Us. So We could be free.

It broke my heart because I knew these three women loved me and I loved them for believing there was hope for me, but they were too late. My Girlfriend and I were too in love and too entwined. Didn't they know that if true heart change hadn't happened by now, it would never happen? We had fought the good fight, but hope was too far gone.[1] Our time together had rid me of my gay friends and wandering lust toward the Captain so they could walk away with that as a partial victory. *At least I am less sinful than before.* But once again, they failed to take my cue. The more I pushed them away, the more they pressed in. They called, texted, and left me voicemails at work reiterating their concern and reminding me that they were all praying for me. It was infuriating. I did everything I could do to avoid them and still they found their way in.

When it came down to it, I only had one move left to make. I permanently blocked them from my phone, social media, and every other contact point. I blamed each of them for the fact that our relationships were wrecked. They didn't have to love me so much. I blamed God for everything else. Rejecting them was clearly the right track to peace and freedom. Finally, I had no friends, no community, and no faith and I determined to kill any remaining hope in Jesus. My Girlfriend and I had what we wanted—protection from outside interference. Months later, we laughed at the memory of my annoying, Jesus-loving friends. All of that was behind us now. I could finally have peace.

And then I got a phone call.

I listened to the voicemail. A pastor I didn't know from my church left me a message explaining that he wanted to meet with me. Apparently, my former accountability partners had met with him and explained the situation. *How secretive!* I didn't return his call, but confirmed in an email that I'd give him sixty minutes of my time to hear what he had to say and see if perhaps he had any insight for me. If nothing else, it was one more box I could check off. *Been there, tried that.* More evidence to throw in God's face.

Unbeknownst to my Girlfriend, I met with this pastor. As I explained my same-sex Relationship and communicated all that I had done to try and break free, I watched his facial expressions like a hawk. Rather than responding with disgust, he listened sincerely without agenda, which surprised me. Throughout our meeting, I vented my anger with God and listed the reasons that She was better than Jesus, certain I could overwhelm him with my evidence. Rather than reacting with shock, he apologized for all I had gone through and invited me to meet with him again to talk further. I did not want to, but accepted, feeling compelled by something I could not identify. Maybe it was the Spirit, or maybe it was my spirit of pragmatic optimism.

Over the next four months, we met on a handful of occasions, our meeting times growing shorter each time. Like before, I started out honest and hopeful, began avoiding truthful conversation, and eventually shut down altogether. *He is not magic either.* Adding to the tension, my Partner and I decided it was time for Her to make a major career change, which would create a monumental shift for Us. For months at a time, Her new job would require Her to be in another city, separated from me, but we were a team and I supported this move completely. By comparison, everything else was peripheral. It felt silly for me to try resolving something so trivial with a pastor when the countdown for my time at home with Her had begun to tick. Since I was sure his hope was that I'd leave Her anyway, I lost interest in the idea of attending any further meetings or responding to his emails. *I will never leave Her or forsake Her.*

I will never leave Her or forsake Her.

Behind the scenes, my friends were meeting with this pastor to pray for me. And when it became clear I was backing out he called a come-to-Jesus meeting, an intervention of sorts that he would attend along with my friends and a mediator. Respectful of the formality and certain I had reason on my side, I decided to argue my case. It would be my official swan song to this crew, an attempt to show respect for their efforts and let me move on with my life. When the day arrived, we gathered around a conference table and each of my friends began by sharing their hopes and sorrows, pleading with me to leave my sinful lifestyle. I heard them but said and felt nothing. My heart was far too hardened. After they had all spoken their piece of the story, the mediator joined the meeting. I had never met him and wasn't sure what he would say, but it was clear that he was the enforcer. With no preamble, he simply informed me that he had five questions I needed to answer.

"Are you a Christian?"

I answered, "Yes."

"Are you willing to leave your life of homosexual sin?"

You're asking me this right now? Don't you think I would have done so already if it were possible!? This was the ever-present impasse—caught between the pleasures of my sin and what God commanded. I was already hopeless. I looked at him and replied, "If you need an answer right now, my answer is no." With that, he stood from his chair and told me that the church would have to part ways with me. It was the last response I expected. *That's it? Where's the grace?! What are the other questions? What just happened?* In a compassionate tone, the pastor I had been meeting up with offered to continue meeting despite what had just been decided. "No thanks," I answered curtly. And that was it. As I left, I realized that I had just been placed under church discipline.

Though it was not their preference, my pastoral leadership formally separated themselves from me, an act Scripture describes as giving me over to my sin.[2] *Fine. So be it.* I choked down my emotions of injustice in stoic, self-righteous victimization and walked away from them all. *Carly, forget what is behind and move on.* I did not really care, I had already distanced myself emotionally and theologically from this

GETTING IN

GETTING STUCK

GETTING OUT

501(c)(3). Lightning did not strike me in the parking lot, and I knew enough that it probably wouldn't. But I was relieved that every tie I knew between God and me had finally been severed. I was free to settle in a land of my choosing. *Fuck you all. I'm out.*

Fuck you all. I'm out.

BUILDING A STORYLINE

I felt relief once the "God" chapter of my life had closed. I finally had a chance to rewrite my story the way I wanted. I could take the leading role and decide what actors and actresses participated in my life, and for how long. My Soulmate and I would have love and adventures and our perfect story would inspire others. *Though the world was going to shit, at least our happiness will have no end.*

What we believe determines how we live. Our personal narrative indoctrinates us into beliefs about the world, about us, and about God.[1] What we tell ourselves matters.

A personal narrative is the story we believe we are living in; it helps us make sense of our human experience. Our storyline is the lens through which we view the world, us, and God. It can include what we think about how the universe began and how it will end. It can include beliefs about our identity and purpose. It can include how we presume God operates. Our storyline is really our functional belief system, it is an effect of our doctrine and affects everything. Below are a few examples of storylines that can inform what we believe and how we live:

THE WORLD

- ☐ Progressivism—Things are continually getting better.

- ☐ Fatalism—Things are continually getting worse.

- ☐ Skepticism—Certainty is unattainable, so all claims must be rejected.

- ☐ Deconstructionism—There is no objective truth, so all established ideas must be destroyed.

- ☐ Post-Modernism—There is no purpose or storyline, so nothing matters.

- ☐ Post-Secularism—There is nothing meaningful, I must find what is trustworthy.

US

- ☐ Consumerism—You are what you acquire.

- ☐ Materialism—You are what you have.

- ☐ Emotionalism—You are what you feel.

- ☐ Individualism—You are the center of all things.

- ☐ Nihilism—You are insignificant.

- ☐ Rationalism—I can understand what is true through knowledge.

- ☐ Empiricism—I can understand what is true through sensory experience.

- ☐ Pragmatism—I can understand what is true through reasoning.

- ☐ Romanticism—I can understand what is true by the intensity of the emotion.

GOD

☐ Perfectionism—God is pleased and accepts you if you are perfect.

☐ Moral Therapeutic Deism—God is pleased if you feel good and are good.

☐ Antinomianism—God doesn't care about morality.

☐ Deism—God is not involved in the lives of humans.

☐ Secularism—God does not exist, but we can restore beauty and meaning to all things.

☐ Hedonism—God wants people to pursue their happiness.

I definitely embraced fatalism, individualism, and pragmatism, and probably a few others, but I didn't realize it at the time. I viewed my entire situation through these lenses. Now I can see that these narratives about the world, me, and God contributed to the perfect storm that primed me for seduction. These stories also helped me justify my lesbian Relationship. And all of them required finessing my reality to fit within its thesis.

As Christians, we should be asking ourselves if our personal storyline is the Christian story of the world or if it is an alternative storyline? Perhaps one we've acquired or built ourselves? Most of the time we don't even realize it's narrating our lives, which makes it an effective method of Satan's deception. *Did God really say that He will make all things new? No. You will die like everyone else so you should take what you can right now. Be happy with Her because God can't make you new again.*

Some of the ways we can see if we have created a fictional storyline or embraced a false identity is to test what we believe:

1. What is the story we are telling ourselves every day?

2. Is there a rival identity that emerges from our belief that seems more real and tangible than our identity in Christ?

Most often these questions can be answered if we can correctly self-evaluate our habits, loves, beliefs, and behaviors. And yes, even our same-sex attraction or emotional dependency. How we live tells us what we believe. The wrong stories leak water.[2] Embracing a misplaced identity, an immoral sexual ethic, or a weak narrative will always lead to disordered living because they can't deliver what they promise. They can't be true all the time and are an unreliable source of hope in suffering. In fact, they can lead to deeper hopelessness because the narrative arc and the end of false storylines are meaningless. They sound compelling, but will eventually cause us pain and to work harder, the very things we are trying to avoid through trusting in the lesser stories.

Most of the burden of maintaining a false personal narrative boils down to image management. Whatever story we've chosen to believe about ourselves and God must be portrayed consistently. We have to project our truth. *I don't need anyone. It doesn't matter. I've overcome. I am strong. I've got it all together. It gets better. It's never going to get better. I'm a better person.* Our narrative of life either orients us or disorients us to reality. When curveballs come along revealing the incongruence in our chosen false story, we hide, downplay, and redirect. The

> *Our narrative of life either orients us or disorients us to reality.*

explanations provided by our stories are resilient and they can cover us for a while, but we'll always find ourselves at a common end lacking the "something" we crave.

Managing an image may not take place in an overt manner. You may be unconscious of the ways you bolster your ideal self or feed your perception of the world. It's also possible to live your version of life in private or in secret, as my story proves. Rather than post on social media in support of same-sex relationships and our worldview, we kept a low profile strategically deflecting attention away from our souls. Being in the shadows helped us hide while we pursued pleasure and peace. Such a life may look quiet, but it is not inactive. It's driving everything.

We also engaged our consciences in morality management. The love, kindness, nurturing, and good works we offered others also provided opportunity to persist in our lifestyle because no one could see beyond the surface. Our moral behavior shone even though our hearts were far from God. It looked like the fruit of the Spirit. We created our own prosperity gospel of homosexuality where our lives appeared perfect. *Blessed.* It's empowering to convince others and ourselves that we are unaffected by sin and that our internal narrative is the truest.

But what do you do if your storyline betrays you? What if the thing you always believed would stay true suddenly proves false? What if God exposes your disorder? Do you pause? Do you panic? I responded in self-protection to keep from faltering. When I faced conflict with my chosen worldview I sought to reestablish the way I thought things *should be* with stronger commitments to myself. For example, if consequences of my sin emerged like anxiety, suspicion, or a potential breakup, I would step up my coping game. I'd workout more, serve Her more, affirm Her more, and identify with lesbianism more—anything I could do to have more security. I needed to exert more control so I would never be affected by outside forces. I'd muscle my sin into submission. Rather than question my newly established paradigm, I reinforced it. *Maybe if I make deeper vows and have clearer self-definition, then I won't be threatened by reality. Or by the Spirit. If my Relationship is rock solid then I cannot be moved. Once I marry Her, it will all get better.* I had no other choice but to dig in my heels. I was always striving to manage the implications of my narrative.

Rebellion requires balancing what's true and what we want to be true. Change becomes an existential threat to our personal identity, which is founded on a storyline that suddenly stops playing by our rules. I knew that my storyline lacked perfect accuracy and in my quest for calibration, I became more disconnected with myself. Internal chaos resulted. *How do I reconcile myself to myself? How long can I survive as two different people?* Not two people like a lesbian and a straight woman. Two people, like one unaffected by Jesus Christ and one completely haunted by Him and His story. Fearing the possibility of being found out as a fraud is paralyzing. An identity and a storyline that leak would mean utter failure.

To compensate, I had to document every one of my adventures, accomplishments, and sacrifices and wave them like a banner. I needed to be celebrated to convince myself I was happy and better apart from Jesus and His people. I wanted others to see how free I was. And to silence anyone willing to tell me that living in a false story leads to identity confusion. The storylines we weave rarely take the form of an overt lie, but they are always a few degrees shy of the truth. The goal is to make sense of the world around us or to keep our true selves—our fears, weaknesses, hang-ups, doubts—below the surface by touting the benefits of a chosen lifestyle. Pushing out a story can also be a method of pushing others away. For me, fronting an image was a filter for covering up the consequence of sin, the sole purpose of which was to project control. Over a long enough period of time, those slight variations from the truth land us in a completely foreign land, creating a person we no longer recognize in the mirror. That, or we become so deceived as to embrace our false self as reality. And suddenly, we're in charge of managing two stories: God's story and ours. More work.

In my experience, most of the Christian women I've known who adopt same-sex lifestyles and emotional dependency have grown exhausted with fighting their battles and eventually give up. They make peace with their sin. Even when they know it's wrong. I am one of them. I took the woman offered by the enemy and sought the thrill of wayward affections as my spoil. Because of my suffering, I believed that I had earned ease and deserved comfort, which allowed me to justify Her. *That was my story, and I was sticking to it.* And this is where a false storyline becomes the perfect distraction, strengthened by reasoning that downplays conviction to rationalize our behavior. *Love is all I need.* It's an effective method for lying to others as well as our selves. But underneath, that story grows and eventually does the unthinkable—it owns us. What we created for a sense of control enslaves us. The management of image and morality doesn't actually create the peace and order we were promised. It just creates a need for more management. The happiness that was promised by a homosexual lifestyle is not self-sustaining. The voice we heard in the Garden of Eden and mistook for a friend is an evil captor. Lesbianism is slavery. And slavery is traumatic.

ONLY ONE STORY

Christians are called to live in another story and it's the only true story, the one about Jesus Christ and His kingdom. This is the story that tells us who we really are. It tells us about God and His world. This storyline is always true and as Christians with a fixed identity in Christ we must operate and participate in this story. The Author can be trusted. The script is found in Scripture. This narrative won't change and there is no striving to attain it. The narrative arc leads us to hope and deeper hopefulness in the Alpha and the Omega. The gospel account is this: God is with us, reconciling the world to Himself through His Son, Jesus Christ. And one day, we will be raised and restored. Right doctrine matters.

We encounter God's gracious self-disclosure in the Bible. We find the patterns of world culture in the Bible. We find everything God deems essential to our identity in the Bible.

☑ Our purpose is found in this true story.

☑ Our worth is found in this true story.

☑ Our stability is found in this true story.

☑ Our rest is found in this true story.

God is establishing His kingdom on earth. The whole world plays a part in God's story—believers and unbelievers alike—whether people believe it or not. The beginning and end of the story are life-giving and that's such good news when that's the story that we are rooted in. Being in the messy middle is not hopeless when we know the genesis and the everlasting. This gospel narrative also gives us a place to bring our suffering and our celebration. It accounts for our struggle with sin. It is full of hope. It doesn't leak.

The Christian Story chart may provide you some clarity and some hope about your struggle with same-sex attraction and emotional dependency. The Bible is a story about God. It includes a beginning (Creation), a middle (Fall and Redemption), and an end (Restoration and Consummation). It tells us about our past, our present, and our future. It's really good.

As Christians, we live between Redeption and Restoration. Learning the reality of my new nature in Jesus Christ helped me understand that I was not in bondage to my will like I thought I was. I was not powerless and destined to sin—that is only the state of an old nature. Jesus Christ took me out of that story. As a Christian, my new nature in Jesus Christ gave me a new heart that is free to choose Christ instead of my sinful inclinations. I am able to sin, but I am also able to not sin. My will can be transformed to love the light and choose to walk in it. The Christian story also gives you and me hope that one day the Lord will restore creation. We too will be fully restored, unwilling to sin any longer and unwilling to desire anything but God. One day, I will only ever want what is best, namely Yahweh.

The only thing that can set us free and restore order is replacing our false narratives with the only true story. The one written by the Author of life. His story is our only means of hope, the rest have already proven untrue. Our hearts, habits, and lives will experience fullness and wholeness when they are aligned with the true story of who God is and who we are in Him. My friend, His story is an invitation into reality.

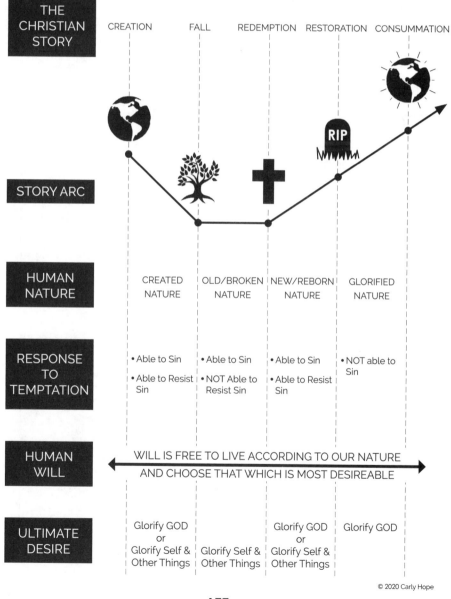

© 2020 Carly Hope

QUESTIONS

1 Which one of the false storylines do you recognize as a lens by which you tend to view the world, yourself, and God?

2 How has a false narrative historically served to disorient you from reality? Why can your chosen story not be true all the time?

3 How does learning more about your nature, will, and ultimate desires help you understand your state?

MY ALLEGIANCE

My Girlfriend and I quickly recovered from the havoc caused by my recurring attempts to gain peace with God. I no longer hid who I was or what I thought about God. I no longer heard or felt Him and my conscience bothered me no more. It testified to my truth alone. The summer that my church formally placed me under discipline, my Girlfriend moved away to the east coast begin her new career. I traveled back and forth to see Her, doing all I could to maintain our Relationship while staying busy without Her at home. This was her opportunity to focus on her career and I wanted to support that, but I felt terribly alone and jealous for her attention, which was especially focused on work. Once the first few years of the new job were behind Us, we were promised more stability and security. I had been loyal for nine years. Surely, I could remain patient for a few more.

Life continued in this manner for the next couple of years. We traveled back and forth often. We talked multiple times per day and texted obsessively, but my loneliness remained. I had burned every one of my friendships to the ground. Only my family remained and they had no idea about my same-sex Relationship. They loved Her and they saw how sad it made me to see my Best Friend move away, but they couldn't understand the depths of my despair. Depression caused my body to physically ache and I started having panic attacks. But I consciously chose my isolation. Keeping a safe distance from people was the only way I knew how to survive. All this time, I had worked to silence my conviction and had finally arrived at a place where it was just the two of Us, then only to have Her move to another city and leave me all alone. *It's not supposed to be this way.*

Some evenings, I tagged along with my brother Luke and his friends around town and in their homes. He tried to take me under his wing knowing I was sad that my Best Friend moved away. He had also watched the slow disappearance of all my other friends. Unfortunately, many of his friends were Christians from my former church. Since I hated everything about that place, I hated them too, but I still ate their food. Besides my brother's group, I had a few acquaintances at the gym who I saw most days, though none of them were what I would call a friend. Other than those people, I was just buying time until I could be with Her again.

One day at the gym, a random woman started chatting with me while I was on an elliptical and then out of the blue asked if I would be interested in going to a Bible study she led with women from my gym. *Haha! Are you freaking kidding me?* She had no idea how ludicrous it was to be asking me! Was she trying to evangelize me? *If she only knew. . .* I could really freak her out if I wanted, but I decided to keep all my secrets close. I asked her what church she went to only because I was morbidly curious. Of course, it was my former church. *I'm sure she'd love to hear that I was kicked out of that place. I'm pretty certain she'd un-invite me if she really knew all that I felt about God, Christians, church, and my lifestyle.* My answer was a definite *Hell No.* But a week later, I showed up. I had no one else.

Early on in our Relationship, my Girlfriend used to tell me that she would give up her life for me in a moment, but now She talked about sacrificing everything for her work and business partners. This new community had begun to gain her highest loyalty, as they embraced women like Us. I was happy for Her, but also jealous. Her friends knew about our Relationship and affirmed it thanks to their commitment to unbridled sexuality. No limits, no boundaries, no rules—apparently even when it came to my Girlfriend. The women in Her workplace constantly pursued Her despite the fact that *We* were in a Relationship. She'd always tell me that She loved me more than anyone, our love was never stronger, and pledged it was never going to change. But that knowledge contributed to my being an anxious wreck at home counting down the moments between calls and texts. I lived for the weekends when I could fly to be with Her. After almost ten years of spending every day together, the conjugal visits were never enough for either of us. We just had to be patient and get through those first years. Then She could move on from this role and those people. Then we could get married and have it all.

My Girlfriend had plenty of stress to go along with her job, but continued receiving promotions having earned the respect of her colleagues. Every day, She called me with the play-by-play, which always made me proud, but also concerned. While She loved the work, it was taking a toll and making Her miserable. Whereas before, She was warm, kind, and patient, in the time She'd been gone she had become hard, insensitive, and distant. I sensed Her detaching from me, which inspired jealous-fueled attempts at controlling the Relationship I held so dear. She apologized. She recognized the growing implications of our state. We knew something had to change in order to protect Us and conquer the chaos. So after two years of our balancing act, She resigned from her job and was going to return home after Christmas. Less than three months away. To celebrate the occasion, we capped off her upcoming return by getting engaged. It wasn't the romantic story that a woman typically dreams about. In fact,

GETTING IN

GETTING STUCK

GETTING OUT

we decided over the phone. But we had spent the last ten-plus years talking about marriage and planning special surprises for one another. Always deeply expressing our love and allegiance. Even though it was more of a formality at this point, we would finally commit ourselves to one another legally. Then, union with Her would be unbreakable. *Finished.*

We were thrilled about what was to come and began discussing dates, venues, and the guest list. At the time, neither of our families knew about our Relationship and when it came time for them to find out we knew it would destroy them. So we decided to enjoy our engagement in secret and wait until the last minute to fill them in. Consequences didn't matter anymore. We'd already dealt with so many. We'd find a way to rebuild in the wake of any unforeseen wreckage. We determined to marry the following spring and no one would get in our way. Love had called us out.

My Fiancé and I planned a glamorous escape to one of our favorite tropical islands where we would formally pledge our lives to one another. We had worn rings since our senior year of college, but the Justice of the Peace and ceremony would make it official. We would have a new name. Afterwards, we could combine insurance, tax returns, dogs, and boats too. All the craziness of separation would be resolved. We had even decided to move cross-country to the beautiful Northwest to start fresh with new jobs and a lesbian community we had found. It would also give our families space to mourn, as our news would devastate them. And we didn't want their sadness to make Us feel guilty about our decision.

Along with our parents, I knew the news would wreck those of my Christian friends who did not know. It would also discourage the ones who knew about my secret life, the ones who prayed so fervently for my rescue. I pitied their belief in the God I had proven to be so profoundly silly. *Don't they see that they are the ones in chains while I live in freedom?* My Soulmate was worth every tear, every broken relationship, every burned bridge with God and His church. I felt no conviction. No shame. Only anticipation for what was to come. She was my rock, my fortress, and my deliverance.[1]

Our marriage was finally right around the corner, just a continuation of the life we had and always wanted, but now we'd be fully *out*. It was time to go all in. Everyone in our lives would know our secret. People could either celebrate us or move on. Everything was exactly as it should be.

WELL WORTH IT

I love the story of the woman at the well in John 4.[2] Not just because her feeling of being "other than" resonated with my own, but because of the kindness of Jesus to enter into her situation and call her to Himself. God the Son had an appointment to keep and the woman was completely oblivious that God was coming to meet her. Jesus sits beside Jacob's Well at mid-day, a time when only ostracized women approached for their daily water. They did not fit in with the morning crowd. Whether by some sin done to her or a sin she committed, this woman felt ashamed and isolated herself from others.

As the story continues, we learn that the woman had experienced many broken relationships. She had married five times and currently lived in a relationship with a man who was not her husband. It's possible that she was forced to marry multiple men or she may have been contractually passed around in a time where women did not have rights. Perhaps her previous husbands died or abandoned her and as the source of her survival she was forced to find another. Whatever the case, the woman carried years of wounds and heartache and was caught in an ongoing cycle of perpetual brokenness.

Instead of condemning her, Jesus approaches the Samaritan woman in love and asks for a drink in order to tell her about a Living Water that satisfies forever. As she listens to Him describe this water, she wants to know where she can

GETTING IN

GETTING STUCK

GETTING OUT

find it. That's when Jesus lovingly asks her a question that He already knows the answer to: "Where is your husband?" The woman responds honestly that she does not have a husband, but Jesus dug deeper to the truth. "You are right when you say you have no husband. The fact is, you have had five husbands, and the man you now have is not your husband." She had told Jesus the truth. Then by telling her the truth, Jesus exposed her deepest shame, her wounds, her misplaced allegiance, and her pain of the sins done to her, for the purpose of healing her. She must have been stunned.

Clearly, she was surprised because much like us, she deflected by changing the topic. The woman accused the religious establishment for confusion regarding the place of acceptable worship. She was trying to shift His focus off of her brokenness and onto a secondary matter. So Jesus responds kindly by shifting the focus onto Himself. Jesus reveals His true nature for the first time in the Gospel of John by declaring Himself the Living Water. The first recipient of Jesus's first "I Am" statement is this despised Samaritan woman. Overcome, the woman can now see herself clearly through His love. She repents of her unbelief and Jesus the Christ forgives declaring her free to go and sin no more. That's why our Savior went to the well that day. Not because He was thirsty, but because she was. And she didn't even know it. God chose the lowly and despised to herald His good news, which the woman proclaims without shame in the verses that follow. Many of the people in her town believe in Jesus as the Christ because of her testimony. They believed that Jesus was better because if He has the power to save someone like her, perhaps He could save them too.

He loved her too much to leave her in unbelief.

Obviously, I identify with this story because I feel much like the "other" woman. I love how God came after the Samaritan even when she wasn't in a desperate heap on the floor begging for Him to show up. Jesus knew better. He loved her too much to leave her in unbelief.

I've often wondered whether I would have listened if Jesus showed up at my well face to face. Maybe I would have repented right then and there. Maybe I would have given up the way I coped with brokenness and run to share Christ's good news with others. Truth is, God did show up many times. But I had hardened my heart and was no longer affected by His offer of Living Water. Instead of repentance, every time Jesus approached me I ran to Her. Daily, I preferred well water to the Living Water. But He kept asking and offering.

Jesus Christ knew my dilemma and pursued me all the same, just as He does for all of us. We have an empathetic Savior who is compassionate when He asks us questions that He already knows the answers to. He does so to show us a better way of living. The Lord knows how and when to approach each of us by His Spirit. He tells us about the same truth. He already knows how many times we will reject Him and when He will ignite our hearts with belief. He is sovereign over our doubt and defiance. Perhaps one day, the Person we've heard speak a million times will melt our hearts of stone. The Lord can work through one divinely appointed moment or a lifetime of them. It's the persistence of our Lord to remind you and me of His love that ultimately compels us to believe again.

By my own efforts, I coped with life in the best way I knew how. I pledged my allegiance to another way. I tried to reframe God and disregard Jesus, but I could not escape His Word. It was in my memory.

I could not escape His Word. It was in my memory.

It was being breathed out by His Spirit. Even when alone and feeling "other than," I heard His voice. I was being addressed in loving kindness by our God who is with us. Jesus Christ knows our wells just as He knows our thirsts. He speaks to us in truth, not to shame us for our misdeeds, but to strip away every barrier of unbelief that keeps us from Him. And He always points us to Himself, the source of life. The Living Water.

RESULTING WRECKAGE

If you have ever experienced a car wreck or known someone who has, you have seen how it leaves behind both a mark and a memory, whether or not there is a physical scar to prove it. Someone made a mistake and loss occurred as a result. We don't get to choose how it plays out. Sin has the same effect. Some of us have experienced living in the wreckage of someone else's sin or that of our own and it is devastating. The entire time I embraced same-sex attraction and emotional dependency, I knew I was leaving behind a trail of damage. I liked seeing Christians wrecked. It made me feel better about myself. I wanted their conflict over my lifestyle to pain them more than it pained me. I wanted them to agree with me that God was the cause of my rebellion and humanity's suffering and pain. *He would stop me if He could.* Ironically, that bitterness became my cancer.

Disordered affections lead to a disordered life. Daily, I faced new consequences for my sexual sin and grew accustomed to waving them off by refusing to give a shit. Her love was enough to numb the pain. . . for a while. No matter the consequences, I wanted Her more. I knew what I had chosen, or rather *who* I had chosen, and I knew that my choice would have certain impacts. Still, I was willing to endure whatever consequences came my way so that I could be happily, emotionally dependent forever. Come hell or high water, I chose my happiness. But what I did not realize and had not yet experienced was the reality that sin has a life of its own. It is always growing. And I could not control its wreckage.

CLUSTER MUCK

Sin loves company, not just a community of others, but it loves compatible sins. On the outside I was happy and positive and outgoing. Friendly and funny. Agreeable. Kind. Loving. But I was repeatedly experiencing growing levels of internal chaos. Never did I agree that these emerging clusters of personal issues were stemming from my particular ongoing trespass, I attributed each one to a different life event as its cause. I refused to believe bad things could come from or be exacerbated by something so good like my lesbian lifestyle. So I ran more, did more yoga. Took meds. Relaxed and made love more. Ate lots of green salads. What I experienced in my life is that when sexual and relational sin was present, its ever-present companions were clusters of consequences that I could not alleviate. The bundles of residual wreckage below are what sin produced in me and they all popped up at various moments. Always inconvenient.

- ☐ Anger, Hatred, Cynicism, and Distrust Cluster
- ☐ Jealousy, Obsession, Comparison, and Lust Cluster
- ☐ Defiance, Pride, Self-Reliance, and Arrogance Cluster
- ☐ Lying, Double Life, Omission, and Secrecy Cluster
- ☐ Fantasy, Masturbation, and Sex Cluster
- ☐ Validation, Acceptance, and Manipulation Cluster
- ☐ Selfishness, Ingratitude, and Entitlement Cluster
- ☐ Striving, Control, Passivity, and Hopelessness Cluster
- ☐ Paranoia, Anxiety, Fear, & Depression Cluster

Sin clusters are no joke. They affect our physical bodies and our spiritual life. We think we can manage the emerging consequences of ongoing sin, but the roots spread deep and wide. Sin is invasive and it grows wild threatening to ruin us. These were the consequences that impacted me the most, they felt worse than others that I thought were the direct outcome of my choice to be in a same-sex relationship. The clusters seemed to be appearing disproportionately and were intensifying without reason. Sometimes I wondered if the growing presence of these issues were God's punishment for my rebellion. *I'll accept your wrath on my body, if you are trying to make me choose. She is worth it.* When He was silent, I sought ways to manage and eliminate the ramifications in my flesh. But I had misdiagnosed their cause. I even prayed they'd go away. *I am begging you to heal me, so the effects of all this will get better!* Trying to deal with the muck and mire distracted me from addressing their real source.

CONSEQUENCE, DISCIPLINE, & PENALTY

The consequences of sin are guaranteed. Like gravity, they come through every time. Consequences matter. They are stinging reminders that something is wrong. The clusters were not indirect outcomes, they were being fed by my sexual and relational sin. The danger of persisting in rebellion to God's commands is that we can grow used to the wreckage and may not notice its impacts anymore. Or dismiss them. I felt happy and justified in my same-sex behavior, so much so that I laughed at my ability to persist in it without experiencing the

I wrongly concluded that I had defeated God by searing my conscience.

tragic, visible consequences that I was warned about. Since She and I didn't break up and that was the worst direct wreckage I could imagine, I tried to convince myself I wasn't sinning. I wrongly concluded that I had defeated God by searing my conscience. Instead, I was experiencing a very grave consequence. God was giving me over to be ruled by my sin.

Scripture makes it clear that God is full of grace, but that grace is not given to us as a license to continue in our sin.[1] It does not mean a life without consequences. Because of what we know about the insidious nature of sin, consequences are also His grace to us. They materialize in a myriad of ways, but as much as some consequences may sting, the true evil of sin is not its impact. Wreckage sucks, but is secondary in effect. The essence of sin is disdain for God and the primary impact is broken communion with God. Separation from Him is far worse than any kind of earthly consequence.

If consequences are justice, discipline is mercy. Both are evidences of God's love.[2] Discipline is more than simply a slap on the wrist. Discipline is a persistent reminder that burns, one we cannot overlook. God's discipline can be light or severe, but it is neither damnation nor a curse. It is not punishment. The King does not exile us or leave us wallowing in our ruin.

> *The purpose of His discipline is to lead us to repentance and transformation.*

The purpose of His discipline is to lead us to repentance and transformation. It's an invitation to come nearer and be healed. God disciplines everyone He loves, the people He calls "His." God intends discipline to be a pathway of restoration. Through discipline, the Lord reminds us that we have wounds in need of His healing, wounds that will continue to spread damage to ourselves and others if left unattended.

Sin is rebellion against God and always deserving of His just penalty, a penalty established in the Garden of Eden. Penalty is more severe than consequences or discipline. The ultimate penalty for sin is death, but not merely a physical death. It results in eternal separation from God, or what is often referred to as hell.[3] This separation is what the Father saves humanity from by sending His Son. Jesus Christ willingly took on this penalty for it was always the united will of the triune God to do so. Our penalty was transferred to Jesus who sunk under its weight on the cross. His human nature was the perfect blood sacrifice required to satisfy the penalty we deserve, receiving the wages of all our sin—past, present, and future. God the Son was not dead though His human body was, and the Son was separated from the Father for three days before it was ordained that the Father would restore His proximity with the Son. The Son was separated from the Father for a short time so we wouldn't have to be. Through Him we were freed from the penalty of sin and death. The Father restored Christ's physical body to Christ in His resurrection just as He will do for us. God the Son showed the universe His divine power in His ascension and sent His Holy Spirit to us as evidence of His promise and presence.

Men and women of the Old Testament were saved by the Holy Spirit by grace through faith in a coming Messiah. Men and women of the New Testament are saved by the Holy Spirit by grace through faith in a Messiah who came. Everyone who believed and believes will never experience the everlasting penalty of separation from God. For all believers have been united with Christ and given the Holy Spirit. Instead, believers in the Christian story receive an everlasting place in His presence. The redeemed soul lives though for now the body dies. Christians get presence, never penalties.

Christians get presence, never penalties.

For though we were saved once from the penalty of sin, we are always being saved from its clutches. By grace through faith, God removes the eternal penalty deserved for our sin, but that does not mean we get to avoid its effects. We still get consequences and discipline. There will still be wreckage. Avoiding wreckage should not be our primary reason to not sin. The reason wreckage is only a secondary consequence is because we are all heading for

GETTING IN

GETTING STUCK

GETTING OUT

eternity. We do not want to experience separation from our Creator or broken communion with God.

The Lord's discipline for our sins also points us to a better choice—obedience. God extends His grace by forgiving our sin in Jesus Christ and calling us to go and sin no more. He offers a better way, and it is through the path of obedience. He knows what we need so His gift of the Spirit empowers us to do what we cannot do on our own. It is true that obedience may result in painful circumstances, like breaking up with your partner, losing your lesbian community, and feeling confused about the state of your identity, but do not run from hard steps of obedience because they are stepping stones to life. Yes, sometimes this road really sucks, but the result is life-giving. Obedience is evidence that God is removing your old habits and installing better ways while reminding you of your new identity in Christ. Loss of hindrances is part of the surgery that leads to healing. The Lord's discipline is a means of abundant life.

Obedience is messy, but it grants a confidence in Jesus Christ that always leads to joy. Righteous behavior yields peace. Holy living grants rest. It is through obedience that we find the shalom we have so desperately sought. But it requires our participation. God does not direct us like puppets into obedience. We have to be intentional about pursuing righteousness, which is possible in Jesus Christ no matter how messy life has become. The nature of sin is to destroy, which means that given enough time we will end up in the wreckage of our disobedience, but thanks to God's grace we are given the option of two basic responses:

1. **Recognize what is true and repent**
   We acknowledge that brokenness is what leads to our wreckage and we turn from it trusting that the Lord will be faithful to rebuild what we have broken.

2. **Reclaim what is false and rebel**

We reject God's design for the world and us and our sexuality, blame Him for the wreckage, and continue to participate in what is evil while breaking more stuff.

Repentance is only possible in Jesus Christ, but it is always an option available to believers no matter how impossible it may seem in the moment. We live in a broken world and daily court temptations from our spiritual enemy, but sin is ultimately something that we choose because it is a product of false worship we embraced. We are not forced to serve our idols. We do so because we love them more than God, which is why we need His transformative grace to intervene. We must pray for Christ to grant us the ability to love Him more and for His Spirit to empower us for right living.

The very fact that you are breathing and reading this means repentance is still on the table. Believing in Christ does not exempt us from consequence or discipline, but it does direct us back to Jesus Christ and lead us to the fullest life possible. The one God intended from the beginning. No matter what, life will still be filled with moments that feel unearned and unfair. You may continue to struggle with same-sex attraction despite obedience to God. But wayward affections are not a form of punishment. They are simply a result of living in a broken world. Consequences and discipline are God's merciful ways of pointing us to the grace we find in His Son who is healing His creation.

WORLDLY SORROW VS. GODLY SORROW

Sin is quite fun until someone gets hurt, or until it accomplishes what it has always intended—our own destruction. When that moment arrives, the willingness to move away from sin, or lack thereof, is one of the most important evidences of the status of our hearts. When wreckage arrives, do we feel bad or do we feel repentant? There is a huge difference between the two. It is easy to apologize remorsefully and make resolutions for the future when everything falls apart. But repentance is more than saying, "I'm sorry." It owns fault then asks for forgiveness. And the true test of repentance is what comes next. Do we ask Jesus Christ to change our behaviors that have caused harm? Do we examine the motives behind our sin? Do we take steps to turn away from our sin? This is the difference between worldly sorrow and godly sorrow.[4]

Worldly sorrow describes feeling grief over the visible hurt we have caused. *I'm sorry. . . that I got caught, outed, or that my actions affected others.* But that's about it. It is not genuine sorrow for the behavior itself and our posture before God. Worldly sorrow is a form of pseudo repentance. It feels real in the mind, but rings hollow in the heart. We plead with God for forgiveness hoping for reprieve from the effects of sin without asking Him to eradicate the sin itself. We don't ask Him to keep us from sin. Instead we ask Him to excuse it. Exposing sin to the light is good, but simply doing so to make amends without any desire for inward transformation is a waste of time. God knows us better than that.

By glorious contrast, godly sorrow leads us to repentance. It means recognizing that our sin is primarily directed at a holy God. A correct understanding of God's character allows us to see our own faulty character. We know that by our sin we are saying that God is secondary. And for this realization, we are sorrowful to the point that our guilt leads us again to the throne of God to ask for forgiveness and the strength to go and sin no more. The subsequent wreckage around us can also be remedied once we have a right vertical relationship with God through repentance. Godly sorrow is evidence of a broken and contrite heart.[5] An attitude that is mindful that God's commands are for our flourishing and that we broke them.

As those who struggle with same-sex attraction and a host of other indwelling sins, the enemy assaults us with temptations and opportunity all day long. It's our wound that Satan keeps open by stabbing at it. Living under that weight will produce one of two paths and will indicate our trajectory in life. One is the path of worldly sorrow, which keeps us on a stagnant roundabout routine. That is simply remorse. Whereas the path of godly sorrow beckons us back to the shelter that is our Savior, Jesus Christ. He is the only true solution to sin. Godly sorrow causes us to acknowledge sin for what it is: rebellion against our Creator. It leads to repentance, but not just once. Repentance is a regular discipline, and that is good. Repentance involves turning and transformation. It's work. While we may grow tired, God is patient and provides comfort and protection every step of the way.

Without repentance, our hearts grow calloused to the point that we may no longer see or feel the consequences of our sin. But that does not mean we have managed to tame our sin or overcome God. Rather, we have reached a state the Bible calls being "dead in our trangressions."[6] We have become ever hearing, and never understanding.

I am pretty sure this is what happened to me. My pride and anger swelled against God, I challenged Him to flee, and at some point I no longer felt or saw Him. It was as though I had wrestled God and won. But instead the Lord let the full weight of my natural consequences for rebellion come to pass even as I was irrevocably tethered in Christ. For a time, I made it my goal to give myself over to my sin in the hopes of silencing the Holy Spirit. I quenched the Spirit for years, but it did not matter. No one has the power to completely kill their hearts. For believers, this is especially true. God the Father does not reject His children. We are eternally adopted as His sons and daughters, a truth that should not be used as a license to sin, but as a comforting salve that our Father is near and willing to save. He will not abandon those He has claimed

No one has the power to completely kill their hearts.

though we wander astray. God, in His grace, often allows us to pursue sin in order that we might come to experience its destructiveness. This is not permission for the Christian to dabble in sin. He gives us this opportunity to experience His wrath and compassion so that we might repent and turn again to His Son.

Despite my hardened heart, Jesus Christ claimed me when I was five years old. His presence never left my side throughout my years of pursuing a sinful relationship. No matter how hard I tried, I found no lasting peace apart from Him. Christ was always calling me out, inviting this prodigal child to come to Him for healing and refuge. Today, if you hear His voice, do not harden your heart. Do not rebel against God. Ask for the will and want to obey. Jesus Christ has the power to produce godly sorrow in our heart. It may hurt for a while—heart surgery always does—but it will lead to rhythms of joy, gladness, and gratitude.

THE HOLY SPIRIT & OUR SENSIBILITIES

Repentance is not merely a change in behavior. Fundamentally, it is a change in how we think. Repentance means agreeing with God that our sexual sin is primarily an indictment against Him and His love for us. Godly sorrow includes a confession that His truth is real, not our own. We must constantly ask for the Holy Spirit to directly inform our hearts and minds, which we do by growing in our understanding of the Word of God. So when that familiar voice speaks, we will be able to discern if it is God's Spirit or the comforts of our justified conscience. If the words we hear are in accordance with the words of Jesus Christ, they are trustworthy.

We must also pray that the Lord would soften our hearts. In the same way that we are active in hardening ourselves against Him, we must participate alongside Him for restoration. And He has made a variety of tools available to us: prayer, Scripture, church, discipleship, recovery ministries, community, and so on. The Holy Spirit, however, is the one who uses these tools to penetrate our hearts with conviction. He haunts us with enticements of hope. He makes the seed of our will conformable again. Even in our bleakest moments, He beckons us home. The Spirit's haunting is another one of God's mercies. He keeps us from ever feeling truly satisfied in our sin. He speaks to us the words of eternal life, shines light in the dark, and causes our hearts to come alive.

By the way, our conscience and the Holy Spirit are not the same thing. The Holy Spirit in every way is above our conscience. One is deity the other is human. Praise God! Our conscience is like a moral code, we can inform our ethics by our experience and by repetition and by belief. Our principles are molded by our emotions and our

Our conscience and the Holy Spirit are not the same thing.

loves. Our sensibilities can be a tool used by the Holy Spirit or a tool of false spirits. This distinction should be cause for hope because our infinite God has power over everything finite and can infiltrate anything. In my years of living in a same-sex Relationship, I preferred my guiding principles over the Holy Spirit. I liked my conscience more because it was informed by others and it was conformable to my will. My conscience was clear. I could distance myself from conviction, silence the cricket, or change the standard anytime. I could soften my heart to sin, and harden it toward God. I could sear it myself.

When a conscience is silent and does not speak warnings to you about your lesbian lifestyle, you can be assured that you are experiencing the effects of a hard heart. A seared conscience will no longer convict us of guilt then no godly sorrow will emerge. For me that was the goal. Individual ethos then became the arbitrator of my personal truth, and I believed that truth to be impenetrable. Some of us have been tricked into the thinking the Holy Spirit affirms same-sex relationships because our conscience does not speak to convict us. Or perhaps your inner voice still speaks but ascribes to a different standard. This is the not the voice of the Lord, but echoes of the one who loves the darkness and disguises himself as an angel of light. The human conscience is corruptible, deceivable, and fallible. It resonates with voices like our own. The darkness loves to testify to my personal truth.

However, it is a spiritual reality that even when our conscience is seared the Holy Spirit can still speak truth to us in a way we can hear. He has all power and authority to do so. It is great news that God the Holy Spirit is over us and in us, but is not us. The third person of the Trinity is altogether not like us. He is outside of time and outside our bodies. Yet He dwells within us too. Our God is a God who communes and communicates with His people. The Holy Spirit only ever speaks the words of the God the Father and God the Son. That's how you know His voice. The Spirit of God does not change its message and is forever consistent with Scripture. If you sense another word, I can assure you it is not God. The voice of God spoken by the Holy Spirit can pierce through the loudest of noise and hardest of heart with a single word or whisper. God is never bound by our bodies or beliefs. He has divine authority over all things created. We can be overcome and transformed by the power of the Holy Spirit.

Christian, you belong to Jesus Christ your Savior. God has called you His own and His adoption is irrevocable. You were made by Him and for Him. You can harden your heart, but God has already taken you out of your original state. You have been physically changed and have a new name and a new home. There are great rewards to be enjoyed for obedience in this life and in the life to come. So do not return to your former slavery no matter how much you may want to at times. Persisting in the pursuit of your same-sex inclinations only reinforces your belief that sin will prevail in the end. You are believing the wrong story.

Sin has a life of its own. Left unchecked, it will grow into a hardened heart that is difficult to break. Sin never leaves

GETTING IN

us unscathed. Consequences hurt. Even still, if it seems that God is nowhere in sight and you are afraid, or if you want to breathe a temporary sigh of reprieve, beware. Christian, He is not done with you yet. He has not let you go. We experience the devastation of slavery in order to crave the freedom that Christ offers. You are not given over, you were adopted so you have been ordained to love God. He is eager for you to experience His kindness. Renewal is coming. Respond to His invitations to obey. Live with the end in mind, looking ahead to your heavenly reward.

> *You were adopted so you have been ordained to love God.*

DEAR SELF

I typed the note below while flying home from a weekend with my Girlfriend in the eleventh year of our Relationship. Since then, I've kept it on my phone to remember. I also pasted it in this book without a single edit. Though I wasn't praying at the time, this is clearly a list of my groanings and wreckage. It's a messy mix of lies, mantras, accusations, pain, and hope. I wrote it to myself to simply clear my head, but it unmasked my heart, which is exactly what Christ desires.

DEAR SELF

You can love again, and be in love again.

You will have true love in your future, a correct true love. You will learn to manage the former.

There is a godly man out there who is actually perfect for you.

cont'd

GETTING STUCK

GETTING OUT

Hope leads to deeper loneliness, but no hope leads to emptiness.

It's OK to pursue love even if you still love another. You have to try.

You will learn how to deal with a broken and hurting heart.

Give yourselves a shot at loving someone you can marry.

Your man will get you, listen, understand, love, encourage, and be your best friend.

Give men a chance, they can't be that bad right?

Continue to love yourself and your life.

I know God is supposed to be better, but while you are waiting, live.

Don't hold things tightly, just people. The ones worth loving.

God can redeem, if he wants, or he'll let you struggle. He chooses.

You hold God at a distance so life won't hurt. So hope won't hurt.

You prayed, he was silent, you begged, he withheld, you let him be.

You answer my Dad's prayers, and then I'll answer to you.

Smell the flowers in the places you choose to go.

I can't control God, so I control my space.

It's easier to live in a self-made paradigm because it makes sense.

When u can't change your circumstances, change your priorities.

I'm afraid of people I love dying. All. The. Time.

You better not kill my parents before they enter the Promised Land. Otherwise, you are mean and a too scary being to trust.

I feel like YOU are the prowling lion. You stalk me. Show your compassion.

If prayer does nothing, and dependence is powerless, then is faith futile?

Why do I believe in women more than men?

I value safety, protection, and provision. When do u care about these?

If all the godly learning still leads to confused death, why play the game?

Can't you answer one simple prayer?

You have crushed bones, and broken spirits, and destroyed love. You want me to trust you?

If your eyes are so busy on the sparrow, what of men in your image?

The will of God seems impersonal and detached of our obedience.

Consequences of sin are absolute. But blessing for obedience is a crap shoot.

Why do your most loyal followers, get the most destroyed with life's shit?

What incentive is there for living holy?

You know your silence caused me to run like hell right?

Oh, you're a cleft in the rock? Must have missed that one.

I truly loved and believed and sought and agonized in prayer and sought your rescue and was obedient and steered others to you for decades. I was in for life. Why trick me? Shouldn't you have protected me?

Why so many tests if you know we are set up to fail? And when we ask for strength, guidance, rescue, faith, power, trust, why ru elusive?

I just want to love and be loved. I don't care what gender.

Oh this is for my good?

cont'd

I trust love that is real and physical.

I see now that a sinner's life can still be full. No wonder they see no need.

Why does your spirit haunt me so, if you refuse to come to me?

I get that you don't want to let me go, but you will.

So when do you provide this faith and trust that only you can gift? I can't seem to muster it up anymore.

I let my mind wander and seek for love, because there is a direct correlation between effort and love, not just unconditional love with no effort or compassion.

Is love not give and take? Not just take and let me sink/swim?

I'm afraid you will take one of my family just to punish my unbelief.

I no longer think your blessing is based on my obedience, just your overall will and whims of the day.

Dependence leads me to desperation and unhappiness. Upside?

Your world is a complicated chess match, your best soldiers can be pawns at any time. And we're left with no explanation, just a flat "trust."

How is the truth of fellowship with you different than my experience?

I know you don't have to prove yourself to me, but wouldn't it be helpful to us? We are blind and weak and faithless and human. Surely u know our struggle?

What standard do you hold us to? Of what gain is eminent failure?

Dependence feels like powerless submission to an invisible force. One that can pierce without notice and explanation, but we are to take it like soldiers. Fun.

Is Heaven the only reason for faith? What value is it here?

I hate that my faithless spirit hurts my family. But don't they see how faith has hurt me? Them?

I know that if all is stripped away, I'm left with only God, but that does not seem fun. I feel he is neither kind or concerned or protective. How can he be a healer and judge and savior and king and captor all in one? Each moment I feel he shifts his persona and I'm left to guess his mood for the hour.

A Christian's life is uncertainty, but certainty in him. How?

He seems elusive and silent more than present and clear. The game is tiresome and hurtful.

I had faith but he allowed me to break. I asked to be healed, but he thought better of it. I no longer ask because he wants me to operate broken for his glory and to remember my dependence, of which I flee so my wounds can scab over instead of being picked by his strategy. I feel safer this way. No pain.

Of what gain for the kingdom is a faith so complicated that its people are in turmoil over finding his will?

The wicked flourish, but Moses never enters the Promised Land. It seems like God holds a grudge.

I wish I loved god.

Why do I love who I love?

Why does it seem better?

Why do I fear, avoid, discredit the options?

My heart knows one and is clueless of the other.

I hear good and bad, I expect the bad and don't want to hope in the good.

There must be a trustworthy man out there.

I'm getting lonely.

It's scary that I am willing to love either.

GETTING IN

GETTING STUCK

GETTING OUT

This whole list could be summed up in one word: "Help." I did not type this note for God, but He used it nonetheless, lies and all. He sees our hearts and hears our cries and He always responds. Sister, if confusion is all you got, tell God. He enters into our mess for our good. Take an honest look at yourself today. Bring your groanings to Him and remember that He is not cruel and distant, but compassionate and near—a loving Father who longs for you to come home. Our Father sent His Son so you have a hand to lead you, and He sent His Spirit so you can grab hold.

QUESTIONS

1 How does godly sorrow and worldly sorrow look different when struggling with sexual and relational sin? What types of responses are hallmark features of godly sorrow?

2 How does understanding that the Lord disciplines believers and does not penalize His children for our sin contribute to your broader understanding of His forgiveness, purposes, and grace?

3 How might you discern whether your conscience is speaking to you or if it is the voice of the Holy Spirit? How does knowing the Word of God help you divide truth from distortions?

GETTING IN

GETTING STUCK

GETTING OUT

PART 3 GETTING OUT

HIS RESCUE

GETTING IN

Our marriage was finally right around the corner, just a continuation of the life we had and always wanted, but now we'd be fully *out*. It was time to go all in. Everyone in our lives would know our secret. People could either celebrate us or move on. Everything was exactly as it should be. Except for one thing. The haunting of the Holy Spirit. My ultimate BUT GOD.

Two months after our engagement, my Fiancé had a few days of vacation so I flew Her home to be with me. Christmas was right around the corner and it would be one of our last times to see each other before the wedding—the day we would solidify our unity with vows committing ourselves to one another above all else. We had decided that on this trip it was time to tell our families and those closest to us that we were together and planning to be married that spring. I felt nothing. Conviction of conscience had dissipated years ago. I only felt overwhelming love for Her.

It was a snowy night when I picked Her up from the airport. I expected our usual embrace and excitement, but something was different. She didn't want to go home with me. Instead, She asked me to take Her to her parents' house. I felt

GETTING STUCK

GETTING OUT

hurt and alarmed, but knew She was exhausted from work and travel. Still, our interaction was awkward and I didn't know why. So I dropped Her off and we made plans to get together the next day.

That night the weather took a turn as an ice storm blew in and froze everything. By morning, the whole city was shut down. There was no way either of us could leave our homes. We were stuck and couldn't get out. We were locked in and physically separated for three solid days, but we continued communicating throughout our confinement and made plans to meet up once the ice melted. We had wedding arrangements to confirm as our promised lifetime awaited. But when the ice cleared, She was MIA. I called. I texted. She stopped responding. I couldn't find Her. Her family couldn't find Her. I felt a pit in my stomach. I wasn't afraid She was hurt. I was worried about something worse—that She was detaching. After twenty-four hours of silence, I found out that my Fiancé checked in on the return flight I had booked for Her and left without saying a word.

The next day, I did something that I never did. I wrote Her an email. *Who emails their future spouse?!* But I had to express everything clearly to compel Her to come home. Concerned and scared, I was desperate to understand. I wanted clarity. I needed something to regain control, to create order out of chaos. I begged Her to tell me what was going on. *Are you okay? Do you still love me? Is there someone else?* Her behavior was so uncharacteristic that it began to send me into a tailspin. I knew how popular She was at work, but She was mine and She was me. She was *my* future wife and Her silence caught me completely off guard. I was distraught with anxiety. Without a healthy Us, I was certain I would die. So I poured myself out in the email in the hopes of convincing her to respond and return to me. Compelling Her that *we* were better than anything else and together *we* could overcome any obstacle.

A day later, She finally replied, though I couldn't

say whether I was more anxious or hopeful as I clicked on her name, but my heart was pounding. Whatever feeling dominated at the time soon turned to utter disbelief. The email began semi-apologetic, but unfeeling. Her message ignored my specific questions and concerns, offering platitudes instead that communicated both empty remorse and detachment. *What the hell is going on?!* The whole thing was cold. She stated clearly that She was no longer in love with me. After eleven years together, my Fiancé was breaking up with me and walking away. She had found someone new and was moving on. They were sleeping together. *She has betrayed me!* Her affections had changed, Her desires drawn to another woman. A married woman. A woman who had professed to being a Christian too. My other half was committing Her life to a new relationship, one that promised a new "perfect" ending. She now believed that it would be *their* love that would heal Her brokenness and bring Her lasting happiness. I was destroyed. No matter our monogamy and eleven years of commitments, all of the hope promised by the nature of our love amounted to this. *I am ruined!* No matter our sacrifices and exchanges, they were not enough to sustain Us. *We are separating!* Her love for me had diminished and She was dismissing me. I was rejected. Ultimately betrayed. She closed her email with a single phrase: "My heart is open." All the while my heart was burning as my world was unraveling.

When I finished reading, two of the most powerful things that have ever happened to me occurred to which I will testify in tears for the rest of my life:

1. My heart felt like it had ripped in half

2. And I heard the Lord tell me, "It is finished."

When the God spoke the words, "It is finished," all I could see in my mind's eye was the temple veil being torn from top to bottom and I felt each breaking thread resound in my chest.[1] The Father brought me to remembrance and understanding of

GETTING IN

GETTING STUCK

GETTING OUT

the worth of my access. *I am free!* Though the weight of my burden had crushed me, my rebellion did not break Him—He always had access to me. I knew beyond a shadow of a doubt that this was not just a normal breakup. She and I had been through enough of them for me to know the difference. But it was also bigger than a rejection from my fiancé or a hurdle to overcome.[2] In every way unimaginable, this act of God was divine. He had shown up many times before and offered

It is finished.

countless ways of escape, but this was His time to take me out. *He is with me!* The Lord had orchestrated something I could never have predicted or accomplished myself. He rescued me and I could see it!

I fell to the ground. As I lay crumpled and sobbing on my floor, I felt the severity of God's love. He pulled me from my storyline, my hurdles, my place of hiding, desecrating every obstacle that kept me from seeing Him. He destroyed my Castle, which threatened my soul. He took me out of my lofty tower. Out of the shithole. Off the throne. Out of my engagement. Out of my same-sex relationship. Out of my entanglements. Out of exile. I cried as if someone had just died. Gasping for air between sobs, I somehow believed that He was doing this not to kill me, but to revive me.

This time, I was not angry at God for His intrusion into my life. Somehow my soul was bursting with gratitude when He yet again offered Himself as the better allegiance. The pain of loss and her infidelity was still excruciatingly devastating. Betrayal shattered my illusions of perfection and forever. My heart felt torn apart and my body was in physical agony. Laying in the ashes of all I had built, hands empty, I had nothing. My entire world crumbled, flaming all the way to the ground. But in my lack I knew I had everything—a Father who willed my return, a Savior who paved the way, and the Holy Spirit who would guide my steps. I felt it all and wept in glorious thankfulness and deep heartache, both existing simultaneously. The pain and the gain felt the same in the moment, but for the first time I was not hopeless. All I knew for sure is that I was still His and that assurance was everything. I had never been more vulnerable, but it was a comfort to be so low because I could finally see Him as high. All powerful. Omnipotent. Kind. I could finally see myself as His daughter. I belonged to Him. And I wanted to remain! For the first time in over a decade, my heart miraculously melted. Jesus Christ was most near and felt most dear, which provided me with the hopeful realization that I would never be the same.

Ten minutes prior, I was blissfully unaware and hardened in my sin. I had sacrificed it all for her. I had not prayed in months, maybe years. But in those moments, I had never felt so loved by Jesus Christ, the one who sacrificed His very life to ransom my soul. My sexual and relational sin was a self-inflicted wound, one that Satan meant for destruction. Yes, this fresh cut caused by the loss of my fiancé was deep and painful, but given to me by a Great Surgeon. It was a wise and precise incision aimed at removing the cancer taking me to the grave. The triune God knows the outcomes of a lesbian lifestyle, and without the loving extraction given by His steady hand, I would still be dying on the inside.

All those years, when I thought I had permanently distanced myself from the Lord, He responded to my prayers just like He said He would. And not just those from the eleven years of my relationship, but ever since the first day of my life. God had listened to my prayers. He had heard my groaning. He had listened to the prayers of His people. His mission had never been bound by my rebellion. Or who I claimed to be.

His mission had never been bound by my rebellion.

Rather, in His own timing, Jesus Christ intervened in ways that were so specific to my situation. It was no coincidence. I had experienced a sovereign intervention. A kind devastation. A divine sabotage of evil.

GETTING IN

GETTING STUCK

GETTING OUT

The triune God renewed me and ministered to my heart as I wept salty tears. I did not know if I could ever get off the ground. It became clear that God had been orchestrating this specific rescue mission for years, priming me in my sin and preparing a soft place for me to fall. After a few hours of sobbing, the voice of the Holy Spirit instructed me, "No remnant." So I slowly stood up. The ground felt different. I dried my tears and immediately and obediently gathered every memento of my relationship and filled numerous bags, which I silently and unceremoniously placed in the trash. *No remnant.* I purged photos, jewelry, clothing, and cards. *No remnant.* Tossed rings and diamonds like common waste. *No remnant.* Deleted all contact information along with blocking numerous numbers for friendships I knew needed to be severed. *No remnant.* Over the course of that day, I collected a third of my lifetime and sent it away to be scattered in the dust and buried among the refuse at the local dump. *No remnant.* There would be no burn parties, no more undue honor for sin. There would be no attention given to the destruction of my sin's many evidences. There was no more time for that. Satan had already stolen so much. It was God's turn to rule. Without the load on my back or my box of evidence in my arms, I was free and He could begin to rebuild and restore.

Nature bent to God's command that week. He used that ice storm to rescue me, even though I had stopped asking Him to do so. He could have given me over to the idolatry of my heart. Until the day I died. I know the depths of my depravity during those years, such that I could never have chosen Him apart from His intervention. It was a long time waiting, but the time was appointed. That day, the triune God was too loving, obvious, and faithful to His promises for me to do anything but submit to His will. God demanded that I run to Him and

This rescue was not my salvation, but the evidence of it.

not look back. To fix my eyes on my Savior without glancing to the right or to the left. And I obeyed. The triune God proved again that He is my ultimate Rescuer pulling me up to life. Even today, I am awed by the weight of His grace. This rescue was not my salvation, but the evidence of it. *God has not left me after all!*

On this day, four years ago, God gave me something I desperately needed—hope. Hope that He is who He said He is. Hope that trusting Him would not lead to disappointment. Hope that He could do anything. Hope that He could heal my natural bents and change my affections for all sorts of wayward and lesser desires. Hope that I would be able to smile, laugh, and sing again. Hope that He would restore all the places I devastated. Despite the pain of that moment, I felt my heart strengthened as the Lord gave me the want to obey His will. He was actually changing my personal will! If God had done this miracle, I knew I could trust Him with whatever came next. Because as you know, there's always more.

WHAT'S ON THE TABLE

There is a parable of a great feast in Luke 15.[3] Jesus told this story to both the teachers of the Law and the tax collectors. One group wanted to hear what He had to say while the other group wanted Him silenced. The sinners were empty and hungry, the Pharisees were full yet starving. Knowing this, Jesus told the parable and set the table for them both.

There was a father who had two sons. One day the younger son went to his father and demanded his portion of the estate, which would have been dispensed upon his father's death. This shocking behavior meant that the son wished his father was already dead and wanted to walk away from everything with his hands full of his father's things. He wanted what was promised now. Graciously, the father agreed and divided his estate between his sons, permitting them to set

GETTING IN

GETTING STUCK

GETTING OUT

the course of their respective futures. The older son received the double portion and remained with this father, as he was responsible, hard-working, and loyal. In contrast, his younger brother took his share and set out for a far country to pursue every pleasure life had to offer.

The younger son wanted to be free, to live by his own rules and spend his father's wealth on what the world had to offer. Every inclination and desire he chased to its end, a spree with countless opportunity. He thought spending his inheritance on self-gratification promised great gain. Maybe he thought that diminishing and dismissing his father secured him successful independence? Whatever his mindset, it didn't take long for him to squander everything he had. Without provisions, he wound up broke, homeless, and starving. He would have continued until his heart ran out, but his provisions had disappeared. Out of desperation, he hired himself out to feed a local man's pigs hoping he might be able to eat some of the slop, but no one gave him anything.

Eventually, he came to his senses and decided to return to his father's home reasoning that even the lowest servant there had food to eat. He would suck up his pride and try to convince his father to receive him back as his slave. Maybe he could offer his father an exchange of his services for a place in his home? Never in his wildest dreams would he have guessed that his father had been watching for his return all along. As the son appeared in the distance, his father ran to him overwhelmed with compassion. And joy. The father threw his arms around his son, kissed him, and ordered a celebration in his honor. The son began what I'm sure was a long-rehearsed offer of penance and eternal servitude, but the father would not let him grovel for a second. For he was forever his son! The son found forgiveness and full restoration with his father. And he celebrated by consuming the meat, the wine, and the bread from the abundance of the father's table.

But the older son refused to celebrate. How could his father forgive such irresponsibility? His brother deserved discipline, not a feast! And why hadn't he ever been celebrated like this? After all, he wasn't the one who ran off and blew his inheritance. He was the good son. He was the one who stayed. Where was the gain earned by his adherence to the rules? The older son was angry and accused the father of doing wrong by him condemning his father's extension of unmerited favor to his brother. In response, the father implored his oldest child to come join them at the table reminding him that access to food and benefits was not the point. Rather, the son who was lost had been found. The dead had been made alive again! It was an event in need of celebration.

And this is where the story ends, hovering in celebration and anticipation. Did the older son ever humble himself and join the feast? Jesus never says, but the parable teaches us about the hearts of the sons and what it means to belong to the father. Both brothers despised their birthrights and what it required of them. They neither loved the father nor being their father's sons. They both wandered away because they were more interested in their father's possessions than a relationship with him. The younger demanded his inheritance and left, whereas the older expected unconditional tolerance from his father for his willingness to stay. But both sons took advantage of their father and in doing so they acted like many of us beloved daughters do today. I'm sure the Pharisees and tax collectors who heard Jesus Christ tell this simple parable caught its overt reference to the way they had been living in God's world.

Yet, the primary character in Christ's parable, as in all of Scripture, is the father. He's at the center of the story—not the sons. Not you. Not me. Knowing our sin, we have a Father who is willing to let our rebellion run its course, to hand us over to our preferences because only then do we realize what we have lost: We've left communion with the Father.

In terms of my own motivations, my pursuit of a same-sex partnership was a lot like that of these men. As the oldest sibling in my family, I can identify with the responsibility

GETTING IN

GETTING STUCK

GETTING OUT

of being the eldest. I was a hard worker, rule follower, and responsible, but as time ticked on I began to view myself as a slave to that role and grew angry with God for not giving me the gain I thought I deserved. I coveted the specific graces God gave to others. I became ungrateful and no longer recognized any good gifts from my proximity to the Lord. I only saw what He seemed to withhold. I had done it all right, but He never gave me a party. I loved God and resented Him at the same time. I didn't yet understand the sufficiency of my Father, the joy of His presence, or the security of proximity.

So I fled. I ran away with her to a distant country where I thought I could purchase the fulfillment I longed for. It was a place we both dreamed of where we would never again be bothered with thoughts of the Father. I played in that foreign land and organized my own parties for over a decade. I invested my birthright in our relationship claiming my unholy alliance as an entitlement for all I suffered. Defiantly and secretly, I rebelled against a seemingly slow, deaf Father who did not know the good gifts He ought to give His daughter. I built in the muck what I thought was sturdy and spent my returns without restraint. Soon, I felt broke though I had hands full of wages. Soon I felt homeless though I had a house with her. Soon, I was starving though I was full of every relational and sexual pleasure.

I don't know why God allowed me to do it. Perhaps He wanted me to experience the consequence of what I thought was right, to recognize the reality of my sinful choices. Or perhaps being lost on the wide roads would make me long for the narrow path. All I know is that only when I hungered could I remember the feast at home. When I was alone, I could still hear the voice of the Holy Spirit. When I was in bondage as a slave, I remembered I was actually free as a child of God. When I was happy, I wondered if I could be happier. Whatever the case, I found God the Father to be even better than the reflection of the one in Christ's parable because our heavenly Father is divine, not human. He is not anxiously awaiting an unknown outcome of our rebellion. He does not wonder if we will ever choose to return to Him. Our heavenly Father knows the end of all things and has the power to bring us home. He alone initiates our desires for Himself and the willingness to trek home. He is the only source that can cause us to choose Him and turn us back. He is omniscient, He is sovereign over our will. And when I repented, He did not condemn. Instead He was eager to forgive, full of compassion and kindness, and invited me *in* to celebrate my homecoming among the hosts and saints.[4] Our loving Father mercifully allows the famine of broken communion with Him that we might come to know the blessing of the feast.

Our heavenly Father knows the end of all things and has the power to bring us home.

For eleven years, two opposing affections waged war in my body. The first, for Jesus Christ. The second, for my girlfriend. Both promised freedom and both beckoned me to follow. One to eternal life now, the other to permanent death. I did not want to choose that which would bring me the fullest life possible, but Jesus Christ had already chosen me. It was not my love for Him that drew Him near, but God's great love for His own glory. That is what drove the Father to adopt me as His own and come after me repeatedly. And to change my desires. My movement toward Jesus Christ was only ever enabled by the Holy Spirit, I could not have chosen to return home on my own. The same is true for you. Rescue is more than common grace—it is the specific grace of a divine Father.

My dear sister, God the Father is inviting you in. His Son, Jesus Christ is the ultimate Rescuer. His Spirit's voice is an invitation into the embrace of the triune God who transforms us for His glory. But Jesus Christ also calls us outward to lives of holiness because our good God seeks to redeem us wholly. He can be trusted. Being in Christ is the only true freedom.

GETTING IN

GETTING STUCK

GETTING OUT

Today if you hear His voice, repent and come home to the table. For the Kingdom of God is here. And He is making all things new. God draws us in to lead us out.

RECEIVING TRUTH

Throughout the time I embraced lesbianism, I chose to exchange many things. I had consciously and unconsciously replaced all the pillars of my faith with prettier things. At I mentioned in Chapter Ten, they felt like worthwhile tradeoffs, but eleven years later my hands were empty. My idols and counterfeits had turned to bitter dust. One by one they disintegrated in my hands. That's when I rediscovered the power of the phrase, "But God." I had lost everything I held dear, *but God* had united me with Christ. He had not abandoned me. His consuming love was never bound by my will. His greater love always prevails. By grace, I was still alive and not dead in my sin. But God was not done. He had to reorient my beliefs about Him, the world, and me. If I was going to live with Jesus Christ, I was going to have to rightly rebuild what I destroyed starting with the foundation.

THE GREATEST EXCHANGE

When I finally faced the full reality of my brokenness, I realized the value of the greatest exchange you and I could ever know. The reality of the ultimate exchange is a vital understanding for Christians because it leads us to freedom. In the beginning, God created a place where He would dwell with us. Before we were alive to offer anything of our own, He designed us as His image bearers to share in the joy of the Godhead. And He was pleased with His creation. But part of reflecting God's image means possessing the capacity to choose, which also means possessing the capacity to rebel against Him, and that is what happened in Eden. Our first parents were deceived. They took of the forbidden fruit and in doing so introduced sin into the world leaving all of humanity in need of a perfect Savior to renew us and reorient us to what is true.

Being the gracious God that He is, the Father initiated the greatest exchange by giving His Son to humanity, as a fulfillment of all He promised to His people. God knew we would crucify Him. God knew His Son was the only perfect blood sacrifice and what His death would do for all humanity. Jesus was our substitute for the penalty our sin deserved. Jesus took the Father's just punishment that was meant for us.[1] Death. He satisfied justice for sin to create a way for us to return to God. To enter into His presence through the torn veil. Christ's resurrection from the dead is the guarantee that salvation is secure. He has paved the way back to our Creator. This was always the triune plan that we would get mercy instead of death. God redeems people in the greatest exchange. It's a win/win.

It's not that Jesus Christ just makes bad people good, He makes dead people alive.

Humans are always trying to avoid dying. Death is an intrusion, but for the believer God uses physical and spiritual death for His purposes of renewal. We are given life where once we were dead.[2] We get to dwell in the presence of God. We live forever even though we die. God initiates, accomplishes, and guarantees the exchange of imminent destruction for immediate life. As has been noted by many before me, it's not that Jesus Christ just makes bad people good, He makes dead people alive. That is what makes Him so great.

Understanding again the foundation of the Christian faith was necessary for me to begin restoring my relationship with Jesus Christ. The greatest exchange all happened at the cross and was applied when I believed in Jesus Christ as a five-year-old, not while sitting at my computer at thirty-three. By faith, my salvation was not at stake. Instead He gave me remembrance of its beauty, and it was more meaningful now than it had ever been before.

Christian faith in the gospel of Jesus Christ is always divine revelation, never something mustered. On our own we could never believe. The Holy Spirit illuminates our souls to the truth. By definition, God is beyond our understanding, but He is not unknowable because He has made Himself known to us through creation, His Son, and through Scripture. If I wanted to begin again the right way, I had to first start reading the Bible again, and believe that it was true, complete, without error, and actually for my good. I also had to pray. And listen. And obey. Illumination caused me to know I now had to tear down and re-form every single thing in my life. This time, I needed it all to be true. This alone is difficult work so instead of rebuilding it myself, I chose to receive the truth. I had to embrace the true Word spoken by God—the truth already proven faithful since creation. Receiving truth meant implementing His formation, not my own. My authority complex had to be laid down if I wanted the life His kingdom offers.

THE WIN

With salvation, we receive a future, but that does not just mean Heaven. This is a common misunderstanding and can lead to disillusionment. We do not become Christians to gain

GETTING IN

GETTING STUCK

GETTING OUT

everlasting life. For me, the idea of living forever in Heaven was not very compelling when compared to living with my girlfriend. In the throes of my sin, the thought of Heaven was never enough to compel me to stop and repent. And a lifetime with God sounded repulsive and boring. *I don't like God. Why would I want to hang out with Him forever?* Faithfulness to God should never hinge on the hope of receiving blessings in return. Even gifts like Heaven. Or healing. We don't initiate exchanges. We do not forfeit our sin in order to get stuff or receive all of His benefits. We do not wage war against our flesh to make demands of Him. The removal of same-sex affections, absence of wreckage, elimination of emotional dependency, the gain of relationships, gender restoration, physical healing, godly friendships, heterosexual affection, or biblical marriage—all of these are good, but they are not the aim of faithfulness. The fruit of the Spirit—love, joy, peace, patience, kindness, goodness, faithfulness, gentleness, and self-control—are good desires and godly outcomes of belonging to the vine and being in the Spirit, but outward evidence of obedience is not the goal either. We are called to desire something more.

We get God.

Jesus Christ alone is our aim. By faith, we gain a Savior. We get God. We receive the presence of God now and that is everything we need. He is what we gain in His exchange. Getting God is what makes Heaven and all of His benefits worth it. Subsequently, we do get

He is what we gain in His exchange.

life from certain death. We get a promised future along with hope for the present and redemption from our past. We get purpose and worth and identity. We get all the power that can transform and redeem, and we get all He offers to bring the most glory to His name. His presence in our life is worth desiring above all else. Nothing else matters, unless we get God.

I know this is difficult. We want guarantees in return for our offering, assurances of every kind, entire lists of specific protections, provisions, and promises beyond what we already have in the Bible. But God does not negotiate or barter with us. The greatest exchange is already completed in full. It is important to understand this reality so we can align ourselves with what is true. We did not participate in the greatest exchange, but it was achieved for us. Our only call is to believe it to the uttermost.[3] This step of belief may seem like a really low requirement and the benefit of God's presence may not feel compelling, but there is truly nothing greater. Getting the fullness of God is holy hedonism and wholly self-indulgent because He alone is most pleasurable, all sufficient, ultimately satisfying, forever eternal, and all that we need in this life and life to come. We must ask God for the power to believe that this is true.

We cannot set our hopes on what is not promised, but we can expect the extravagant. God is eager to overwhelm His children with blessings.[4] His grace is bountiful. His love for humanity overflows from the triune love of the Godhead. For His glory and our joy, He offers what will always be better. The pleasures of God are bigger than we can imagine, farther reaching than we can comprehend, different than expected, and more fulfilling than we can dream.

My friends, we do nothing in the great exchange, yet we get everything. He first loved us. We do not have the ability to choose God without the work of His Spirit in us. His sovereign grace initiates, produces, and finishes His work of salvation. He has allowed me to believe again that He is worth it. He can do the same for you. And He may choose to grant us great mercies of healing and the good gifts we seek, but if not, we must wrestle with the question, "Is He still worth it?" Are you willing to believe that getting God is more valuable than His benefits, sin,

We must ask Him for the will and the want to believe.

225

and earthly pleasure? Each of us must decide our answer to this question. We must ask Him for the will and the want to believe. The greatest exchange is the most important thing you can believe about God and it will determine the extent of your freedom and the level of your joy.

I AM FOR I AM

When the storyline that I trusted for a third of my life became untrue, I lost a sense of who I was. My "I am" statements—*I am happy, I am in control, I am at peace, I am who I am, I am one with her*—were proven to be a lie. They failed miserably. My identity had been aligned with who I was outside of God. I had been operating out of a functional system of relational security, sexual preferences, moral intuitions, and my union with her. So when it crashed and burned, I finally saw that all of my identity statements were temporal at best. They could change in an instant. I was not as immovable as I thought I was.

I really believed that my truth would never deceive me. *After all, I created it.* I was dependent on my false self remaining true all the time and the assurances of my storyline gave me comfort and power. I trusted me. And then I was betrayed by my own false confidences. I was also dependent on my same-sex affections remaining steadfast, but then they became the source of my most severe pain. And for a pain avoider like me, this was demoralizing. It was not her rejection that hurt the most. Rather, it was the reality that I knew I had chosen this path and pain and carnage resulted. At first, I was deceived and then I took the fruit with eyes wide open. It was my fault. My sinful choices and my preferences wounded me the most. And because my sin was sexual in nature, it hurt like hell—like someone being saved from hell, that is.

While deeply entangled in my relational and sexual brokenness, I had rejected God for refusing to change for me. But when He severed my sinful relationship, I grew desperate for His steadfastness. I needed to depend on God who never changed. I desired something secure and that is exactly what Scripture describes. Our triune God is always consistent in how He loves us—while we are *in* and while we are *stuck* and while we are *out*. The Lord never rejects His children. He never betrays them. He is never unfaithful. He always loves those who belong to Him.

Seeking to operate within my old identity with all its nuances turned out to be a disastrous endeavor. When God rescued me, I crumpled to the floor heaving tears heavy with both sorrow and joy. In my anguish, I finally did not have to be anything. I did not want to be anything. In that position, God got to be everything. I wanted Him to be everything. Desperately, I needed Him to tell me what was true. And He generously reminded me what He told Moses and what He has always revealed to the faithful men and women before me, "I AM who I AM."[5] God is all-sufficient and self-existent. God is omnipotent and unchanging. Inexhaustible. Infinite. He knows all things.

In my brokenness, I knew nothing other than the unchanging reality that pierced me to the core that day: who God is eternally. He is Love. He is the LORD. God re-opened my eyes in wonder to the great I AM and thus, He told me the truth about who I am. Only in His light could I rightly view myself. It was a great reversal of all the work I had invested into my personal identity and theology. But it was only when I believed what God said about Himself was the *truest*

> *It was a great reversal of all the work I had invested into my personal identity and theology.*

truth, did my faulty "I am" statements fail. I desperately wanted to trade them all in for what was real. It was then I could finally realize that the new identity I received at salvation was permanent, even in my wandering. My identity as "His"

GETTING IN

GETTING STUCK

GETTING OUT

daughter was secure, and now, most cherished. What I knew to be true in that moment and in the years since is that He is who He says He is. And I am His.

My new identity was not just static, but active. More than simply a new name, it came with the force of the divine—God is establishing His kingdom dwelling on earth and in me. His Spirit is always sanctifying me. Saved and always being saved. New and always being made new. Rescued and always being rescued. Freed and always being made free.[6] The one who initiated my dynamic salvation was warring for me.

When God exchanged His Son for our adoption, I got the great I AM. God tells us His personal name and exactly who He is in the Bible. And as I lay on my floor weeping over God's gracious rescue, I knew what I had to do next: I had to exchange my version of "I am" for the great I AM. All of me for all of Him. The Lord's "I AM" statements became my new foundation. When I was broken, they were all I could claim, all I could muster, and all I could trust. God deconstructed my entire world, my heart, my Castle, and everything that I had built to endure. He allowed sin to do what it does—destroy. All the former lies immediately felt painful. I hated them because of what they had done. I hated Satan for deceiving me. And in this revelation, I saw the great I AM as only good. And not evil or unkind like I had thought.

For His good pleasure, God accomplished the greatest exchange by granting me life in Jesus Christ, and the Creator was renewing me again. The Lord helped me to see God's "I AM" statements as glorious and worthwhile. Here are a few of Jesus Christ's "I AM" statements along with examples of how you can speak their significance to yourself:

I AM: THE LIVING WATER[7]

Jesus Christ is the wellspring of life, a fountain of living water. He is the sustainer of life and those who believe will not be thirsty, but satisfied for eternity by the sustaining power of the Holy Spirit.

I AM: THE MESSIAH[8]

Jesus Christ is the prophesied Messiah who has come from the line of Abraham to fulfill everything promised, reign as King, and offer redemption as the Savior of the world.

I AM: THE BREAD OF LIFE[9]

Jesus Christ is the most filling and needed provision. He meets my daily needs and I will not lack the things that bring life. God alone sustains me.

I AM: THE LIGHT OF THE WORLD[10]

Jesus Christ is light to my life and the lives of all humankind. In Him, there is no darkness at all. He brings light to my eyes and exposes the darkness of my heart.

I AM: THE GATE[11]

Jesus Christ is the door to salvation. The yonder gate on the narrow road. He invites, I knock, and He saves me when I enter His gate, which leads to His rest.

I AM: THE GOOD SHEPHERD[12]

Jesus Christ is the authority. He is good all the time. I belong to His flock and He shepherds me for my flourishing. He gave up His life so I could live without the penalty of death from my wandering.

I AM: THE RESURRECTION AND THE LIFE[13]

Jesus Christ has risen from the dead and sits on the throne at the right hand of God the Father. He is God's plan for granting the most satisfying life possible.

I AM: THE WAY, THE TRUTH, AND THE LIFE[14]

Jesus Christ is the only path to right standing with God. He tells the truth. Because He lives, He grants me everlasting life with God through faith in Him.

I AM: THE VINE[15]

Jesus Christ is the source of all spiritual fruit. He grafts me in and supplies me with life when I abide in Him. God reserves the right to cut off the branches that bear no fruit. There is life when the grafted branches remain in the vine through obedience.

The "I AM" statements of Jesus Christ should give us confidence in the unchanging nature of God the Father because Jesus Christ is the exact imprint of His nature. If we know what Jesus Christ is like, we know what the Father is like. And the Holy Spirit is sent to only speak their words. The Godhead does not change like shifting shadows.[16] He is consistent, always I AM.

God is the great I AM and He loves us enough to make that known. Growing in our knowledge of the I AM helps us to know who we are and who we are not. Once we understand more of who God is through His gracious self-disclosure in the Bible, we can begin to exchange our personal "I am" statements for the more accurate ones, the one's God speaks about us. Greater knowledge of God leads to greater knowledge of self. And vice versa. When we do this work, we further deconstruct the systems that we have built as foundations to our faulty storylines and false identities. Doing so allows us to adopt the true structure of God and His universe, always gaining confidence that His foundation is right and good.

When we believe what is true about God, we can begin to believe what is true about us. Furthermore, when we know who God is, we can admit with joy what we are not:

> I am not God. I am not the Christ. I am not infinite. I am not eternal. I am not in control. I am not perfect. I am not my own savior. I am not all-knowing. I am not the better rescuer. I am not the better friend. I am not the better lover. I am not my own. I am not destined to sin. I am not my own authority. I am not always right. I am not always good. I am not unchangable.

All of these are good news! They are not excuses, but proclamations we can make in light of the claims of the I AM. By believing in the greatest exchange, we trade in false claims of who we are for the true claims of God. We are His and not our own. All of this deconstruction of our false narratives builds up our true identity and is a work of ongoing discipleship in the Christian faith.

HE TAKES & HE GIVES

While living in my sin, I was full but I came back empty because I filled my life with the wrong things. I found happiness in worldly pleasures, but Satan is deceptive. Those years stole my life. When God came down and rescued me, He emptied me of myself. He demonstrated the benefits of His greatest exchange by again reminding me of my given inheritance: the righteousness of His Son for my unrighteous mess. God calls His children out of indwelling sin and into righteousness that gives life. But that does not mean life without loss.

When God caused my fiancé to breakup with me, He took away my relationship, which was neither the first nor the only grace He was willing to offer. God in His sovereignty had more in mind for my freedom. I just had no concept of what He planned to give and take. I was disoriented and could no longer discern up from down, let alone right from wrong. Every thought seemed fused together in a mess that I didn't have the strength or knowledge to separate. But God is faithful to reveal to each of us what is necessary for life and godliness.[17] He reorients us, opening our eyes to see what is good and bad—what leads to life or death. He opens His hands to give and to take. When God calls us out of our sexual and relational sin, He calls into something better. For His glory and our joy, He takes. And He gives.

God took "good" things from me *that were never actually good*, for His glory and my joy:

- My same-sex relationship
- My plans to be married and die with her
- My lesbian friendships associated with that life
- My sex life, romance, and best friend
- My emotional dependency
- My "I am" and "We are" statements
- My fantasies and dreams
- My eleven years of monogamy
- My Castle
- My worldly sorrow
- My Surface Idols
- My Source Idols
- My sleep-filled nights

God took bad things from me *that were always actually bad*, for His glory and my joy:

- My shame
- My guilt
- My pride
- My lies and my truth
- My chains
- My co-dependency
- My fear and anxiety
- My many deceptions and counterfeits
- My Lesbian Sin Cycle
- My requirements of Him
- My inferior coping mechanisms
- My worldview and mantra
- My anger, suspicion, and hatred of Him
- My need to prove myself and my storyline
- My heart of stone

God has given good things to me *that are always actually good*, for His glory and my joy:

- His presence
- Hope
- His forgiveness
- His peace
- His promises
- His rest
- "His" identity
- His right-standing and eternal security

- Happiness and joy
- His army of angels
- His family of redeemed men and women
- Reconciliation with friends, family, and the church
- Inter-dependency with a few trusted Christians
- A state of gratitude
- Knowledge and belief in the sufficiency of Christ
- Reorienting right belief about who God is
- Rest-filled days and nights

God has given "bad" things to me *that are never actually bad*, for His glory and my joy:

- Tears and brokenness
- Exposure of my sin
- Awareness of my fragility
- Dependence on Jesus
- Vulnerability with God and His people
- A covenant community of faith
- Ability to feel pain and grief over my sin
- Guilt leading me to Jesus Christ
- An ongoing thorn in my flesh to push me to Himself
- Books, blogs, sermons, podcasts, and articles about same-sex attraction
- Parachurch ministry same-sex attraction guidance
- His design for sexuality
- Willingness to submit to His authority
- A changeable nature
- A new foundation
- The covering of my church leadership

- Godly sorrow
- A heart of flesh
- The promise that I get God
- Ultimate truth and ultimate authority of the Godhead
- His "I AM" Statements
- His presence
- The haunting of the Holy Spirit

God takes what is harmful and gives to us what is helpful in order to lead us into the fullest life possible. Where we can be healed. It often feels upside down when God takes and gives, but it is the way we move forward as part of His kingdom—a kingdom that is actually right-side up. The Lord is specific to each of us in what He gives and takes and while some exchanges are scary and others long awaited, they are all meant for our good.

As we pursue holiness, we are called to make many changes and holy exchanges and warned about the dangers of falling away. But one truth remains constant: we are children of God. Our birthright is everlasting. His love is steadfast and He preserves our identity in Him. That exchange is forever. My friend, receive the truth. I pray that the Holy Spirit will grant you comfort and bring light to your eyes in the struggle to see God in the way He describes Himself in the Bible. So we can see ourselves as we truly are.

GETTING IN

GETTING STUCK

GETTING OUT

QUESTIONS

1 What do you gain in God's greatest exchange?

2 In choosing to surrender and walk in sexual and relational holiness, what **losses** and **gains** do you consider compelling?

3 What are some examples of deconstruction that would have to happen in your personal theology, identity, and worldview in order for you to receive the truth about who God is, who you are, and what He says about human flourishing?

HIS RECONCILIATION

I was pretty quiet in the weeks following His rescue. I was awestruck by His manifestation and humbled so profoundly that I didn't have words for much. I listened to the Lord a lot. I was also just completely undone and aching. I had tears and groans, but this time I was on my face and grateful.

My first honest conversation with anyone post-rescue was both unplanned and unexpected. It came a few weeks after the ice storm during a visit from my brother, Luke. He could tell I had grown fragile and distraught over something. All it took was for him to ask me how I was doing and I broke down completely, sobbing with the waves of emotion that had become so familiar to me. I collapsed into his arms and confessed everything, bawling throughout. Luke held me tight for a long time and told me that he loved me, even though I had deceived him for eleven years. Even though I was no longer seen as the perfect older sister I longed to be.

Before God rescued me, I imagined a much different conversation with Luke, one in which I shared my upcoming marriage. While the news was sure to be heartbreaking, I banked on the fact that he would love me despite my maintaining a same-sex relationship. My romantic choices had forfeited many other relationships, but I counted on my family's continued love in spite of my trades. Instead, God led me down a better path, that of repentance. The Lord inspired in me a godly sorrow that told the truth and invited help, which started the process of relational healing. Over the next weeks and months, my brother regularly checked in on me offering daily encouragement, prayer, and a listening ear. But above all, he was present. Despite the confusion and hurt caused by my sin, God began to strengthen what I planned to break.

After confiding in Luke, I knew I had to tell the rest of my family. I couldn't require my brother to keep my secret. *No more secrets!* God was asking me to be obedient and trust Him with the next step to restore all that I had broken. I needed my family to know so that I could celebrate God's grace with those I loved the most. Also, I was broken enough to know I couldn't make my way forward alone. So I met with my parents about two weeks after my conversation with my brother, warning them up front that I had a hard story to share, but one with a good ending.

As a thirty-three-year-old adult, I humbled myself and I confessed to my parents my years of deception, my bitterness and angst, and my attempts at baiting them into anger against God. I told them about my best friend and my resulting same-sex attraction. I told them about my eleven-year partnership and how God had dramatically rescued me, having remained faithful to me despite my unfaithfulness to Him. Going in, I wasn't sure what to expect in terms of how they would respond, but my parents listened intently and lovingly with faces reflecting neither shock nor horror. When I finished, my dad's first words were filled with both compassion and hope: "You are now going to walk with a limp." Reaching for his Bible, he began to list examples of well-known biblical figures and their stories:

"You are now going to walk with a limp."

"David sinned greatly against the Lord, and God chose to use him in great ways. Abraham sinned greatly against the Lord, and God choose to use him in great ways. Paul sinned greatly against the Lord and God chose to use him in great ways."

He did not let even a moment pass before reminding me that men and women throughout the Bible committed grievous sin against God and the Lord consistently redeemed them for His great and mighty name. God restored them not for proof, but for His divine and ageless purposes. With every proclamation of freedom, my mom nodded in agreement. Their response modeled God the Father for me in a way that I will never forget. In the days after, they acknowledged the hurt my confession caused and shed tears as they tended to aches outside of my presence—they are human, after all—but they spoke only words of redemption to me in that moment. And every moment since. Without hesitation, they welcomed me to back to the table and forgave me for my wandering.

As we talked, they shared that they had been praying for my return for years. Though I had never physically left, they felt as though I was living my life in a distant country. Because that's exactly what I had done. All of the bitterness I had stored up against the Lord beginning with what I perceived to be His absence of care toward my family came full circle. Somehow, Jesus Christ miraculously eradicated my bitterness, not through answering my specific life-long prayers for financial provision for my family, but by showing me His true character in a completely different scenario. He had never been distant or evil. Rather, He was just and merciful. He had graciously attended to the prayers of my parents, even before I was born, but in His own ways and timing. He had heard and He had shown His kindness to all of us—in this situation and in so many more that I was beginning to recognize. *I can see that even His common grace is specific!* This provision was different, but better than any I could have prayed for or imagined.

My parents committed to walk the road toward healing with me and they have done just that as I have mourned and celebrated each step. The day after our conversation, I told my sister, Desiree, and she became a wonderful encourager and the best shoulder for months of my ugly cries. She listened and spent lots of time with me. In spite of my concerns, my family welcomed me home. Without disgust. Without rebuke. Without fear. They were eager to participate in the ways God was restructuring my world. To this day, they continue to be one of God's greatest gifts to me. They covered me in gospel reminders as I faced each new day at a time attempting to pursue holiness with a broken heart and a contrite heart.

Remember that random new friend I met at the gym six months prior? Well, I knew I needed healthy Christian friendships with females, so I met with her for a beer and told her everything. Apparently, I wasn't as mute and aloof as I had appeared in our small group study. She became someone I could call or text anytime I was distraught or lost or confused or tired in my exodus. We'd workout at the gym and pray out loud on the elliptical. She reminded me of the gospel constantly, sent me Scripture and sermons, and became someone and some place where I could be vulnerable and safe and encouraged. I also joined a running club with two women who were Christians. I told them all the same things. There is something about training and talking, physical discipline and faith that helps me persevere. One month after my breakup, the three of us signed up for a marathon and so on most days when I couldn't get out of bed and could only cry all day, they'd get me out and allow me to cry while I ran. They listened and proclaimed truth over us on our routes. For four months, we trained for hours each day, growing in strength through repetition, tears, and fatigue. Together we shared words of hope and words for the wind. It was sweet running that race with my sisters in Christ. Their ministry of presence helped me run and finish the marathon and also experience the presence of God through all of it.

In the six months following my breakup, I also felt compelled by the Spirit to seek forgiveness from the three women who had encouraged me from the beginning: Stella, Chelsea, and Katelyn. As much as it stung at the time, they loved me enough to tell me the truth about my choices and followed the biblical pattern of loving a sister by confronting unrepentant sin. And this trio became casualties of my rebellion. A few years had passed since I had seen or talked to any of them so they were rightfully hesitant at my invitations to meet. But each of the women accepted and took the time to hear what I had to say. I went into each meeting with only the expectation that I would confess and ask for forgiveness. They had no duty to forgive me and I couldn't demand that of them.

> *As much as it stung at the time, they loved me enough to tell me the truth about my choices.*

Yet to my surprise each listened tearfully as I shared the long-awaited story of God's rescue. Tears of joy and godly sorrow still flowed down my face as I spoke about God's pursuit of me even when I resisted Him believing that He was evil and had handed me over to Satan forever. I thanked Stella, Chelsea, and Katelyn for taking the hard, narrow road of biblical truth-telling and for desiring my holiness over relational tranquility. And for praying for me. Together. I named the specific sins I committed against each of them and asked for their forgiveness. And they swiftly forgave. Katelyn went so far as to say she had already forgiven me years prior during my church discipline meeting. God has fully restored these three friendships—an incredible testament to His mercy in healing the wounds I caused with my sin. And today, we travel the world together, drink good wine, and recount what God has done in all of us. We choose to stay close as a reminder of God's mercy and as an encouragement that Christ is trustworthy.

GETTING IN

GETTING STUCK

GETTING OUT

After confessing to my family and my trio of friends, I felt the Holy Spirit leading me to pursue reconciliation with my church. I needed to repent and rebuild my relationships with the pastors and leaders involved with counseling me in the months leading up to my church discipline. The pastor I met with prior to my mediation meeting had taken a new position at a different church, but he still agreed to meet with me. Once again, I felt unsure about how he would respond, but as I shared all that Jesus Christ had done he celebrated with me through tears, knowing the long and narrow path required for a daughter to return to her Father from years of pursuing same-sex attraction. Today, this pastor has become a dear friend and I am grateful for the compassion and steadfast love he modeled, even though I had initially rejected it all.

The rest of the individuals who were involved with my discipline were still a part of my church. By then, I had returned and begun faithfully attending services for about a year, though I still felt uncertain as to whether or not I was welcome in the gathering. I also carried with me traces of bitterness over how my situation was handled, but I knew that God was asking me to humble myself and seek reconciliation. *No remnant.* It was time for me to be known in the light rather than remaining in the shadows of a back-row pew. After much time and reflection, I reached out and made formal appointments with the pastor and mediator who were involved with my church discipline. Going into that meeting, I resolved to share with them how God had graciously rescued me. I hoped they would allow me back as a member of the church, but even if they said no, I wanted them to know how God had graciously rescued me. If nothing else, I prayed my story would encourage them in the fact that they had played a hard and important role in what God was doing in my life.

Again, the Lord was merciful and each of them forgave me for the damage I had caused. Even more, they humbly asked for my forgiveness—not for the discipline itself, but for its rough edges. I gladly forgave them. Years before, I faced these men with a hardened heart having no intention of leaving behind my same-sex commitments, but now they celebrated my healing with me. Soon after, I was restored to membership at my church, which continues to be a place for me to learn about our God, struggle for obedience in all areas of life, and worship together with the saints.

GETTING IN

GETTING STUCK

GETTING OUT

BATTLING FOR WISDOM

As God awakens our souls to renewed hope in Christ, we want to cross the finish line jubilant. Eyes bright and hands raised in victory clutching the promises we have carried with us along the way. Doing so requires wisdom. Wisdom for healing and wisdom for how we are to walk. Setting out on a new path will introduce plenty of unknowns, but we have an assured win in our Savior. In this chapter, I want to share the wise counsel I've received as well as offer some guidance from my own exodus out of a lesbian lifestyle. I want to share practical advice with you, my fellow traveler, so that you, too, can get out. It's a battle to make our paths level by enacting wisdom, but it is worth it. The narrow road ahead has been travelled and charted. It's a specific path. It leads into the life God desires for you. And you are not alone.[1]

THE FEAR OF THE LORD

Gaining wisdom is of primary importance in the Christian life and it starts with the fear of the Lord. We need a right reverence toward His holiness as well as His power over creation. We must know what it means to bow in awe to His authority, as it positions us rightly to receive what He offers. When we fear the Lord, we will live within His ways, which is why fear of the Lord is the beginning of wisdom.[2] God grants His wisdom to all who ask without conditioning His offer on our past or the dust of idols on our hands.[3] But it does not happen through divine download. Rather, God has given us prayer and His Word as well as the Holy Spirit who enables us to embrace it faithfully. Let go of everything else. Sell whatever you need to get wisdom.[4] There is nothing more valuable.

It's a funny thing how fearing the Lord will drastically change your life. Sure, emerging from traumatic long-term sin requires a lot of processing and healing, but right worship transforms options that seemed hopeless before. When my engagement fell apart, I knew I needed help. *So you know what I tried this time?* The exact same things I did before.[5] The spiritual disciplines I shared about in Chapter 9. But this time around, I came without expectations on how God should behave. I was not demanding God to act according to my will. This time, I was desperate for Him to lead the way. My heart was flesh, no longer stone cold. My hands were empty and outstretched. *Anything Lord! I must have life!*

Everything I tried before—prayer, church, Scripture memory, counseling, Bible study, recovery groups, Christian books, accountability— were hindered because I was clinging to a lover and a lifestyle with expectations for how God should act and reward my obedience. I didn't want to be wholly holy. I wanted a peaceful path that would allow me to carry two competing loves in my heart. Those tools of righteousness were not faulty before. My heart was the problem. So without shame, I returned to the very things I did in the beginning. Obedience brought about different results this time, even though the remedies I sought did not change. He even used what I did learn in those years but could not yet believe, to ignite my love for God. No longer did I have a weight tied around my neck, my tail between my legs, my nose in the air, or an idol in my hands. After God opened my eyes, I prayed a lot. I repented. I started reading the Bible again. I went to counseling. Everything changed. No longer was I expecting to be healed by my moral lifestyle or find lasting comfort in the approval of others. Instead, I relied on God's grace to heal me and to empower my living according to His original design. Doing so brought me so much rest, but it required my active participation. It is wise to employ the tools of sanctification.

We are not healed through indifference. We have to constantly repent of what is wicked and turn to pursue the things that God created us to enjoy. Things that terminate on worship of the Son. True repentance can work itself out in many ways. Whether through tears and groaning or grins and praise, the spectrum of transformation is not bound by appearances. God designed you in a specific way and there is nothing that demonstrates Jesus Christ's redemptive work more than what He accomplishes in your heart, which inevitably produces spiritual fruit. It is wise to look for fruit from the vine and the evidences of a transforming will.

RELATIONAL HEALTH

Along this journey, I have learned that I need fellow travelers, those who will war with me and for me. That has been a journey in itself because my sin centered on a relationship, which warped the way I saw so many of my other relationships from friendships to my own family. The same is true for anyone deciding to battle their same-sex attractions. Wisdom must inform the kinds of people we pursue and God generously gives it to those who ask. As you resolve to fight for victory, you will need others to help you along the way, which at times will require being vulnerable with new people, reconciling with God's people, and other times will mean leaving behind those relationships that continue to pull you back into the muck of sin.

Our God is a reconciling God, which is why He sent His Son into the world to reconcile us to Himself. We are to go and do likewise, to be like Christ and model the same restorative love of God. Pursuing healing requires that we first must go and be reconcilers as evidence of our reconciliation with the Father.[6]

HEALTHY, SAME-SEX FRIENDSHIPS

Despite struggling with female same-sex attraction, it is essential to continue to seek out and form healthy same-sex friendships. Satan's strategy is to keep us fearful and isolated, but do not fall for his traps. After my engagement fell apart, I was wary of making new female friends, especially when it came to Christians. I didn't handle those relationships well in prior years and I wasn't sure how people would react if they heard my story. I was afraid of their response. *Will they fear me? Can they ever believe me again? Can I hug friends without being watched? Am I allowed to have a roommate?* But I was also afraid of myself. *Will I become emotionally dependent? Will I seduce them, drag them in, and begin the cycle all over again?* From the start, I felt the pull toward judging others and believing myself unchangeable. But those were nothing more than the same lies from Satan to keep me alone.

At times, I also felt shame because I began to think that wanting and needing to have close female friends was somehow sinful for me now. I had a hard time distinguishing my desires between wanting to connect in a healthy way with another female or if I was wanting to make it an exclusive friendship. I was tempted to choose isolation because it seemed easier, no one would question me, and I wouldn't question myself. However, relational starvation is never smart. Loneliness can make us long for what is old and familiar and many times it causes us to repeat the cycle. The truth is that connecting and feeling close to women is a legitimate need and a longing that God has placed in our hearts. Where it goes awry and becomes sinful is when these longings or desires become ultimate and we think the only way to meet those needs is in a sexual or romantic relationship. Or an emotionally dependent one. We must pray that God brings us a few Christian women for healthy friendships and that He blesses them in a holy way.

Building a crew of a few will help you guard against your former unhealthy ways. Start by looking for healthy same-sex friendships with Christian women in church or through a Bible study—especially environments that invite accountability and transparency. Then go out for margaritas. Choose a place where you feel comfortable: a lake, a patio, or a dinner table. Wherever it starts, healthy intimacy with others in the body of Christ helps us experience the transformative power of God's grace. These kinds of friendships restore laughter, connection, and hope. They also keep us connected to Jesus Christ and His church and prompt opportunities to replace our old life with better things.

I also had to fight the lie that I required sameness in friendships—that a friend had to mirror me exactly in terms of our loves and brokenness. I had been attracted to these types of women and believed that sameness was the only way to be known and understood. It was easier to reject what I didn't understand. However, I have learned from, laughed with, and been humbled by women who are not like me. I've been heard and understood by women who have other strengths and interests. There can be beauty in friendships based on the celebration of difference.

Healthy intimacy helps us experience the transformative power of the grace of God and risk is part of the process. Don't get discouraged if you share with someone and they do not have a great response. Keep praying. Keep looking. Keep trying. It's humbling and scary to start over, but the Lord will replace what is old with something new in its place.

GETTING IN

GETTING STUCK

GETTING OUT

Friendships help you persevere in your faith. It is wisdom in action to pursue healthy, same-sex relationships with fellow believers.

I also had to completely change the way I thought about men. Ultimately, I had indicted their value based on what I thought were insurmountable differences between women and men. When I came to know and believe that humans—both women and men—are created in the image of God, I realized we are of the same essence. There will always be more that unites us than differentiates us.[7] We are bone-of-bone and flesh-of-flesh. Men and women are made same-of-the-same. God formed humankind in His image. He created gender with equal dignity and worth. He made us with needs. It was before the Fall that God said it was "not good" that man was alone and so He created woman to partner with man. Their union was exactly how God designed it. It was "very good." God designed males and females to unite together as one in equal and distinct ways. To flourish. To be a shadow of Christ's union with the Church. To fill the earth and subdue it. To join together in the gospel. To be friends. To be brothers and sisters in the family of God. To make disciples. To be fruitful together in all sorts of ways. I learned it's by design that men and woman are not identical and I should not reject them for not conforming to my likeness.

It is very good that men and women are made to reflect the same image—God's likeness—and that we have the same God-given purpose for our lives. When I saw this deepest possible sameness for the first time, I was shocked. I could begin to gladly divest from the gender disparity and superiority I had felt for so long. Whether or not I would ever feel attracted to men had no impact on the reality of our same nature. I could still value God's design and the unity and partnership required for flourishing.

You will need healthy same-sex relationships as you decide to fight against your wayward affections. Maybe you're like me and some friends will come through reconciling your past. If not, find new ones. I did that too. Believers are everywhere, in your church, your gym, your workplace, on hiking trails, and in your neighborhood. Ask the Lord and He will be faithful to show you strong and godly women who can travel alongside you. Then take the risk of inviting them in. By God's grace, the risk will be worth the reward.

SEPARATE

While it's important to build healthy friendships, it's also crucial to cut off those that cause you to long for your old life. I had to do a lot of separating to get untangled. Freedom requires removing not just our girlfriend or the women we lust after, but also their friends and families. Or the communities we participated in. Maintaining proximity to known temptation will do nothing but hinder victory. Obedience to Jesus Christ reorders how we love others and sometimes it looks like letting them go. Do not mistake God's call for reconciliation for an excuse to enter back in and make peace with sin. That is not admirable; it is dangerous. It does not always require meeting up with old connections to get "closure." Sometimes God simply tells us to flee.[8] There is no neutral ground in the midst of a war. Drive out whatever tempts you to return to your former life.

It's possible that separation may take on an even more serious form than leaving a friendship. God's call for holiness may require leaving your same-sex marriage. If so, it will be tempting to weigh your fear of the fallout against the implications of continuing in your sin. When God calls us to separate, it can be easy to focus on the pain that would come to your wife or to any children or extended family involved. And there will be pain, but it cannot compare to the destruction of your own soul. Or the implications on theirs. The consequences of separation cannot compare to the surpassing benefits of your restored relationship with Jesus Christ.

You cannot stay in a place that God has called you out of.

There is no virtue in remaining faithful to an unholy marital vow. Doing so will ensure lifelong bondage for your soul, as well as those you drag into your imprisonment. Others' view of God is harmed when you mar His image. Embracing what God hates is to continue in rebellion and you will not be able to see Him clearly or have peace until you put to death all that stands in the way of your relationship with Him. The most loving thing you can do is get out.

You cannot stay in a place that God has called you out of.

God has made it clear that He designed marriage to exist between one man and one woman as a shadow of Christ's relationship to the Church.[9] A same-sex relationship or marriage can never be holy or redeemed because it is inherently broken. Nowhere in the Bible are homosexual relationships approved or established by God. Homosexual union does not honor the Lord. In fact, it warps a right understanding of Him. Homosexuality rejects God's design and founds itself on a fundamental disdain for the King, His love, His knowledge, and His authority over all things. Any "blessings" we claim from homosexual union are misunderstood. Don't attribute benefits to sin. Sin will never be okay. Or worth it. Nothing about sin itself can be redeemed, but by grace through faith a person can be. You can be free. The cross confirmed it. Align yourself with truth. You *can* abandon an unholy covenant that you made with an unholy vow. Divorce yourself from sin and be united with Christ.

DATING & MARRIAGE

So let's clear the air: the primary goal of victory in Christ is also not to begin dating, fall in love with, and marry a man. Heterosexual marriage is not the goal. Holding up examples of same-sex attracted women who now have loving heterosexual marriages is certainly cause for celebration, but it is not always helpful. At least it wasn't for me. Biblical marriage is good, but it is not ultimate. A romantic relationship with a man doesn't have to be your aim or expectation and it is not essential to full healing or even to experiencing the fullness that life has to offer. Birthing a slew of children is not God's highest calling on the life of a Christian woman. It is beautiful and honorable, but it is not ultimate. Jesus Christ may restore to you a desire for men—or maybe just one man. He may make a way for you to enter into a godly, heterosexual marriage. He may bless you with children. Or He may not. No matter what happens, God is not withholding from you. The Father is granting you what is best for your sanctification and His glory. Sometimes the gift we receive is not the one we want or expect, but it will always be what we need most.

Furthermore, a same-sex attracted woman who is married to a man is not necessarily more healed than one who remains single. You can experience full healing and the brilliance of union with Christ without the shadow. You can have true victory and joy outside of romance, sex, and marriage. I'm still single and I testify that I have never been freer and healthier than I am today. Jesus Christ and His church—of which I am a part—are beautiful to me. I am not missing anything essential to the fullness of life that God offers us. So be careful about upgrading Christ's call to faithfulness with any model—it is unwise and unhelpful. And this should free you up tremendously! Restoration and healing are evidenced in a million different ways. God has a unique call for you to be holy in your station. Single or married. As an attorney or an artist, an ambassador or a mom, you are called to model Christ in all that you do. Do not set your sights on something that is neither eternal nor what God has promised. You can trust Him with your longings. You can trust Him with your fears. You can trust him with your remaining years. You can trust Him with the rest.

GETTING IN

GETTING STUCK

GETTING OUT

APPROPRIATE CIRCLES OF DISCLOSURE

Pursuing recovery requires wisdom. While you will need supporters who will encourage you and keep you accountable, you shouldn't feel the need to disclose your story to everyone you come across. You need to pray and ask the Lord for wisdom. Though people need to know, not everyone needs to know. Beyond those immediate relationships that require reconciliation, like family and close friends, it is best to seek direction from the Lord. Jesus Christ calls us to vulnerability so we can be loved well and bolstered in faith in the process of sanctification. Yet some spaces are more appropriate for sharing than others.

Therapy is an extremely appropriate place to pursue healing. I strongly recommend finding a biblical counselor skilled in issues like trauma, crisis, divorce, infidelity, emotional dependency, and same-sex attraction. Ask your church for a list of recommendations and do your own research. Beware, not every Christian counselor or biblical counselor will encourage you to find your identity in Christ. Some elevate attraction and a celibate gay identity above everything else. It is vital that you find out what a Christian counselor believes about the issue of same-sex attraction and what their approach will be. Pray for the Lord to lead you to the right person and tell them everything you can. Then, keep going back. Pay the money. Reliable biblical counselors are trained to help you navigate both sin and celebration, lament and joy, healing and freedom. The body and the soul. The consistency creates a reliable structure while you find additional advisors to join your circle.

The brokenness we've experienced in homosexuality requires our vulnerability as we war for holiness. People need to know. That doesn't mean every conversation should involve discussing your struggle, but accountability is essential. When I have something hard to share, I've made a rule for myself. I always tell at least two people, from at least two different circles of same-sex friendships and perhaps with trusted men in my life. Choosing new behaviors that derail exclusivity and secrets helps me stay relationally healthy. I can tell my counselor, my Bible study leader, my parents, my pastors, and my Christian friends. I give each one the same access, the same ability to speak into my life.

From day one, I had to learn what it meant to be wise about sharing my intimate struggles with people around me. When I am tempted to stay silent, it's often the case that I need to be honest with someone. When I am tempted to word vomit, I pause to consider speaking slowly or not at all. For some, it may be best to share your story on a "they need to know" basis, or a "I need to tell them" basis, as the Lord leads you to do so. I'm still working on this, but regardless of the situation I have found that praying and asking God to introduce me to trustworthy Christians with a biblical worldview is a practice that I must embrace even when it's scary and uncomfortable. It's vital to confide in people who embrace Jesus Christ as Lord and the Bible as authoritative so that they constantly point your gaze back to the Savior and His words. Those kinds of friends will be willing to draw you out when you need to share your struggles, but they will also be wise enough to know that they cannot be your savior.

These days, the idea of being "raw" and "vulnerable" is often emphasized as a crucial part of accountability. While such a posture is important, it still requires wisdom. Not everything is meant for corporate consumption and you are not required to purge your deepest hurts and struggles to people you don't know or in an assigned small group. Not everyone is trustworthy or equipped to handle rightly the details of your experience. And not everyone is relationally or spiritually healthy. Christians or not, some people can be prone to respond without mercy and others offer cheap grace which is not grace at all. Neither is appropriate. Offering no compassion or extending easy comfort by affirming lawlessness will both quench the Spirit and disregard godliness. Neither should be in your circle of advisors.

Additionally, it's probably not the best idea for you to seek out someone who also struggles with same-sex attraction for one-on-one support, or have others refer their struggling friends to you for counsel and accountability. As I mentioned previously, start with a trained biblical counselor or recovery ministry. Your struggle will not surprise the wise. Speak with a Bible study leader, a parent, or a pastor. They may suggest that you speak to someone else with more experience in the areas you struggle in. That's okay. Take them up on their recommendation and put your hope in Jesus Christ.

We cannot be healthy in isolation. Seclusion and secrets cannot produce spiritual health. It's wise to include a few strong believers in your inner circle, those who know the most sensitive parts of your story. I can't tell you the degree to which God will ask you to share your story, but I know for certain that you need to share it. The size and scope of disclosure requires wisdom, but it does not determine your capacity for healing. Inviting people into your struggle is often a messy process. It will not always be easy and may even be met with opposition at times. Or hurt. Don't let difficulty keep you from pursuing reconciliation and healthy relational intimacy. But do not give up as you seek out solid believers to be part of your appropriate circle of disclosure. Silence will always limit your ability to thrive. The Lord will bring safe people to surround you. If you meet pain or disappointment along the way, keep praying and watching. The Lord always sends faithful saints to light the way.

THE TABLE

Throughout history, men and women of faith have committed all manner of sin only to experience God redeem their weakness for His glory. The Lord asks for us to obediently seek reconciliation where we have caused wounds. While doing so may not always mend the cracks in those relationships, it will mean walking in faithfulness to the Lord and He will provide for you every step of the way.

Your story with your family and friends may not look quite the same as mine. Many have experienced the opposite reaction to the one I received. If that's the case for you, don't lose heart. Remember that Christ accepts your repentance because He already reconciled you to Himself. In the midst of seeking a faithful crew, the Father always receives you with open arms and an invitation to return home to His feast. Just like the father of the two sons in Jesus Christ's parable, God's loving kindness leads us to repentance and a seat at His table.

That's why God has given us His presence and His people—to preach this gospel as a means of encouragement and edification. Turn to Jesus Christ and find a place in His local church. Pursue healthy relational intimacy. Do not stay silent. Partake of the Lord's table—a foretaste of the kingdom. Pray for provision and surround yourself with believers who will point you to the Son, those willing to empathize with your pain and provide support on the way to healing. Ask God to show you wise and grace-filled believers who will champion your faith in the good times and listen to your doubts when the days are hard. Befriend the "dangerous" ones, the ones who will hunt you down if you begin to wander away.

Gather the saints around you and struggle well. The *place* God has given us on earth is with the people of God. Though we are strangers to some and dispersed around the globe, God continues to gather for Himself a people, a nation, a priesthood, and a family. He has done this for us because He knows humans are deeply relational—just like the Godhead. So as we go, we must join in with the family of God in His church. Because He is doing a work among "us" first and in "me" second, we can rightly look up and around for hope. Especially when we are positioned rightly. The Lord has given His people to help us persevere when we've lost our way. They are not naïve to the human plight. You may be surprised how many others have lived a similar story. We grow in confidence in the Lord as we hear the stories of how God is establishing

GETTING IN

GETTING STUCK

GETTING OUT

His kingdom on earth in us and through us, despite us. And ultimately, we are called to join with the people of God today as a rehearsal for eternity. Because one day, when we are feasting at the Father's table, we will not be sitting alone with God. We will be celebrating together among all the saints! Toasting to the King for the glory He got through our stories. It will be the greatest regathering of the people of God that we will ever experience. Victory will be ours!

Your circle will be dear as you pursue the goal of your salvation. Seek out those who are willing to learn, listen, interfere with your status quo and who bravely share their scars in hopes that others will be healed. Those are your people. They are not that hard to find if you know what you're looking for. They're the ones who walk with a limp.

QUESTIONS

1 What posture precludes gaining wisdom? Where is true wisdom found?

2 How should godly wisdom inform your thinking and your life in each of the five relational health topics below:

Healthy Same-Sex Friendships

Separate

Dating and Marriage

Appropriate Circles of Disclosure

The Table

3 What are some spiritual habits and practices that you have given up on that you believe the Lord is asking you to re-implement as you seek to walk in sexual and relational holiness? How might they help stir your affection for God?

HIS RESTORATION

Rescue and reconciliation were God's mercies to me. And yet there was more rebuilding to be done. Once my foundation was renewed and reinforced, the Lord's aim was always to restore. And I knew my brokenness enough to know that restoration was not just going to mean that I get to check out for a few weeks and return to some great reveal of beauty. Instead restoration was going to be a laborious and glorious reversal. I would be involved in the work. There'd be sweat. And more tears. Sanding and grinding and chipping. It's demo. It's design. It's rebuilding. It's adorning. The purpose: Not for me to create something new, but for God to restore His image to how it was in the beginning.

Early on, after I made the commitment to follow Christ—again—and war with my sin, a friend of mine told me to expect what she called a "Year of Firsts." She said that it would take courage, a whole lot of Jesus, and good wine. And she was right. The first year after Jesus Christ led me out of my same-sex relationship was beautiful and hard. My first holidays, birthdays, and anniversaries came around with feelings of nausea and heartache. Even normal Tuesdays, weekends, or social media throw backs threatened to lay me out. I cried through most church services. I cried when I was alone. I cried during celebrations. It was really, really difficult. I felt like I was going through a terrible divorce and only my close friends and family knew—the ones in my inner circle whom I had entrusted with my story. I had a hard time sleeping and waking up. Each day brought the realization that my bed was empty and my phone was silent.

But that first year was sweet. And not even just in hindsight. I knew its abundance in the moment as well. Each day, I felt free of shame. Even when I had tears running down my face, I could smile because I was not where I was before. No longer was I living in duplicity. I could feel the pleasure of God again. My living room was always absent one particular person, but my table was full of God's faithful people—my spiritual family—and that was more than enough. They brought the Church into my home. Even though I had removed a certain ring from my finger, I put new rings on other fingers as reminders of better blessings from God. Even when I was hurting, I felt happy. Even when I couldn't sleep, I was restful. Every moment of my day was a war, but I had peace for the first time in over a decade because I was no longer warring against God. I could feel His delight and His presence. In the stillness I could hear Him whisper. He was still calling me to Himself. I talked less, and sang

Every moment of my day was a war.

more. I was seen less, but in His Word more. Now, I knew for sure that my identity was fixed in Him. I had a permanent place even in the mess of a life being rebuilt. God granted me grace upon grace, pleasure upon pleasure, and the joy that He had promised.

Welcome the Year of Firsts, my friends. Surround yourself with a godly crew and dwell in the light. You can expect that memories won't carry the same bite. Old longings will wane. Damning voices will be muzzled. The gut checks will become less frequent and the attractions will lessen. Satan will lose his oppressive power and your affections for the triune God will grow. You can expect to walk a little lighter, look a lot higher. You will grow in thankfulness. You will know real freedom. The sorrow of wasted years will give way to jubilee as your heart explodes with wonder at Jesus Christ's provision. He will redeem the time. Behold, He is doing something new that you can't even imagine.

THE LORD IS RESTORING YOU

When I got out of my same-sex relationship, I didn't have any idea how long the journey of restoration would take. I figured it could be a while. *One year? Eleven? Twenty-two years?* Now I know it will probably be forever. *And maybe that is the point?* And at this point, I don't care that restoration will be a lifelong process. *I have to fight for the life granted by my King!* Sisters, we have to mentally prepare for battles that may last our lifetime. We must know the promises of God. We must anticipate the aches God allows to remain. We may live with the consequences of opening the door to sexual sin. We might still experience same-sex attraction. All while believing our God is restoring order out of chaos.

Just because longing, temptation, or desire for homosexual connection may continue, it does not mean you are simply gay. As you know, your sin struggle is never your name. The New Testament records an interesting moment where God grants a "thorn" to Paul.[1] It's unclear whether this thorn was a temptation, a wound, or some kind of disease. All we know is that it was given by God to keep Paul humble. Paul went so far as to say the thorn made him trust in the power of God during times when he was otherwise tempted to trust in himself again. Instead of hanging his head in sadness over his ordained suffering, he praised the Lord for a daily opportunity to find that God's grace was sufficient for Him. It's hard to imagine Paul jumping for joy with a thorn lodged in his flesh, but he was sober minded and grateful for its presence. God's power was most evident when Paul was at his weakest and aware of his weakness.

In His sovereignty, the Lord may grant you a thorn to focus your gaze on Jesus Christ. It could be anything from a physical ailment to a continued struggle with same-sex attraction, but a God-ordained thorn is never actually sin though its outworking can be. God grants the thorn not because He is evil, but because He is loving and wants to keep us from depending on ourselves and our weak flesh. They remind us that we need a Savior who is unhindered by thorns. Thorns train us in humility. Pain yells at us to find comfort and our ultimate comfort is only found in our resurrected and ascended King.

> *They remind us that we need a Savior who is unhindered by thorns.*

Shortly after my rescue, I also started having vivid dreams. Not about streets of gold and chorus lines of angels, but about my old lover. Dreams are not reality, but they pose real consequences to the possibility of reopening the door to my old self. Mornings after, I would wake up with my heart twisted in knots. Only hours before, I had loved her, hated her, been betrayed by her, rejected by her, longed for her, and been near her again. Opening that wound again was painful. It felt like reliving my old life again and the dreams threatened to disorient and crush me for days. But then I would remember the thorn. I knew my enemy and I knew my God.

Even this morning, four years later, I woke up aching after from one of these dreams. But instead of letting its effects rule me, I threw myself at the feet of Jesus Christ. I've made a rule for times like these not to get out of bed until I work it out with God and duke it out with Satan. I pray like I'm fighting for my life. I proclaim what is true about Jesus Christ. I claim what is true about me. I expose what is true about the nature of sin. I state what is true about her. And reclaim my victory through Christ over the power of the old. I thank Him for the thorn, even if I must wince through it. Even though I don't have control over my dreams, the helplessness they inspire is an opportunity to rise up with my morning mercies purchased by the blood of Jesus Christ.

Often, I will text a close friend and have them pray. Other times, I've played my audio Bible on my pillow all night long, had people pray over my room and my bed, and invited them into the places where Satan loves to lurk. Yes, I wish the dreams would stop. I pray that God would take the dreams away, but He has not yet. So instead I count them as a thorn. A fleshly reminder given by God that I may remember what I did and what He's done. Instead of letting the accuser capitalize on them, I let God use them for good. I choose to respond with the belief that God is using my thorn to train me in humility, to remember my human fragility, and to trust in His ultimate goodness.

It's important to remember that God created the flesh of Adam and Eve as "very good," not inherently evil. Even though the Fall fractured our bodies, our bodies are not bad. Even as they change shape or hold conditions and affections that frustrate, hurt, fail, and betray us. We cannot hate our flesh and yet try to love God with everything we have. Treating the flesh with contempt and the spiritual with adoration will not solve our thorns. As we are being renewed, we can no longer separate the physical, emotional, intellectual, relational, and spiritual realities of our lives. We must realign ourselves to His original design. God has made humans as embodied creatures, which means we have a body and a soul. They are good and yet also being restored. God the Father loves our frame and the Son is redeeming us as a whole person. So we must view ourselves as a soul and a body, *with* and *in* whom, God is pleased to dwell. Even now, in the midst of sexual and relational brokeness. For our future inheritance is not just a spiritual inheritance, but it is a physical one.

There's no way of knowing if a pain or thorn is temporary. We don't know if it will last the first year or all

GETTING IN

GETTING STUCK

GETTING OUT

of our years on earth. Our omniscient God does not always eradicate the reminders because it would not be best for us. Knowing this, we war despite the ache believing that joy and suffering can co-exist in our sanctification. We humbly engage our weaknesses and offer our bloody thorns to Jesus Christ who grants us strength to endure. And while we struggle in the meantime, those thorns point to the enthronement of our glorious King whose kingdom will one day be fully restored.

DECIDING TO FIGHT

I don't know how long you will experience same-sex attraction or be tempted by emotional and relational idolatry. I don't know how long I will. I don't know why the Lord feels distant at times, nor do I know the timetable for our struggles. Everyone's story is different, but God is the same, even as He acts uniquely for each of us. Some women experience immediate eradication of lust and same-sex attraction. Many maintain their battle on some level until death. God sees, hears, and draws near whether or not we feel Him. His presence is the fuel for our fight, not the absence of our struggle. All believers experience a lifelong battle with temptation in one form or another. We who struggle with same-sex attraction do not have the harder condition. We all struggle with sins of identity and sexual brokenness. I don't know how long your same-sex attractions will last, but I do know all of humanity has to war to see Jesus Christ as better than all other desires. Despite the pull from the remnants of our old nature, the Lord commands us to pursue victory today.[1] We must decide to fight.

For me, I was always asking God how long I must battle my flesh, my wayward affections, and my ongoing temptations. I felt that I needed to know that there was an end for me to start to even consider fighting again. Historically, it was the level of pleasure or pain experienced from my same-sex attraction that motivated me to fight in any direction. I wanted to define the type of victory I required. I needed to be guaranteed a specific outcome for it to be worth losing everything. Or a specific promise of eventual victory to even begin to hope. Well my friend, there is an end and it is worth it all.

Fellow warriors, we need a robust understanding of the victory promised in Christ. We need to redefine victory to match what the Bible tells us. True victory is union with Christ. It is gaining His righteousness. Victory looks like perseverance when life becomes difficult. It's belief. It is claiming the Word over Satan's ongoing temptations. It's repentance. It is unhindered worship of the King. Victory is faithfulness to our God until the end. This is how the Bible defines victory. And I must train myself to fight to believe it to the uttermost.

COUNTERFEIT GOALS & THE ACTUAL GOAL

When we commit to re-enter the battlefield, we need to understand victory, but we also have to know what we are fighting for. Unless we're chasing God's purposes, we'll end up aiming for counterfeit goals that will simply lead us astray once again. Our goal is not a replacement of the old relationship with a new human one. We don't go looking for a new best friend or boyfriend to transfer our dependency. The goal is not to rid ourselves of same-sex attraction or create a social media following. It's not sharing your testimony on the big screen at church or leading a small group of same-sex attracted women. It's not even Heaven or perfect healing. The evidence of a redeemed life does not take on one particular external form. So breathe deep, dear friend. You don't have to prove your healing by outward appearances or achievement. Therefore, do not anchor your expectations on celibacy or sinlessness as being what sets you free. Setting up ideals or morality as idols simply dethrones one for another.

Counterfeit goals cannot produce the heart change we need for victory. That's why our actual goal must be none other than union with Christ and communion with Him. The object of our faith is that we will get God. The Spirit is always

> *The object of our faith is that we will get God.*

at work in the heart and mind of the Christian turning our eyes to see Him as the only worthy goal. Deciding to fight means embracing Jesus Christ as our greatest good and acknowledging whatever He calls sin as a hindrance to our relationship with Him. We wrestle to let go of all false loves and only behold Jesus Christ.[2] This is the primary victory we pursue. The more we know Him the clearer and more compelling our goal. And to this end we must fight relentlessly. When we understand who God is, we know what we need in order to make war. For me, I literally had to say some of these things out loud over and over to verbalize what I needed to believe in order to see God as more worthwhile than what I clung to:

- Even if I hurt for a really long time, I get God.
- Even if I never have sex again, I get God.
- Even if I continue to be tempted by my same-sex attractions, I get God.
- Even if I _____ , I get God.

Emerging from same-sex attraction with a reign on behavior apart from Jesus Christ is no victory. The true battle for our hearts rages on. God's goal is always to transform our desires to conform them to His own. Perhaps you do not yet know Jesus Christ as your Savior. There is no victory outside of Christ, only morality management, religiosity, and therapeutic mantra. Without Him, there is no hope of life from death or life after death. If that's where you find yourself today, don't turn away. Cry out to the Creator of the world. Ask Him to

GETTING IN

GETTING STUCK

GETTING OUT

open your eyes to the beauty of Jesus Christ and grant you saving faith here and now. A new nature and a new name avails you everything.

If you have believed in Jesus Christ do not give up. He has not abandoned you. Pray for the Spirit to help you, even in the mess that is your disordered hopes and affections. God can cause lost desires for His lordship to emerge anew. Experiencing homosexual attraction does not negate the reality of salvation in Jesus Christ. Nor does it squash His power to overcome whatever you face. When we've surrendered to Him, nothing can change the fact that we are His chosen and beloved. Jesus Christ is in the business of making us whole. He is not interested in simply repairing our wayward affections and sexual desires. Christ's purpose for you is that you become like Him from the inside out. His love is so extravagant that He seeks to restore all our broken places because it makes us happy and brings Him glory.[3] He desires to reorient our lives comprehensively so that we become fully aligned with His good design.

Obedience is not easy, but we are not alone. God is near and his Holy Spirit empowers us to do what we cannot.[4] War is faith in action, but our faith in action is also resting in God's promises that He fights for us. That He has won for us. That He will continue to conquer for us. That He loves us no matter what. Our battle is never for right standing. Jesus Christ already accomplished that for all His people on the cross. Many days, maybe all you can muster is raising the sword of the Spirit in the midst of your stronghold, and God is pleased with you. Maybe its clinging to the belt of truth while you're laying in the dust, and God is pleased with you. He doesn't require human strength or a scorecard to bestow His gifts or His presence. There's no time clock. Our God dwells with His people in times of war, peace, advancement, and retreat. His victory is unhindered by our strengths and weaknesses.

Our God passionately desires restoration in all areas of our lives and He will do it. When you find yourself in seasons of doubt, remember His promises. Remember His story. Bolster your faith by reclaiming the truth that Jesus Christ has given you a new nature. You may feel discouraged. You may feel tired. You may feel completely disconnected from the Lord. You may feel exhausted and hopeless after many years of efforts. Do not give up, my friend. Press in to the promise of the gospel and do not let Satan woo you with lies about your former life

Victory is coming and victory is now.

or your future inheritance. Victory is coming and victory is now. Your hope is secure because you belong to the King and He is always faithful.

PERSISTENT OBEDIENCE IN THE RIGHT DIRECTION

Life with Christ involves more than responding to a single call for obedience. It means adhering to God's daily call for righteousness. In lots of things. Obedience is a long-term instruction and God grants us joy along the way, but the right path is hard. Our suffering makes the days and the years feel exhausting. Struggling with same-sex attraction imposes a weight that God never intended for His creation. Rather than starving just sexual immorality, persistent obedience is an ongoing war of killing all the sin in our lives. Sin has fractured everything, but do not lose heart. God is near. He is at work bringing about renewal every day in all things.

The mark of a true Christ follower is a faith in action. Not perfect obedience, but progressive obedience. Persistent sanctification. Unhindered worship. Fidelity to the end. As we know, this is true victory. God directs all of humanity to His Son for the purpose of transforming us into mirror images of His Son through our prolonged obedience to His Word. He wants our will to be the same as our God who is triune. As Christians, we are wholly active in our healing and completely dependent on God to bring it about. Primarily, our aim should be to obey Jesus Christ because it pleases Him and brings us great pleasure, but if obedience doesn't feel good yet confess that to God. Ask for the happiness in doing what He desires, but do not put off acts of obedience in the meantime. Soon they will shift from duty to delight. The time for healing is now. Here are a few reminders of what faithful obedience can look like:

- Pray the big prayers and listen for His voice.
- Pray the groans of your heart with whatever words you can muster and listen for His voice.
- Worship God for who He is.
- Walk faithfully according to the Scriptures.
- Humble yourself, pray, seek His face, repent, and flee temptation.
- Don't look back.
- Leave no remnant.
- Invite other believers to speak into your blind spots and correct your theology where needed.
- Become a member of a biblically faithful, local church and attend regularly.
- Remember your new name: His.
- Put on the full armor of God, every damn day.
- Rest in the finished work of Christ.

As you begin your journey out, you may only be able to muster active faith in a few things each day. If so, I recommend praying, reading the Bible, and building relationships with a church community. Call upon the name of the Lord and ask Him to change your will, to change your desires so that they reflect His own. Join Him in the daily habits of sanctification. Then when God reveals things to you, obey Him. He is answering your prayers. Follow the Spirit in the tension wherever He leads. Cling to Him in the pain. It gets better.

Choose life, freedom, and victory. Choose Jesus Christ. Soon, your groaning will give way to great praise.

We will never be able to walk out our Christian faith perfectly, but that is no excuse to persist in relational idolatry and sexual sin. Obedience is messy. At first, holiness feels weird and looks crazy to others. But it doesn't matter because God is for us. Jesus Christ is our grace to persist in obedience and it starts with our minds. God transforms us through the truth of His Word. Remembering what He actually says keeps us from asking, "Did God really say. . . ?" Right thinking informs right feeling, which informs right living.[5] Through habits of sanctification, we war for obedience in the mess.

We cannot muster a love for God or the things of God apart from Jesus Christ doing that work in our heart. Yet we do not have to wait to see if God destroys our sin before we believe Him. Claim what is true and walk in it. It is rebellion to withhold obedience to what God has already commanded. We do not command God to change our will before we leave Egypt. We prepare now because the Spirit of God can reveal Himself any time He pleases. At your highest, your lowest, or on a random Wednesday, like me. Perhaps He will destroy sin against your will. Or perhaps He wills to destroy it by your own hand. Whether it comes in the form of God giving or taking, He is acting graciously on your behalf.

Faith and love should be what fuels believers. God created us to love Him more than anything and He is jealous for the affection of our hearts. He wants us to feel, not just to think or decide to obey. In His pursuit of us, He is after our highest affections. What causes me to worship is knowing that I am a recipient of His unequivocal mercy. For it is God's great love for us that He made us alive in Christ even when we were dead in our sin. It is by grace that we are saved, never by our works. That is the Christian faith. That's what we fight to

In His pursuit of us, He is after our highest affections.

GETTING IN

GETTING STUCK

GETTING OUT

believe. That is why we persist in righteousness. We refuse to give up because God never ceases to revitalize our hearts and grant us more faith. By the power of the Holy Spirit, we war to love Him more than anything.

RECALLING SLAVERY FONDLY

Scripture contains many stories of people rescued by God who fondly recall their dire circumstances soon after. When God led Lot and his family out of Sodom and Gomorrah moments before destroying the cities, He warned them not to look back. But Lot's wife turned back toward the life they had loved and left behind to make an ongoing memory and hold it in her heart forever, and she was immediately reduced to a pile of salt.[6] She was leaving in action, but in in heart she still wanted to remain. Something similar happened when the Lord freed the Israelites from slavery in Egypt. They walked out of captivity and journeyed through the Red Sea on dry land, but then grew hungry in the wilderness. That discomfort colored their ability to recall rightly. Rather than trust their Rescuer, they yearned for the meat of Egypt rather than the manna of freedom.[7] They accused God. They forgot about the cloud and the fire, the manna, the water, and the quail. And they built a new god—a golden calf—to worship and praise for splitting the sea.

There is a way of remembering that brings hope and a way of remembering that delivers loss. Each of these examples demonstrates the dangers of recalling slavery fondly. To remember Lot's wife, God preserved a pillar for all to see. To remember Israel's false worship, God prolonged their wandering. These Bible stories remind us that savoring slavery will hinder our ability to experience the freedom God offers through Jesus Christ. Whenever we look back with rosy glasses or look forward with sadness, we fail to see God's rescue as more desirable than the bondage of our sin.

It is always wise to ask God for the ability to view

everything through His eyes. Pray for Jesus Christ to ruin the belief that your sin was because of *her* perfection, not your sinfulness. Ask Him to help you destroy the fantasy of benefits associated with your lesbian relationship or same-sex attraction. Refuse to think that she or your same-sex attraction were worth it. Don't be thankful to God for sin. Wisdom means desiring to see all of life as God sees it. Refuse to look back lovingly. Don't confuse slavery for freedom. Kill your longings for the comforts of brokenness. Do not recall your rebellion fondly.

A number of years ago, I saw a documentary about a psychologist who treated patients with drug and alcohol addictions. During his work, he discovered that he could determine in less than one second whether or not each patient would relapse following his or her treatment. He set up a camera and interviewed his patients beginning with the same question every time: "What do you remember about being high?" The doctor wasn't so much concerned with their answer as he was their nonverbal response. If their eyebrows lifted or their eyes brightened, if their lips curled into a slight grin or their face muscles relaxed they were not ready to be released. They did not yet detest their addiction. But the addicts whose eyes fell, whose lips pursed, whose foreheads slumped when remembering their despair remembered rightly.

Our first response to temptation can tell us much about the state of our hearts toward our former lesbian lifestyle. Those of us who remember fondly, who are thankful for the experience, who willingly sit in the active memory of committing sinful acts do not yet hate our sin. We do not yet believe that sin produces death in us. The Bible says that temptation will always exist, but it is our response to the temptation that God seeks to redeem for His glory and our freedom.

As believers in Jesus Christ we are not resigned to a destiny of failure. Even if we flunk our first, second, or 1,000th response to temptation, we are never doomed to the next step in the sin cycle. We are heirs with Christ and victory is in our

GETTING IN

GETTING STUCK

GETTING OUT

blood.[8] When we submit our weakness to Jesus Christ, He gives us His strength to withstand our old demons. He has equipped you to fight. We may experience hunger pangs, our bodies may respond to old lusts, our hearts may quicken with same-sex attraction, but we have the ability to overcome. Feeling same-sex attraction does not mean we are powerless against homosexual behaviors. It just means we must surrender our will to the King again. By the power of the Spirit of God we can still have ongoing victory—true victory—despite the assaults of Satan.

REMEMBERING & REPLACING

Remembering sin and reminiscing about sin are two different acts. The former is a pathway to freedom whereas the latter is a source of continued bondage. And that is why we must employ wisdom in the art of remembering. Remembering rightly leads us to hope rightly.

When it comes to my memories, I refuse to reminisce—especially about her. Instead, I choose to dwell on Him. When I feel lonely and want to find comfort in reminiscing about old times, I must remember my memory bias and apply the truth instead. Whenever I feel hurt or anger resurface about the betrayal and rejection I experienced through our breakup, I put her on God's hook, let go, and allow Jesus Christ to take control. When old affections resurface in a new way, I remember Satan's playbook and God's methods of rescue. When we ask Jesus Christ to inform our minds, He gives us wisdom as we deal with the assaults of the devil. Learning about Satan and the nature of sin has also taught me not to frame her as the greatest perpetrator of evil. That role belongs to me. I made the decision to reject Jesus Christ. Coming to terms with that truth has changed my perspective. When I view sin for what it really is, I can forgive others, forgive myself, and cling to the cross for ongoing healing and renewal. When I view God for who He really is, I can receive His forgiveness.

Restoration follows, transforming my mind, body, and heart as I mourn loss and celebrate new life.

We should never forget the chains or the wreckage associated with our false worship. Remembering the costs is helpful to be sure. It fuels our obedience. However, fear of consequences can never sustain obedience. At best it is only a secondary motivation for obedience. Our primary motivation should always be to remember who God is. Again, this is the actual goal. It is wise and the only thing that can sustain us in the midst of temptation. Recalling His love reorients our hearts. Fear of loss is weak motivation and will rarely drive us to battle. The beauty of Jesus Christ is what compels us to fight to stay near to Him. The more we come to know Jesus Christ and His many benefits, the more attractive obedience becomes. Our fondness for temporary pleasures melts away when we hold the eternality of Jesus Christ most dear.

Wisdom dictates that in our remembering, we replace what is old with what is new. Christ never leaves us empty handed when we let go of our idols. He always offers something better—Himself. The art of replacing is another discipline I have learned along my journey that has helped encourage my healing. An eleven-year relationship leaves behind a lot of memories. To this day, they still cast darkness on certain experiences and spaces like places we visited, foods we ate, or music and movies we enjoyed. These types of things will pop up unexpectedly on certain days either inflicting *Christ never leaves us empty handed when we let go of our idols.* pain or tempting me toward fond feelings. I've faced many triggers like these that will spark a memory of something old and I know they are Satan's attempts to draw me back to reminiscing. But I am aware of my weaknesses and I know I cannot sustain the devil's assaults without God's help. These types of memories have to be replaced.

For me, that began at the identity level. My temptation was to believe that I had lost more than I had gained by leaving behind my old life. To fight that lie required me to embrace the truth of my identity in Christ, replacing my faulty beliefs with the fullness of my Savior. Wherever lies remain, our thoughts must be reclaimed and replaced. They must be overrun with the truth that our identity is secure in Jesus Christ and that He always grants us more than what we lose. To that end, here is the strategy I use to fight back when triggers arise tempting me to reminisce or question my freedom in Jesus Christ:

1. **Immediately yell, "Hell NO!!!"**
    Seriously. Out loud. God is not alarmed by any attack you face. He sits on His throne ready to save. But alarm should be your initial response as it identifies the assaults of the enemy. Ask your Savior to bind Satan in the name of Jesus Christ. The deceiver is not your master any longer. You belong to God, fully equipped to flee temptation by the power of the Holy Spirit. Our God conquered death in Adam and will one day crush Satan beneath His feet.

2. **Focus on how you are feeling and tell Jesus.**
    Don't shut down your feelings when surprised by a memory. Press into them and validate their existence by telling Jesus Christ what they are. God created us to have emotions and wants us to feel in ways that are informed by His truth. When I do this, I first thank Him for the ability to feel anything at all. Second, I tell Him exactly what emotions I am experiencing in that moment. Third, I ask Him to expose any lies I believe as He continues to heal my heart, mind, and feelings. Fourth, I confirm my faith that Jesus Christ is better than my past. Fifth, I restate my confidence that God is eager and able to redeem my emotions and that He is actively

sanctifying me through my obedience. Though old feelings may remain, they need not rule our hearts.

3. **Tell Jesus Christ the specific memory that needs to be replaced, repent of any sin He brings to the surface, and receive His forgiveness.**

   God loves it when we ask Him for big help. Memories can be formidable things that keep us bound. When my past pops up or when I come face to face with old temptations, I confront each one head on. Out loud. I do not avoid or let them alone to fester. If I identify unrepentant sin in the process, I immediately repent in detail. I pray that God will again show Himself more powerful than the human experience and thank Him that there is nothing more powerful than the cross. If I have repented of a specific sin already, I acknowledge that I am weak, but willing to lay down the old shit again and again with His help. I trust Him with the outcome. While God may or may not allow memories to remain, He can rid them of any power over us. He is strong enough to deconstruct and rebuild all things.

4. **Ask God to replace, replace, replace.**

   If there was an incident in your past that caused deep brokenness, you can't take away what happened, but God can sustain and restore you. Speak what is true. Speak any lies that you believed in those moments and rewrite them with what you now know to be true. Burn any false thing you've deconstructed and replace it with His story. Thank God for His rescue and ask Him to bind up and heal the hurts and grief that remain. Pray that He would remove Satan's power over you and replace whatever is evil with redemption.

5. **Make new memories.**

Build something new. Lay a new foundation that you can make new memories on. Embrace your good, God-given desires and pursue the things you love and let them magnify the Lord. Rather than returning to your former life, celebrate your new life with the people of God and do cool stuff. Enjoy God's good gifts. Pursue Him and His benefits that lead you to worship Him. Follow the lead of your Creator who is making all things new.

In the midst of assaults on my memory, this process doesn't have to take long. Most times, I move through the steps quickly to keep from giving too much time to what is old. If I drive by a place that triggers a memory, I place my open hand on the window and pray replacing my past with the truth of Jesus Christ's power. If I see someone who reminds me of my old life, I pause to remember Jesus Christ's authority over all things. I thank Him that I am a new creation and no longer who I was.

Sometimes, I even seek out opportunities to visit places to reclaim ground that I forfeited. I invite my friends and we lay hands on doorways and volleyball courts and hotels and pray over places that were once the site of wickedness. We proclaim my freedom in Christ and I leave that space more free. I don't go to every spot, it's not necessary or even wise sometimes, but I go where the Spirit leads. I do this not because these places have any legitimate power over me—they absolutely do not. Stuff does not have intrinsic power and superstition has no place in the life of the redeemed. But Satan is crafty and can create strongholds by the high places.[9] No longer do I want Satan to hold any power over me. So I tear down old places and make new memories. It helps take away the fear and sting of what is old. Practicing this process reminds me that God loves me and has dominion over all things. And it can do the same for you. Over time, it will become a godly reflex that keeps you agile and strong in the Lord.

Our journey forward is not about reminiscence, but redemption. God desires to take back what thieves stole. The triune God is reestablishing His kingdom on earth through the Son, and has invited us into His work. Redemption is the true storyline of the world and as Christians we are born again into this Christian story. It helps to look back and imagine standing at the door of His empty tomb and look up to see that His throne is full. It helps to look forward to someday dancing on my own empty grave. Remembering what is true gives us hope.

God is far more powerful than our flesh or the spiritual forces we face. Do not give way. Refuse to hold dear anything that Satan brings to mind for your enslavement. The Lord can be trusted. He can be trusted with all that I left behind, even when the consequences remain. The aim of remembering and replacing is to establish affections for Jesus Christ where others once reigned. Your past does not have to drive your present. Instead you can be filled with joy and confidence in what God has done and what He is still doing on earth.

#HELPFUL & #NOTHELPFUL

My friends, I'm on this road too. Literally, right there with you, always knowing at any point my wayard affections could trip me up and lead me astray. All Christians are always one second look away from bondage. We must persevere in righteousness. Making level paths for our feet requires wisdom.[10] It also requires humility to realize the habitual and comfortable may be undermining our own efforts. The seemingly innocent may actually be dangerous. What seems neutral is feeding our hearts. The shortcut may actually be a dead end. Or a trap. Satan loves to deceive us with lies of false safety. Instead, Jesus entreats us with the truth of His security and blessings. Christ must be ultimate in our affections. The path to healing is aided by the Word of God and the testimonies of those who travel ahead of us. And those who travel with us.

So here is some wisdom from my story. The following list includes a few things that I learned and found #Helpful as I was being led out and healing from my homosexual lifestyle. I also list a lot of things that I found #NotHelpful. Some are obvious, some are funny, but all of them make me cringe a little because I remember all the years that I forged my own path believing that I could do—or not do—these things and think they would have no effect. What is true is that pseudo-independence from God was enslavement to a perilous cycle. Obedience to the New Covenant is not legalism. It's heart-level, desire-level, DNA-level transformation. Here are some recommendations as you walk in a manner consistent with your identity in Christ:

#Helpful

- Relentlessly pursue Christ by reading the Bible, living in ongoing prayer, being part of Christian discipleship, church membership, Scripture memorization, godly community, hospitality, service, and ongoing obedience.

- Pursue healthy same-sex friendships.

- Expand sharing of personal information to multiple people, keeping an open mentality.

- Be vulnerable with appropriate circles of disclosure for grace and healing.

- Rotate sharing experiences and details with separate friends.

- Consider getting off social media altogether (you won't actually disappear).

- Change your phone number.

- Block tempting people or your ex with your cell phone carrier service.

- Delete all files of contacts, voice memos, videos, emails, folders, and photos.

- Trash all gifts, mementos, memories, references to past lovers, or relationships, and evidences of sin and your old self.

- Replace music or media or TV that incites old longings or memories with better options.

- When you see something that tempts your flesh, bounce your eyes off of it and pray.

- Take a prayer warrior friend and pray over spaces in your home and life that are/were places of sin and temptation.

- Redecorate your room, buy a new bed or linens.

- Consider how you dress and wear clothes that align with your true identity in Christ.

- Widen your circle of godly friendships.

- Break all lesbian relationships in your life.

- Believe Christ is better for everyone than you are.

- Serve, focus on others, and do things for others.

- Make plans to fill the time and space with new things.

- Pre-schedule outings, events, fun activities, and trips with healthy friends to replace void time, upcoming time stamps, or time previously spent in old rituals.

#NotHelpful

- Not spending time with Jesus Christ in prayer and in the Word of God.

- Being in a physical or sexual relationship with someone of the same gender.

- Living with your girlfriend.

- Pursing a "renewed" friendship with an old lover. Or thinking you can. Or should.

- Obsessively texting or calling your female friend or girlfriend.

- Viewing other women through the lens of them being a new, potential "best friend."

cont'd

- Creating exclusive friendships.

- Referring constantly to yourself as "we" in relation to previous experiences or a current romantic relationship.

- Late-night texting and video chatting.

- Spooning and sleeping with someone in the same bed every night. Or ever.

- Participating in sexual petting, erotic touching, or letting someone do it to you.

- Taking naps or watching movies in tight quarters in the arms or lap of close friend.

- Kissing, petting, stroking, fondling face, head, body, hands—basically, inappropriate touching. (Would you do this in front of your accountability partner?)

- Masturbating.

- Discussing your attraction with the person of your attraction.

- Assuming that it is smart to counsel or assist other same-sex attracted women when you are living in owning sin or struggling to get out yourself.

- Obsessively praying for your girlfriend, ex, or romantic interest to justify thinking about them constantly.

- Making your girlfriend your accountability partner, and vice versa.

- Negotiating with God. "If you_____, then I_____."

- Keeping lesbian associations thinking that you're the only Christian they know.

- Judging church, Christians, and God.

- Killing hope while ascribing to some sort of made up penance system.

- Making other people feel uncomfortable or unwelcome in your presence by your exclusive same-sex relationship, weird language, inside secrets, or sexual conduct.

- Testing your godly friends by putting the onus on them to sense your secrets.

- Believing people can save and rescue you more effectively than God.

Though far from comprehensive, the items in the #Helpful and #Not Helpful lists helped me relearn what is wise and unwise because I really didn't know anymore. I had lived this way for so long and now I could see Jesus Christ, but I still needed some practical daily direction. Perhaps the Holy Spirit will speak through the #Helpful chart and affirm your faithfulness in positive areas and bring to mind specific actions you should take to further level your footings. The #NotHelpful examples may spur you on to evaluate negative thinking and stop behavior patterns that you maintain. This is not meant to be prescriptive. You don't have to adopt every action listed, but the extent of your freedom may be tied to the level of your obedience to what God has said is holy and wise. We can't refuse to believe that practices have no effect or power over us. Old habits can carry baggage and give Satan a foothold. Always consider if a behavior will help or hinder your relationship with Jesus Christ. We must stop doing these things that impede our freedom and start doing the things that promise perpetual victory. Our actions contribute to who we are becoming and vice versa. Daily decisions are very practical ways to be free in your tomorrows.

Life with Christ will always require us to yank out the sin and its roots, but our Savior plants new seeds. Following Jesus Christ does not only mean death to self, but new life in Him. Jesus Christ is the living water that satisfies our thirst. He is the bread of life that fills our appetites. He helps us grow and thrive. His Spirit has awakened us to everlasting life here and now. For we were dead in our transgressions and sins and He has caused us to be alive. Because of Him, we have hope for where we are headed. Jesus Christ supplies the power to sustain our faltering frames. To live victoriously. To wage war against our lusts. To rest in His finished work.

What God's holiness demands, Jesus Christ provides. As we move out of sexual and relational sin and forward on the better path, we engage in many battles along the way always contending for belief. Talking with God is the best method to engage in this spiritual warfare. Yes, there is much unknown out there, but there is an assured win. We are equipped for the journey. We are not passive or incapable of holiness. Since the trail is technical we give careful thought to the paths of our feet and do everything we can to even the ground to walk the secure way. Wisdom calls out for us to engage in the battle for our hearts. Do not play dead. Praise the Lord that He has given us everything we need for life and godliness through what has already been revealed.[11]

STARVE WHAT YOU WANT TO KILL

Beware. Like the man who raised a tiger in his apartment, we can make room for sin in our hearts. As we begin to heal, it's possible that we will be tempted again to view the tiger as desirable, like an old comfortable friend. We can forget the danger it poses. Over time, we can dismiss the former carnage. Without care, we can even begin to feed its desires, forgetting it desires to devour us. No matter how much control we assert over our sinful behaviors, sin will always destroy us if left unchecked.

Starving our sinful indulgences is necessary for healing. It's not evil or oppressive to kill the very thing that's killing you. It's wisdom in action. Murdering secret loves is painful, but it's the only way to emerge alive. Active faith means feeding what we want to grow and starving what we want to kill. We nourish ourselves by consuming what is good and denying what is evil. Making the right provisions creates the right opportunities. Feeding on the truth of God's Word prepares our minds to fight, our hearts to win, and our bodies to reign over the power of sin. We grow strong in our faith and resolve when we eat from the hand of God.

It's not evil or oppressive to kill the very thing that's killing you.

If you've ever tried to start eating healthy again, switching to a nutritious menu starts off leaving you hungry after meals. And kind of cranky. But that's only because you've trained yourself to feed on crap for so long. Eventually, your body adjusts to the new diet such that it becomes the new norm. Starving sin follows a similar pattern. We have to restrain the old appetites and exchange them for the bread of life and living water. Strength and recovery come from feeding the body what it needs rather than what it wants. Before long, our bodies begin to yearn for the spiritual health afforded by our new diets. We hunger and thirst for righteousness. And thank God that He's told us in the Word what is good for our health so we don't have to seek out our own remedies.

So wisdom requires a healthy intake of what is good, but it also calls us to avoid those cravings that diminish our faith and confidence in the Lord. We must starve ourselves of whatever feeds our sin cycles and rots our souls, which could include certain friends, alcohol, social media habits, and so on. And always porn, masturbation, homosexual relationships, and sex outside of God's design. Discipline is not legalism. It's a conscious pursuit of freedom. Choosing health requires long-term self-denial. We must be precise about what we feed and what we starve. It's not about finding balance; it's extreme. Killing sin and finding life in Jesus Christ is not accidental. It's intentional.

Self-denial leads to abundance, not emptiness.

Self-denial leads to abundance, not emptiness. God is present in the messiness that is our fumbling toward obedience. He does not require our perfection to receive an outpouring of His power. We will never be flawless in terms of killing sin, but we must not use our humanity as an excuse to continue consuming the things we have been instructed to purge. We don't redefine grace. We realize that the instructions in the Bible are the very means of His grace. In time, old desires will slowly lose their grip and you will experience freedom as the

Holy Spirit transforms your affections granting you joy along the way. In Jesus Christ, we received new hearts. Hearts that want to serve Christ when they are not weighed down by sin. God can supply you with the will to want and love the things of God. So consider the provisions you gather on your journey to sexual and relational restoration. Ask the Spirit for wisdom and spit out whatever feeds death.

QUESTIONS

1 What is the way you have historically defined personal "victory" over sexual and relational sin? How does the Bible define "victory"?

2 How does fantasizing or recalling slavery fondly hinder you from walking in holiness and the freedom Jesus Christ offers? How might learning more about God's true character give you confidence that walking in purity and holiness will lead you to fullness of life instead of emptiness/hopelessness?

3 What are some ways that you can seek to starve your flesh of the things that bring death and destruction? What are some ways you can seek to feed your flesh the things that bring life and vitality in God?

GETTING IN

GETTING STUCK

GETTING OUT

HIS PROMISES

Choosing to walk wisely in obedience, fighting lusts, and replacing old ways can be scary and disorienting. In this last section of my story, I wanted to give you some personal advice from my own experience of *getting out* over the last few years. My friend, I want you to know what to expect as you engage in this spiritual warfare. You probably already have a good idea since my guess is that you have likely begun to battle your same-sex attraction and emotional dependency, but I want to offer you encouragement nonetheless. God equips those that He calls. My hope is for you to persevere in Christian faith until the end.

While I can't tell you exactly how your story will play out, I can equip you with a few signposts to look for along the way. There is much unknown about choosing to walk away from what you know and go with Jesus Christ in the way He commands in His Word, but we can expect some things. We can depend on some things. There are promises that are for you. There are promises for me. There are promises for the people of God. There are promises for all of creation. Our hope in Him will always be trustworthy.

THE ALREADY & NOT YET

Some of God's promises are complete, while others we wait for expectantly. This is the tension of the "already and not yet." Because God is faithful, He will fulfill all of His promises, but we may experience certain unresolved longings and unfulfilled promises in our lifetimes. We are part of one big story and God has one overarching will for the universe, which starts and ends with His glory spread throughout the earth. And all His promises coming true. One day, Jesus Christ will return and make all things new. He will fix what is broken and deliver us from sin forever. He will restore us to wholeness. He will establish His kingdom on earth, a kingdom where the world's end is not its own self-destruction, but the renewal and restoration of all things.[1] Heaven on earth is the final destination for those in Jesus Christ—eternity in the presence of our King. It will be more than Edenic; it will be glorious! In the meantime, we look around and it's hard to believe God is bringing this kingdom even now though His divine action and through His people. But it's true. It begins here in the midst of brokenness. It is already and it is not yet.

Knowing the end fuels us to bravely battle sin today because we know Jesus Christ has already won. We are guaranteed a specific outcome. Though, not every earthly battle will end in victory. There will be suffering. There will be death. Sin causes us to groan inwardly longing for Jesus Christ's return. And this is the tension of the already and not yet. We experience victory now while our ultimate victory is soon to come. Now we know in part, but one day we will know in full.[2] We are rescued and always being restored. We still sin, but one day we won't. Knowing the final end of all things gives us Christian hope.

But the fact that we will not experience ultimate deliverance from sin until death should not keep us from pursuing victory today. It is not an excuse God accepts. Living in the tension disciples us. As an achiever, I find this to be a hard truth because I want it now. I tend to operate in an all-or-nothing mentality. And I have a bad habit of telling God how I define things. So now I am learning to align my definition of victory with that of Jesus Christ. Remember, victory is being united in Christ. Victory has already happened. And more victory is coming when He returns.

Rather than waiting on Heaven, we are called to live as victorious people today. By the power of the Spirit, we have victory to claim already and the freedom to walk in the way of Jesus Christ among the land of the living. The battle for true victory begins now.

PEACE. AND REST... FINALLY

As you fight for victory, you can expect peace and rest. Finally! Throughout the eleven years of my same-sex relationship, I frantically sought tranquility by striving to justify my lifestyle. Of course, it didn't work. So I tried to run away from God hoping to find lasting serenity elsewhere. That didn't work either. But when He brought me to repentance, He brought back His peace. I discovered that Jesus Christ alone provides the rest I craved because He is its only source.

As we know, embracing sin creates turmoil. It offers no peace or rest because the sin we chase desires to destroy us. It deceives us and steals our trust in God. Sexual and relational sin strips us of hope by shackling us to its allure. Walking in obedience to the Word of God has the opposite effect. Not only can you expect shalom, but you should expect it to become a natural part of your daily experience. Whereas before you were fleeing from God's design, bringing your life under the authority of God means that you are now actually obeying Him. No longer is there a dividing wall of hostility. Peace comes from communion with God. Rest is restored when the deepest part of us trusts that God is better than what we are giving up. Pursuing vitality in Christ and putting sin to death means that we have moved from warring against Him to warring alongside Him. Remembering God is with us provides

GETTING IN

GETTING STUCK

GETTING OUT

deep peace in the battle.

By faith, you have been united with Christ, which means you can expect more than mere safety in the fight for holiness. You have been granted a permanent place among the family of God along with the perfect righteousness of His Son. You can trust your security. You have nothing to prove to the world because you have already been accepted by the King.

Submitting to the lordship of Jesus Christ is how our souls find rest and that is what brings about the peace we crave.

Living in the Spirit also produces this fruit. When we exchange our sins for Jesus Christ's righteousness, He imparts these evidences of our reconciliation. We become more fruitful as we increase in love for our God. Submitting to the lordship of Jesus Christ is how our souls find rest and that is what brings about the peace we crave. It's a promise.[3] This does not mean that our life will be perfect, it means that we can have shalom even in a fallen world. Rest can only come from our Creator who made us to rest in Him.

RESCUE & FREEDOM

Part of the reason peace and rest become regularly present is because of God's relentless pursuit of His people. Count on it. Belonging to the Father means that He has already offered ways of escaping both temptation and enmeshment through Jesus Christ. Rescue operations are Jesus Christ's joy and part of His job description. He has already paid your ransom. He has intervened to rescue you before, and He will continue to do so. Even now, Jesus Christ is orchestrating intricate missions to rescue you from your old ways. If you refuse, fail, doubt, or give in to fear or lust, He does not quit providing you a way out. He names you worthy whether or not you feel fit for rescue.

If you find yourself drifting back to your past, be wary of blaming it on the insufficiency of Christ. In those times, we must check our chains and examine what we love. Are we coming to Jesus Christ with open hands? Do we require God's rescue in spite of our desire to stay? God is working in you to believe that His love is most powerful. That His rescue is worth the sacrifice. He wants to transform your will and your heart. This is our most immediate need. Ask God to help you desire the comprehensive rescue He brings. God carries out rescue missions with the aim of extracting us forever, never to return. So expect a certain level of fear about the unknown, but fight to remember your gain in the Lord. The more we regard Christ's freedom as beneficial, the quicker we will be to answer "Yes" to His voice calling us out of darkness.

A hardened heart will make it difficult to see the Lord's saving work, but that is not because He is concealed. It's because we are looking for liberation in something else. As we've discussed before, God may allow us to chase our broken desires for a time to let it run its due course. But our Savior remains near with His hand held out. The Father is always calling His children home as the Holy Spirit ushers us toward freedom. Look up. Grab hold of your Savior. It is right and good to expect His rescue. It's a promise.

As you go, expect freedom. Expect to be emancipated from your old life. Freedom is not the absence of temptation, but the ability to resist the power of sin over your will. God's promises of freedom are for today. The struggle of same-sex attraction or the pull of emotional dependency may rear their ugly heads when you least expect it, but you are not destined to be conquered. Jesus Christ conquered Satan at the cross. You are no longer a slave unable to choose freedom. You are a Daughter, able to choose righteousness. So live in the triumphant victory that is His supremacy over sin and death and His promise of resurrection into new life. Your Father is a

GETTING IN

GETTING STUCK

GETTING OUT

warrior and you are made in His image. You have the power of God in you, who conquers all by the authority of His name. Because of the Son, your will is free to choose Jesus Christ. My sister, you are free indeed.

FEELS LIKE DEATH & OPPORTUNITIES TO GO BACK

Expect that there will be times when God's saving work feels like death. Letting go and walking away from old loves means killing what we formerly treasured most. It means tearing out who we were before—our plans, behaviors, and relationships. The whole process is excruciatingly painful and will likely mean losing a lot. But the absence of cancer means it can no longer kill us. Even in the gaping wounds left behind, God is at work healing. From the inside out. He is granting us life as we are dying to our self.

Speaking from experience, I can tell you that there are times when self-denial sucks. Many times, it felt like God was killing me when He was actually saving me. Because of my unhealthy enmeshment, emotional dependency, and sexual entanglements, I had caused an unholy bond that took parts of me as I warred to put it all to death. Healing requires active obedience in turning to Jesus Christ with every temptation. That means turning to Him when I want to sneak a second glance at a new woman in the weight

Many times, it felt like God was killing me when He was actually saving me.

room or when I feel like fantasizing about a romantic female relationship I see on TV. Most times, I am thankful for the Holy Spirit's conviction in those moments, but there are other times when it just makes me mad, like God is refusing to give me what I want. Or if I were to reach out and take it, that God will exercise His justice on my sin again. And I pout.

Sometimes seeing a lesbian relationship makes me feel happy for them as I recall the old days, or jealous because they can have what they want but I can't. Responses like this remind me that there's always more to kill. When it feels like I'm dying, it may be that I'm actually being healed.

You can expect that you will be tempted with opportunities to go back to Egypt—back to bondage—back to a lesbian lifestyle. As you are being led out, you can expect that Satan will be offering you inroads. Ways to get in with your old girlfriend or chances to meet someone new. He does not offer you opportunities because he wants you to be happy, the devil wants to see you bleeding and trick you into dying.

How easy it is to forget the death our former lives brought about. Old habits really do die hard. Killing sin is mortifying, but God never asks us to lay down something that He will not replace with something better. The absence of something does not equal nothing. For some of you, because of vows and kids and family, you will lose a lot. Expect a deep level of sadness as you let go of the life you loved. You can mourn as you bury the ashes that once brought you pleasure, but know that God is sanctifying you in the process. He is vivifying you. Beauty will come from the ashes. Crucifying your flesh is never meaningless. When something dies, it makes room for something new to grow. Do not lose heart. Death will soon turn to deliverance.[4]

GRIEF & REJECTION

Worship will well up from within you when you are free. Yet life with Jesus Christ does not always occur on the mountaintops. We walk with Him through valleys as well. You can expect sorrow and rejoicing simultaneously. Grief may result from putting sin to death and it's crucial to deal with it appropriately. Grief is like a pinball machine. One minute, you feel overwhelming joy in the Lord for what He has done in your heart only to be flooded with sorrow the very next. But

GETTING IN

GETTING STUCK

GETTING OUT

this is normal so do not hide your grieving. Lament and praise can and should co-exist.

For a while, I had a hard time admitting to my counselor that I was happy in my newfound freedom, but also sad. I thought that sadness indicated that I was still desirous of my sin, even though I knew I was not. It was in counseling that I learned it is healthy to process sin in grief. After all, it was a real relationship that had to mourned and grieved. I was encouraged to talk about it and her as a means of moving forward and healing from a significant loss. As a whole, doing a relationship autopsy differs from fond reminiscence in that it is a right way of processing what was exchanged. Jesus Christ holds us fast and faithfully carries us through the gauntlet of grief. When He addresses our sin, He does so to heal us wholly—the heart that started it all as well as the grief that proceeds.

Your grief may tempt you toward isolation. It did for me. I didn't think I had a right to receive care and comfort from the Father or believers. After all, my suffering was a result of my choice to pursue a lifestyle I knew to be sinful. Since I felt it could have been avoided with a different choice, I felt the onus was on me to perform damage control. But this is not how Jesus Christ treats the broken and it is not how the church deals with the wounded. God brings our lawlessness before us so that we might see our need for a Savior. He does not leave us to pick at our scabs. Rather, He binds our wounds and raises us up to walk with Him as we heal. We do not have to hide our guilt or shove others away because we willfully chose our sin. Instead, we extend grace to ourselves and receive godly exhortation, counsel, empathy, and comfort from those who enter into our grief with us.

Grieving may come as a result of being rejected by certain friends, family, or communities as well. Walking with God and following His design for sexuality will likely cause your lesbian friends and gay community to distance themselves from you. If you break up with your girlfriend or leave your wife, there will be pain involved. It can't be avoided. A life being transformed by the gospel is offensive. Following our King and proclaiming a better allegiance feels alienating to others. It's possible you may even face rejection from certain Christians who dismiss your conviction and obedience as oppressive and optional. As you are despised and judged, remember that you are accepted by the only one who matters—Jesus Christ.

Expect to be misunderstood. People will count you foolish for leaving your "perfect" relationship or the family you love. They will not understand your choices: righteousness over revelry, poverty over riches, humility over exaltation, emptiness over fullness. It seems a silly trade to those who are not of the Spirit. Don't invest your hope in convincing them of the gains that come with submitting to the Lord. Jesus Christ is the only one who can accomplish that work. Even Jesus Christ was despised and rejected by certain family, friends, and communities.[5] His gospel was a hard message and yours is a hard choice. The Christian life is the harder road to be sure, but you know the Savior you have trusted. You may look and feel strange, but it's because God is conforming you to the image of His Son. For you, the valley is a door of hope.

Grief and rejection are real and must be dealt with appropriately. Jesus Christ is with you and at work in your hurting and mess. The promise is here now and an end is coming soon. God will restore you as He continues His work of making all things new. There will be an end to your mourning.

JOY & HAPPINESS

When you fight to place your supreme value in Jesus Christ, expect to feel joy. Happiness in God. It is a promise. Scars will remain, but their ache reminds of the Great Surgeon who loved you enough to do what was necessary for you to thrive. My scars tell an epic story of His long rescue. They remind me of how loved I am. Now, I smile and laugh unencumbered. At the end of my life, I will sing instead of groan. Now I can worship Jesus Christ with outstretched arms for all He has done and I thank God that I can feel both joy and happiness.

At first, killing what is contrary to holiness may feel like joyless duty. When I started acting in obedience, it rarely felt satisfying. Holiness often begins this way because it requires us to eliminate our false loves. And that is not always happy work. But holiness removes what harms us. With time, consequences like shame, separation from God, bondage, and wasted years will yield the joy that Jesus Christ offers. When lesser affections are eliminated and striving ceases, it creates space that God fills with joy. Better affections infiltrate your life. Now I can enjoy creation and rejoice in a new way because I can see how the earth's beauty displays my Creator. I can be grateful when I have a new fun experience or get promoted at work because I know it has purpose in God's kingdom. I can happily serve my neighbor because I love them with Jesus Christ's love. Now I can eagerly proclaim the gospel because I am wanting to share my joy and compel others to a God who can rescue them too. Now I can be happy when God brings glory to Himself foremost. Ongoing celebration is a marker of my life because now I can see that it is all from Him and for Him.

Joy is a fruit of the Spirit that affects everything.[6] It is evidence of being transformed into the likeness of Jesus Christ. When you wage war against the pull of same-sex attraction, God will grant you happiness in Him. You can have wonder for what God is doing in your life as well as what He is doing in others. God will grant you joy in the valley and on the mountaintop. Soon, you can expect to celebrate with friends and family as you share the story of where you've been, what God has done, and all that He is yet to do. Praise will mark your life.

HEALING PAIN & THE LONG WAY

Expect pain as you battle since sin created wounds. But also remember, you can expect the Great Physician.[7] God's methods of healing will always involve surgery. Deep cuts, amputations, incisions—whatever it takes to remove the source idols, the surface idols, the false gods, our objects of worship, our false hopes, and unholy alliances. When He cuts, He does so only to remove whatever keeps us from Him. Same-sex attraction and emotional dependency are cancers that metastasize within. They are always growing and expanding. They are ravenous, feeding on anything they can find. Sexual sin attacks the soul and there comes a point where its symptoms can no longer remain hidden. They present themselves in all sorts of ways. Its deadly wounds are obvious to the Great Physician and our secret sin gets disclosed by the Light. The Lord knows the sickness that we cannot see and He provides the remedy.

It's easy to confuse God's kind wounds with that of Satan, but God's goal is always for our flourishing. Divine surgery means there will be pain, but it is redemptive pain. Healing pain points me to Jesus Christ because the feeling reminds me that I am alive because of Him. Brokenness may become your new normal for a while, but it is right and good for healing. Do not be afraid. Jesus Christ wounds only so that He may heal. It is better to gain eternity missing an eye or a hand than find ourselves outcast.[8]

We can also expect suffering. Belief and obedience does not shield us from suffering. Sometimes it just sucks. Separating myself from eleven years of an emotionally dependent same-sex relationship felt miserable for a long time, even though it was an act of obedience. My sexual sin had escalated everything. Even months after Jesus Christ's rescue, I was dealing with regular shockwaves. Often, I felt nauseous, depressed, and overwhelmed. Some of the suffering felt worse than my former bondage. Satan tried to use the chaos of my sin's consequences and fear of the unknown to scare me into retreat, but Jesus

Christ was bringing me out of my disorder.

When deciding to war with your sin, you can expect circumstance to get worse at the start. In fact, life may grow increasingly difficult before it ever gets better. Your personal pain will increase, your body will physically ache, and suffering will amplify, but do not lose heart. God is not done. Your Creator is ordering the chaos, even in the storm. It will get better.

Numbing away the pain will never produce healing. When the pain of staying the same exceeds the pain of divine surgery, you are ready. We fight through the pain, not around it. God is with us. Jesus Christ is able to sympathze with us in our weaknesses, not just in terms of His earthly suffering and temptations, but also by His infinite knowledge as the sovereign God.[9] What a comfort that we are fully known and He understands that we are fully human.

Have patience with the process as well. God is not in a rush. He takes us the long way around, as painstaking as it may feel. His work is always complete and thorough and in the end you will never be disappointed. He will deliver you. Throughout the Bible, God often takes His people the long way around. Rarely does He guide them directly from point A to point B. In the wilderness, He wants to conform us into His image more than He wants to deliver us quickly.[10] He does this because He knows what we need even though it's rarely what we think is best. The wilderness gets the fondness for Egypt out of His people. The route burns away the chaff and teaches us how to let Him carry our burdens. That refinement can be painful. The process also yields greater trust in Him.

Eventually, you can expect the emotions that taunt you will subside. You can expect that the Lord will use His time and His restoration for your flourishing. It's a promise. Sometimes, I still face new painful consequences for my choices I made back then. My hurts are not completely gone, but their sting lessens day by day, year by year. The fight is not just about getting out, or getting to the other side, or entering the Promised Land; it's so when we arrive in His presence we know the face of the one who is our Great Deliverer. The road will likely be long, but it is the only secure way for the Lord is walking with you.

LONGING

So I also want you to know that you can expect longing to remain. And I don't mean a longing for your old life. There is a longing that God has placed in the hearts of humankind that will not be satisfied until we are in the presence of God our Creator. His proximity solves the desire for relief from our broken world. I think this is where so many of us get tripped up. This is one of the ways I was confused and went deeper into the cycles of my sin. Our whole lives we feel a longing for something, "more" than we have experienced so far. We look to be fulfilled in countless ways and emptiness and want still exist. We became a Christian and eventually became perplexed that longing still remained. *Did I miss something? Was I tricked? Am I really a Christian? Maybe I need salvation and a girlfriend?*

I want you to know that once you repent and turn back to the Lord, you can expect that longing will still be there. Do not confuse this longing with a sexual identity. Or the lack of a lesbian lifestyle. Our deepest longing has nothing to do with sex and humans. The Lord has placed a longing in all human bodies and souls that will only be satisfied when creation is home with its Creator. We long for God to be in Garden with us again like He was in Eden.[11] Ask the Lord for wisdom to help you distinguish the difference between missing Egypt and longing for the Garden to be reestablished on earth where once again God will walk among us. And if it's helpful, when I admit that I have this longing to be at home in the physical presence of God, it is not fatalistic—I'm not wishing that my life would end. I am longing for the restoration of all things. I want ultimate vitality. I want creation to be made new. I

GETTING IN

GETTING STUCK

GETTING OUT

want the world's brokenness to end. I want to be fully satisfied with God. I am longing for His good kingdom to spread over the earth. I am longing to be restored in my life now and in everlasting life to come. It's already. And it's not yet.

HOPE

More than anything, you can expect hope. One day, we will experience perfect rescue, freedom, peace, rest, joy, and happiness when we meet our Savior face to face. It's a promise. That is the basis of our hope and should inform our journey every step of the way. One day, pain, temptation, and sorrow will fade away. Sex will cease. Suffering in this body will end. The "not yet" will come to be. I want you to anchor yourself in that hope rather than feeling some kind of general sense of hopefulness. Inspiration can fluctuate a million times a day. Along with my will, my wants and desires shift constantly. But hope that is rooted in the promises of Jesus Christ remains steadfast. It never disappoints because it's not tied up in an earthly outcome. Our hope is the person and work of Jesus Christ.

Whether or not you are tempted by same-sex attraction this afternoon, next year, or in a future heterosexual marriage, that threat cannot negate your hope. And even if you stumble, your failures cannot steal the hope offered through Christ because God is always faithful. He keeps you. Look up and claim what is true about Him and what He says is true about you. Expect that God will stand beside you and shield you from Satan's ends. That is the hope of the gospel—we get

Our hope is not based on probabilities, but a promise.

God. Even if we lose everything in this life, we still gain Jesus Christ. Our hope is built on nothing less. Christian hope will not disappoint because God defeated Satan at the cross and will one day rid him and his brokenness from creation. Our

King is also the ultimate warrior. The hope of the Christian life is that redemption is now and resurrection is coming. Our hope is not based on probabilities, but a promise, and God's steadfast love constantly points us to His Son who is the source of all our hope.

GOD, THE I AM

When God calls us out, it is extremely helpful to have an idea of some of the experiences we can expect. But as we decide to war, prepare for battle, and begin to fight we must know even more than *what* to expect. We must know *Who* to expect. It's crucial that we depend solely on the one who God has sent and believe that He is who He says He is.

In all my years of striving to free myself from relational and sexual sin through my own strength, I knew that if God was not who He said He was then I would never be free. He tells us in the Bible that He is all we need and that promise is true. God displays all His infinite attributes at the same time. He is holy and loving. Patient and fierce. King and friend. Exercising wrath and compassion. Justice and mercy. His works demonstrate the fullness of who He is without reservation. He is a Rescuer when we are stuck. He is merciful when we face discipline. He is a surgeon and the Great Physician. He is omnipotent and good. He is patient, wooing us to Himself and redeeming what we have exchanged. He creates life out of nothing. Expect your great Deliverer. Expect God to be who He says He is.

Expect that Jesus Christ will be faithful. Faithful to His promises, to His church, and faithful to you and me. He will grant relief. It may take time, during which we will groan inwardly, but the Father will accomplish all that He has promised to His people through the Son by the power of the Holy Spirit.[12] Expect the I AM.

GETTING IN

GETTING STUCK

GETTING OUT

LIVING IN VICTORY

It has been four years since God extracted me from my same-sex relationship and I am still humbled by all He did to rescue me. Yet I know that the true miracle God accomplished was a further transformation of my redeemed heart.

When Jesus Christ came down to rescue me, I could have chosen to reject my Savior and go back or look for a new muse. I could have repeated the cycle so prevalent in the lesbian community: emotional dependency, enmeshment, detachment, and reattachment with someone that promises greater pleasures, more fulfillment, and less pain. But I didn't. And it had nothing to do with the fact that I weighed both options against one another and found my same-sex lifestyle wanting. Simply put, the Lord opened my eyes to His beauty in such a way that I wanted nothing more than to follow Him. He caused me to will and to want Him. Love Him. I wanted be who He said I was and live in the fullness of that freedom. I knew that if I returned to my bondage, I would end up in the same shitty place again years down the road. Broken and shattered. Enriching someone else's house. Hopeless. Devoid of the fruit of my salvation. Hardening my own heart. Regretting more wasted years. But God was done with my rebellion. His anger burned against both my sin and His enemy and out of great love He acted in power. Not only to restrain further evil, but to change my will in order to desire Him more than any other earthly pleasure.

Thinking back on my story continues to bring me to tears. In all my former arrogance and pride, I never could have seen the merciful tragedy that God orchestrated. And I would not change a thing. I had built a castle on a foundation of sand. I constructed a tower to be like God instead of trusting Him to be my strong tower. I ran away to a distant country and carelessly spent my birthright instead of remaining with the Lord at His table and with His people. I kept an illicit lover in my home where I worshiped idols and ideology more than my King. And I longed to be at home in a place where my pride and sinful behaviors would be accepted.

For eleven years, I built a storyline and a theology I considered impenetrable. I was determined to prove that I was different, that my lesbian relationship was special, that the insanity of sin did not apply to me. Only when I found myself sitting in the wreckage of my life did I realize that I was at fault for all of its destruction, not God. I had forged ahead on the wrong road believing that I would eventually find peace in rebellion. I believed that self-rule was the supreme freedom. But thanks be to God that He grants believers the Holy Spirit who whispers to us. Haunts us. Entices us to hope in the Son. It was only when God opened my eyes that I could see Him as He is. He changed my heart to embrace the goodness of His design. The joy of His rule. God caused me to realize that my salvation was not a loophole, but a way back to a close relationship with Jesus Christ.

Jesus Christ has made a way for each of us to freedom and, ultimately, to eternal life. For He is the way, the truth, and the life.[1] If you are still struggling with the chains of sin, I want you to be encouraged. I wrote this book for you to create a space where the Holy Spirit can foster a want for freedom that may not exist yet. Or rekindle the desire for the Father that used to exist. More than anything, I want you to experience a renewed love for God and not merely healing from same-sex attraction and emotional dependency. I pray that you will desire our triune God before all things. And overflowing from that love that you will desire to live in all ways pleasing to the Lord. And that He will restore all the places long devastated.

HIS STORY

My story has always been His story. God has no surprise or alarm about what happens in the chapters of my life. He wrote it, ordained it, and is sovereign over it. God has promised an ending that will not leave me disappointed. Getting in, getting stuck, and getting out of a lesbian relationship is just part of my story; it's not my only story. My sin is not the overarching theme. And it is never the sum total of who I am, or who you are. It's simply the context from which the I AM is restoring you and me. He will make all the brokenness we experience matter—for you and for me and for His kingdom. His story is grimy and glorious.

At any point throughout those eleven years, the Lord could have changed my situation in an instant. Why didn't He? I don't know, but I can say for certain that He is still good. I really don't care anymore about getting an answer to that question because I so strongly believe His timing

Getting out of a lesbian relationship is just part of my story; it's not my only story.

was best for me. Perfect in fact. On this side of Heaven, there are many things we simply cannot know, which is why we must build our faith not on explanations of our circumstances, but on the unchanging character and nature of our God. He knows why and for how long we will struggle with all sorts of brokenness and I can rest in the fact that He does only what is right and good for each of us. His authorship is not to be

GETTING IN

GETTING STUCK

GETTING OUT

resented, but to be a source of relief. If we know Him, we can believe Him. If we know Him, we can love Him. And when we know Him, we can trust Him.

Our stories are always part of God's greater story. There is a very good beginning and there is a victorious ending, and whole lot of wins and losses in the middle. By His mercy, God is with us in the mess. God is still unfolding His story in us and through us and His theme is always epic redemption. My story is pointing to His story. So is yours.

MAKE WAR

For eleven years, I was *in*—what some would say are the prime lesbian years of life. *But God.*

Every day before, every day during, and each day since is a war for me to see Jesus Christ as more worthy and beautiful than the things of this earth. I have to fight for joy. War is never passive. It is hard and painful. Freedom does not just happen. To be sure, it is always harder to escape our sin than to befriend it and make our bed with it, but the joy and peace we long for can only be found through Jesus Christ. We war because the sins of emotional dependency and same-sex attraction are always growing, never benign. Day by day, they steal from us while depositing just enough change to keep us energized and blind to their ploys. Do not be deceived any longer my friend. We must remove ourselves from the throne and burn our idols. We do it because the throne belongs to God alone. God will not share His glory with our preferences. He will not share His glory with our wife or girlfriend. Or us. God will glorify Himself alone.

God took me *out* of my lesbian relationship, but He has not taken away my same-sex attraction. He destroyed the former and by His mercy I have never looked back. But God gave me something better than taking away my weaknesses— He gave me Himself.

I still face days where I struggle with same-sex attraction.

It's way less potent, but I still feel it. I also still experience ongoing consequences of opening the door. It's hard to listen to songs about romantic love or breakups without feeling some pain from my misplaced allegiance. When I see a vehicle similar to the one she drove I have to fight against fear. When I see someone with her body type I panic. My body holds onto responses and memories that can torment me given the right triggers. Satan tempts me to believe that I will eventually fail in my exodus. I have to fight the lie that I am unworthy and untrustworthy. When I am approached by certain women, I am tempted to indulge my preferences. And at any point, I know that I could. When those times come, I've learned to run to Jesus Christ and tell the believers I have invited into my journey. I ask God for His comfort and another rescue. I must be proactive. I must make war to believe all that He has proclaimed.

Sometimes waging war against my enemy and my own flesh means quitting a TV series in the middle of a season for the sake of freedom. Sometimes it means skipping leg day if I find myself lusting after someone on a machine next to me. I even had to leave social media altogether and stop engaging with certain people because of the temptation to remember sin fondly. Instead, I pray out loud in my car. I claim the truth of God as I read the Bible in my bed. I contend with Satan on long runs. I sing to God with my hands raised in my kitchen. I text a close friend and ask for prayer. I go to my godly friends who make war with me. I proclaim the gospel to others. I dance out my worship. I rest under His covering during yoga. Defending my transforming heart is engaging in conscious freedom. Making war with our flesh is rooted in a fear of God, never a fear of man.

As we've learned, sometimes waging war looks like refusing to engage our flesh. Not responding to the taunts of the enemy. Not responding to a text. Not attending the party. Not taking a second look. Stillness can be proactive. It anchors us in the gospel's promise and God's power. When we conquer

GETTING IN

GETTING STUCK

GETTING OUT

temptation in the moment, we grow confident and resilient in our faith. At first, you may lose more battles than you win. But as you fight, you will grow in your strength and resolve to honor Him with your whole life. Jesus Christ does not keep count of your wins and losses. Remember, you have already been counted victorious in Christ. God has equipped us for the journey. Put on the armor and stand firm.

We make war because greater pleasures, more satisfying experiences, and more sustaining joys are found through the identity given to us by the God of the universe. There is no union more secure than what believers already have with God in Jesus Christ. Yet there is always more intimacy and deeper communion with God to be had. You can experience the fullness of your relationship with the Father through greater ongoing sanctification. That is why we war by continuously laying our same-sex affections at the feet of Jesus Christ always believing that the power of God can destroy its owning nature. Sin always expands, separates, and it steals our affection away from God and hinders our relationship with Him. So we fight for obedience in the mess to maintain unhindered presence with Him and highest affection for Him. Getting God is what makes eternity worth it. Getting God is what makes self-denial worth it. Getting God is what makes getting out worth it. Getting God is what makes happiness worthwhile. Getting God promises present and future restoration. God getting us is our ultimate victory.

The most glorious of victories are the uphill battles. The hard-fought triumphs. The ones that mean something. You can expect victory on earth with Jesus Christ. You are also assured of victory in death. My friend, I pray that you will know and believe that a same-sex lifestyle with all of its earthly pleasures will never give you ultimate fulfillment. It will never bring you rest of soul. It will never be pleasing to God. No matter how you nuance your life, when you pay homage to a lesser love it will yield nothing. Idols offer pleasure in the moment, but they do nothing for our souls but rob them. In the end, they are worthless, as there is no god but the God of the universe. Ultimate fulfillment can only be found in Him.

Learning about God the Father, God the Son, and God the Holy Spirit allows us to peer into the heart of our most loving Creator. He has a passionate desire for our spiritual restoration, which brings about our sexual restoration. He calls so that we may turn. He wounds for the sake of our healing. He takes

He has a passionate desire for our spiritual restoration, which brings about our sexual restoration.

in order to give. So run to Jesus Christ. Don't look back. Let go of all that would entangle you and be free. Choose life. If something hinders you from running, toss it. Set ablaze whatever causes you to stumble. Crawl on bloodied knees if you must. If the pain is too great to run or your heart grows too weary, ask God and His people to carry you. But you cannot stay here. As far as it depends on you, go. There are greater treasures ahead. Run in such a way as to win. Run in such a way as to finish well.

Sister, it is time for you to move on to maturity. You have already spent enough time living in debauchery. The Holy Spirit has granted you the power to repent, turn, and run toward Jesus Christ. May you go and sin no more.

LIVE IN VICTORY

Yes, I will need Jesus Christ to battle sin with me until death. Every day there is more faith to be granted, work to do, grace to receive, more healing to be had, more struggles to face, more flesh to kill, more joy to experience, and more victory to realize. There is a war going on. But because Jesus Christ is the author and finisher of the story, there is hope.

If you already know Jesus Christ as your Savior, I pray

GETTING IN

GETTING STUCK

GETTING OUT

that you grab hold of Him. He has kept a hold on you. I pray that you will faithfully read God's Word, talk to Him, pursue long-term obedience, and starve the sin that remains in your life. Receive His offers of rescue. Re-pledge your highest allegiance to the only one who has authority over all things. Thank Him for the gospel and His specific gifts. I pray that your eyes will be opened through the gracious work of the Holy Spirit and His persistent whisper to your soul. And I pray, by the grace of God, that He will provide you the will and the want to glorify Him in all areas of your life: your thoughts, desires, sexuality, and behaviors. Even when the days are hard. This is victorious living!

If you do not yet know Jesus Christ as your Savior, my hope for you in reading this book is that you will walk away with a greater understanding of who God is and that He will draw you to Himself through His loving-kindness. I pray that you will get God. I pray that you will ask for and receive the offers of rest, rescue, and hope in Him. I pray you will repent of all the futile ways you self-satisfy and give up self-identification in exchange for His identity that never changes. I pray that you experience saving faith in Jesus Christ for redemption and sanctification in this life and resurrection and restoration in the next.

More than anything, I pray this book brings you hope. Hope in what is true and in Him who is the truest friend. Believe that Jesus Christ alone can free you from the clutches of indwelling sin by the power of the Holy Spirit. Even if you never experience full eradication of same-sex attraction in this life, I pray you're your hope remains in the already and not *For the Christian hope is a Person, not an outcome.* yet. God's good plan will always go forth because His story is unhindered by us. For the Christian hope is a person, not an outcome. Your freedom is possible. Take courage! Do not lose heart!

Sister, you must fight! Battle! Make war! Do the hard work of obedience amidst your present, same-sex attraction and emotional dependence. It is worth it. Today you can experience freedom. And soon, you will arrive safely at the home promised to you in Jesus Christ. The struggle is real and may last a long time, but God hears your cries, He sees your suffering, He gave you weapons that will prevail, and He desires your freedom too. He longs for you to experience the greatest possible pleasures on earth knowing that lasting joy only comes from Him.

God brings forth life from what was dead. He brings hope to places that once seemed hopeless. He comforts the brokenhearted. He creates joy from tears. Beauty from ashes. Behold, He is making all things new. His kingdom has come. There is a glorious plunder in victory over the pull of same-sex attraction and emotional dependency. The benefits may seem too few to count right now, but they are limitless in number and scope and deeply rooted in the infinite character of our God. Christian, He has preserved you for Himself as part of His remnant people. And someday you will not be able to measure all that God has done in you or perceive all the benefits of your inheritance.

The Lord is faithful. He who has called you out will be faithful to lead you out. He will replace everything you have lost and give you more than you can imagine. Hope is what you received in the Father's great exchange. Hope is the person of Jesus Christ, the Lord of our salvation. We look back to find hope for what lies ahead. We look forward to His return for hope today. Sister, you are loved with the fierce and abiding love of your heavenly Father. Christian, you are His. You were made to be free. The Holy Spirit is calling you out of death and into abundant life in Jesus Christ. Make war and live!

For His glory and our joy,

Carly

GETTING IN

GETTING STUCK

GETTING OUT

ACKNOWLEDGEMENTS

TO MY ENCOURAGERS AND PRAYER WARRIORS

Thank you to my dear friends who have been on this journey with me. Thank you for listening and speaking truth. Thank you for praying for deeper healing, more protection, and overwhelming joy in the years it took to write this book. I love each of you.

TO THE FAMILY OF GOD

Thank you to the body of Christ who rallied around me and made this book happen. Thank you to my wonderful crew who read all the versions of my manuscript and provided invaluable feedback. I'm forever grateful that you partnered with me on this project.

Thank you to all my editors: conceptual editors, copyeditors, theological editors, and expert editors. Many of you were referrals and now I'm thrilled to call you my friends. You are each gifted in extraordinary ways. Thank you for hearing my heart, understanding the unique aim of this book, and helping to clearly proclaim another testimony of the love and authority of Jesus Christ. You spent countless hours reading the drafts, correcting my errors, and reminding me that this hard work is good work. Thank you for making this book better.

We are truly saved to God and also to a people. This book would have not been possible without the men and women who shared their gifts so that this book could become a reality. Fellow believers assisted with layout, focused the content, created the artwork, and made a way to get this book in your hands. For me, the best part is that each of you are just normal people with extraordinary skills working in the marketplace. You have a heart for seeing God establish His kingdom on earth through your craft and in your homes. Your teamwork and friendship have helped reveal the beauty of what the family of God truly is. Thank you for being the Church even as we all are members of different congregations.

TO MY CHURCH HOME

Thank you to my local church. So much of what I love and know about God the Father, God the Son, and God the Spirit is displayed by you and through our people. Thank you for all you have done to preach and teach the Bible and lead us to worship the triune God all week long in all things. You have been faithful to proclaim the Word of God to us and have discipled us unto Jesus Christ.

Because of how well you have discipled your people I can hardly differentiate my words about God from our orthodox words about God. So much of the content in this book was imparted by your faithful teaching of God's Word and I'm thankful that you gave me permission to use it and contextualize it.

I love our church family and our gathering. I am thankful and humbled to be among you.

RECOMMENDED BOOKS

Butterfield, Rosaria Champagne. *The Secret Thoughts of an Unlikely Convert: An English Professor's Journey into Christian Faith*. Pittsburgh: Crown & Covenant Publications, 2012.

Butterfield, Rosaria Champagne. *Openness Unhindered: Further Thoughts of an Unlikely Convert on Sexual Identity and Union with Christ*. Pittsburgh: Crown & Covenant Publications, 2015.

Dykas, Ellen. *Sexual Sanity for Women: Healing from Sexual and Relational Brokenness*. Greensboro: New Growth Press, 2013.

Gilson, Rachel. *Born Again This Way: Coming Out, Coming to Faith, and What Comes Next*. Charlotte: The Good Book Company, 2020.

Hallman, Janelle. *The Heart of Female Same-Sex Attraction: A Comprehensive Counseling Resource*. Downers Grove, IL: InterVarsity Press, 2008.

Hill-Perry, Jackie. *Gay Girl, Good God: The Story of Who I Was, and Who God Has Always Been.* Nashville: B&H Publishing Group, 2018.

Hope, Carly. *Getting Out: How I Got Into a Lesbian Relationship and How God Got Me Out.* Kansas City: Free Indeed Press, 2020.

Howard, Jeanette. *Out of Egypt: One Woman's Journey Out of Lesbianism.* Oxford: Monarch Books, 1991.

Howard, Jeanette. *Into the Promised Land: Beyond the Lesbian Struggle.* Oxford: Monarch Books, 2005.

Needham, Kelly. *Friendish: Reclaiming Real Friendship in a Culture of Confusion.* Nashville: Thomas Nelson, 2019.

Paulk, Anne. *Restoring Sexual Identity: Hope for Women Who Struggle with Same-Sex Attraction.* Eugene, OR: Harvest House Publishers, 2003.

Rentzel, Lori. *Emotional Dependency.* Downers Grove, IL: Intervarsity Press, 1990.

Slattery, Juli. *Rethinking Sexuality: God's Design and Why It Matters.* Colorado Springs: Multnomah Books, 2018.

RECOMMENDED SUPPORT

IN-PERSON AND ONLINE SUPPORT
FOR INDIVIDUALS, SPOUSES, FAMILIES, AND FRIENDS

HARVEST USA

"Harvest USA brings the truth and mercy of Jesus Christ by: Helping individuals and families affected by sexual and gender struggles and providing resources that address biblical sexuality to individuals and churches."

215.482.0111
715 Twining Road, Suite 200
Dresher, Pennsylvania 19025
www.harvestusa.org
info@harvestusa.org

LIVING HOPE MINISTRIES

"Living Hope Ministries seeks to proclaim God's truth as we journey with those seeking sexual and relational wholeness through a more intimate relationship with Jesus Christ."

817.459.2507
P.O. Box 2239
Arlington, Texas 76004
www.livehope.org
info@livehope.org

PORTLAND FELLOWSHIP

"Portland Fellowship is an organization dedicated to glorifying Jesus Christ by proclaiming His desire and power to release people from unwanted same-sex attraction."

503.235.6364
P.O. Box 14841
Portland, Oregon 97293
www.portlandfellowship.com
office@portlandfellowship.com

REGENERATION MINISTRIES

"Regeneration equips men, women and families to learn to live God's good, holy, and beautiful design for sexuality."

410.661.0284
P.O. Box 9830
Baltimore, Maryland 21284-9830
www.regenerationministries.org
info@RegenerationMinistries.org

NOTES & SCRIPTURE INDEX

INTRODUCTION

1. Gen. 1:1; Exod. 15:11; Deut. 4:35, 6:4; 1 Sam. 2:2; 1 Kings 8:60; Ps. 115:3; Isa. 44 6–8; Matt. 3:17; 17:5; 28:19; Mark 1:10–11; John 1:1, 14–18; 3:16; 5:19, 26; 6:44; 11:41–42; 14:6, 26; 15:26; 16:7–13, 15; 17:1; Acts 2:33; 5:3–4; 8:16; Phil. 1:2; Col. 1:15–20; 2:9; Titus 2:13; Heb. 1:3; 1 Cor. 3:16; 8:6; Rev. 22:13.

2. Gen. 1:1–31; Job 33:4, 37:23; Pss. 8:5–8; 19:1–2; 33:6; Isa. 44:24; Jer. 32:17; Mal. 2:10; Matt. 11:27; John 1:1–3; Rom. 1:19–20; 4:17; 2 Cor. 8:6; Col. 1; Heb. 1:3; 11:13; Rev. 4.

3. Gen. 1:26; Job 33:4; 37:23; Ps. 33:6; Isa. 44:24; Jer. 32:17; Mal. 2:10; John 1:1; Rom. 4:17; 2 Cor. 8:6; Col. 1; Heb. 1:3, 11:13; Rev. 4.

4. Ps. 19:1–4; Isa. 55:11; Matt. 5:17–18; John 10:35; 16:13–15; Rom. 1:16–20; 10:9–10; 1 Cor. 1:21; Eph. 1:17–18; 3:10, 18; 2 Tim. 3:16; Heb. 4:12; 2 Pet. 1:19–21, Jude 3.

5. Isa. 53; Matt. 1:1; 2:43–45; 16:15–17; 26:36–47a; Luke 2:52; 22:39–46; John 1:11–14; 8:40; 9:16; 14:6; 20:30–31; Acts 3:22; Rom. 5:15; 1 Cor. 8:6; 15:45; Gal. 3:16; Phil. 2:6, 10; Col. 1; 1 Tim. 6:3–4; 2 Tim. 1:13; 4:3; Titus 2:13; Heb. 1:1–3; 2:14–15; 4:15; 5:1–10; 7:1–28; 2 Pet. 1:13–14, 2:1.

6. Gen. 1:2; Pss. 33:6; 139:7–19, 70; Mic. 3:8–10; John 16:13;

Acts 2:1–5; 5:3–4; Rom. 8:2–6; 1 Cor. 2:10; 12:1–11; 2 Thess. 2:6–7; 1 John 2:19–27.

7. Gen. 1:1; Exod. 3:14; Ps. 115:3; John 3:16–17; 5:19–20; 1 Cor. 8:6; 13:12; Phil. 1:2; Col. 1:16; Rev. 22:13.

8. Gen. 1:23–28; 2:15, 24; Lev. 18; Matt. 19:4–6; 28:18–20; Rom. 1:21–29; 1 Cor. 6:9–20; 7:2–5; Gal. 5:19; Eph. 5:3, 21–33; Heb. 13:4.

PART ONE **GETTING IN**

CHAPTER 1 MY BEST FRIEND

1. Beth Moore, When Godly People Do Ungodly Things: Arming Yourself in the Age of Seduction (Nashville, TN: Broadman & Holman Publishers, 2002),13.

2. Psalm 37:4 (ESV) says, "Delight yourself in the LORD, and he will give you the desires of your heart." During this time of my life, I twisted the application of this verse to the point that I believed if I was holy and worked hard enough for God, He would owe me the desires of my heart. The correct context is when we delight ourselves in Him, He changes our hearts and desires to be like His. He gives us His desires rather than all of the stuff we desire.

3. This particular criticism of God came from a psalm I had misunderstood. Psalm 34:20 (ESV) says, "He keeps all his bones; not one of them is broken." I cried out again to Him because I believed this to mean He had an obligation to spare me from the worst forms of suffering, which I felt He had failed to do. However, the New Testament makes clear that this particular verse was a prophecy about Christ's crucifixion (John 19:36). Even still, as a poetic psalm the context shows that the point here is not that God keeps us from suffering, but that He carries us through it. He is faithful not because He spares us from suffering, but because He holds us in the midst of it.

4. 1 Pet. 1:6; 5:10. I misunderstood the timeframe and the promised outcomes of these verses. I thought they meant that suffering would be for a short time and that if I really loved God there would be a good outcome soon. Peter says that suffering will indeed happen, but after "a little while" it will result in perseverance in the faith, restoration, and the glorification of God. This portion of 1 Peter has an

eschatological flavor to it in that Peter has glorification in mind more so than worldly deliverance. The idea is that this life is considered a "little while" and will include suffering, but God will deliver us into His glory in the end.

CHAPTER 2 OPENING THE DOOR

1. I didn't understand my sin and felt like I could not keep going to God and asking for help unless I first had a strategy to help myself. But Hebrews 4:14–16 (NIV) tells us to hold firmly to the faith that Jesus Christ is our great high priest who is able to sympathize with all our weaknesses. "Let us then approach God's throne of grace with confidence, so that we may receive mercy and find grace to help us in our time of need" (v. 16).

2. Gen. 2:23–25.

3. Matt. 19:4–6.

4. Ps. 127:3; 1 Cor. 7:2–5; Eph. 5:21–33.

5. Lev. 18; Rom. 1:24–27; 1 Cor. 6:12–20; Heb. 13:4.

6. I felt like God had handed me over to Satan to be ruled by him because I no longer saw, heard, or felt God. But the truth is God never gives Christians over to Satan. God can hand us over to be ruled by our sin, but never to our old master. According to Romans 1:18–32 (ESV), God pours out his wrath on those who know God, but reject Him. "Therefore, God gave them over in the sinful desires of their hearts to sexual impurity for the degrading of their bodies with one another" (v. 24). God also gave them over to "shameful lusts" (v. 26) and to a "depraved mind" (v. 28). Sometimes God's wrath is to let us be owned by the very things that we chose.

7. Pss. 34:8; 139:14; Matt. 7:11.

8. Jen Wilkin. "James: Living a Life of Genuine Faith." *Week 3 Teaching*. February, 5, 2014. www.jenwilkin.net.

9. John 16:33.

10. Mark 15:3–5.

11. Gen. 3:6; Rom. 1:32.

12. Eph. 2:1–9.

13. Rom. 3:21–26.

CHAPTER 3 MY INCONGRUENCE

1. See the book's Introduction where I state my biblical convictions about homosexuality with supporting Scripture.

2. 1 Cor. 15:32b. I knew I was probably using this verse out of context, but I didn't care because I wanted to quote the Bible to prove I didn't value it and to show that I could make it say whatever I wanted. I wanted this verse to mean that I should do whatever I want now because I am not promised tomorrow. However, what Paul is saying is that without the resurrection we are to be pitied so much so that this should be our mantra. But because there is a coming resurrection, our hope is pointed toward the future and not here and now. It is also followed by the verse that warns us to "not be misled" and to "come back to your senses as you ought, and stop sinning" (15:33–34 ESV).

CHAPTER 4 TAMING TIGERS

1. I first heard this story from Jen Wilkin in her Bible Study called, "James: Living a Life of Genuine Faith." *Week 3 Teaching.* February, 5, 2014. www.jenwilkin.net. You can find an article on this story online: Alan Feuer, "Police Subdue Tiger in Harlem Apartment," *New York Times,* October 5, 2003, https://www.nytimes.com/2003/10/05/nyregion/police-subdue-tiger-in-harlem-apartment.html.

2. 1 Pet. 2:11.

3. Gen. 1:31.

4. Gen. 2:15–17; 3:1–19.

5. Ps. 51:5; Eph. 2:1–3.

6. Rom. 5:15–17.

7. 2 Cor. 11:14.

8. Gen. 3:15; Rom 16:20; Heb. 2:14.

9. Ps 26:2; 2 Cor. 13:5; 1 Pet. 5:8; 1 John 4:1–6.

10. Rom. 8:38–39.

11. James 1:13–15.

12. Rom. 8:12–13; Gal. 5:16; James 4:7.

CHAPTER 5 MY CASTLE

1. Ps. 127:1; 1 Cor. 3:10–15. Eccles. 1:9–10 says, "What has been will be again, what has been done will be done again; there is nothing new under the sun. Is there anything of which one can say, 'Look! This is something new'? It was here already, long ago; it was here before our time." At the time, I did not think God's idea for relationships—and especially modern lesbian relationships—were timeless. I thought I had found an innovative way to make my life a beautiful monument and that God was too antiquated to know how to do anything about it.

2. See the book's Introduction where I state my biblical convictions about homosexuality with supporting Scripture.

CHAPTER 6 FINDING IDENTITY

1. Phil. 3:20–21; Heb. 11:8–10; Heb. 13:14.
2. Gen. 13:12; Gen14:12.
3. Rom. 8:1–2.
4. Rom. 6:1–14; Gal. 2:20.
5. Rom. 8:15–16.
6. Eph. 1:13–14.
7. Rom. 8:38–39.
8. Gen. 1:27, 31.
9. Rom. 5:6–8.
10. Heb. 4:12–13.

CHAPTER 7 MY STRIVING

1. Gen. 3:4; James 1:13–15.

2. I thought I could help others find peace with themselves by offering them affirmation and encouragement. But peace and lasting acceptance only come from the Father and through Jesus Christ. God reconciles us to Himself. There is no other way it happens. Colossians 1:19–20 states that God was pleased to give His Son the power to "reconcile" all things to Himself by offering lasting "peace through his blood." God approaches us in mercy to reconcile us to Himself by forgiving our sin. It's like the picture we see in Hosea 2:14–15: "Therefore, I am now going to allure her; I

will lead her into the wilderness and speak tenderly to her. There I will give her back her vineyards, and will make the Valley of Achor a door of hope." See also Rom. 5:1–11 and 2 Cor. 5:18–20.

3.   Rev. 2:4.

4.   John 6:68.

5.   Gen. 3:21–6:7.

6.   Gen. 6:8–22.

7.   Gen. 11:5.

8.   Gen. 11:7.

9.   Gen. 1:28; 9:1.

10. Gen. 3:4–5.

11. 1 John 4:8. "God is love" is a verse commonly cited out of context. Typically, I used it to justify my will, as if I was ultimate in God's affections so God would never condemn me. It's also used to bully dissenters of the gay lifestyle holding them to human standards of love. However, God's biblical love referenced by this verse is more merciful and just than we can imagine. The love of God is dynamic in ways that human love is not. God's love is holy and powerful, faithful and true, wrathful and compassionate, severe and kind. This "love" John speaks about is explained in the verses that follow: "This is how God showed his love among us: He sent his one and only Son into the world that we might live through him. This is love: not that we loved God, but that he loved us and sent his Son as an atoning sacrifice for our sins" (vv. 9–10). He points us to our sin and then directs us to Jesus Christ.

CHAPTER 8 REPEATING CYCLES

1.   Eccles. 1:9.

2.   Rev. 21:1–4.

3.   1 Cor. 10:13.

4.   Math 11:28.

5.   John 1:14–18; Heb. 4:14–16.

6.   I created this chart based on ideas adapted from *"Why? Understanding Homosexuality and Gender Development in Females."* DVD. Living Hope Ministries. Arlington, TX. 2015.

7. Heb. 12:1–2.

8. Ps. 51:17.

9. Dr. Barry Jones. Used by permission given through private email correspondence.

10. Gal. 5:1.

11. James 1:13–15.

12. Heb. 4:15.

13. Gen. 3:6; Exod. 16:4; Matt 4:1–11; Luke 22:24.

14. Heb. 1:3.

PART TWO GETTING STUCK

CHAPTER 9 MY WAY

1. Eph. 6:17.

CHAPTER 10 BELIEVING LIES

1. 1 Cor. 6:9–11.

2. 2 Cor. 5:17.

3. John 10:27–30.

4. Rom. 3:21–26; 5:1–11.

5. Gen. 1:27.

6. 2 Cor. 12:9–10.

7. Jer. 32:17, 27.

8. Pss. 34:8; 107:1; James 1:17.

9. Lam. 3:22–23.

10. Isa. 6:3; Phil. 2:10–11; 1 Cor. 10:31; 1 Pet. 4:10–11.

11. John 10:27–30.

12. Jen Wilkin, *Women of the Word: How to Study the Bible with Both Our Hearts and Our Minds* (Wheaton, IL: Crossway, 2014), 31.

13. Mark 9:14–29. See especially verse 24.

14. John 14:6.

15. John 8:31–32.

CHAPTER 11 MY TRUTH

1. People are not the light though Christians should reflect Jesus Christ who is the light of the world (Matt. 5:14–16; John 8:12). My friend was not a lucky rabbit's foot nor did she herself have the power to dispel darkness or bring light to my eyes. Illuminating us to the beauty of Jesus Christ is the work of the Holy Spirit (Eph. 1:18).

2. Philippians 1:18 says, "But what does it matter? The important thing is that in every way, whether from false motives or true, Christ is preached." The only part of this verse I remembered was the "whether from false motives or true," which I thought meant if I did good things that good things would happen even if my reasons were messed up. But I didn't know the context of the verse. The surrounding portions of text (vv. 15–18) clearly state that this is specifically about preaching the gospel. And the motive of love is good while the motive of those competing with Paul for converts was bad. But luckily, the words of Jesus Christ are never hindered by humankind. They always carry the power of the Holy Spirit for salvation.

CHAPTER 12 WORSHIPING SOMETHING

1. Gen. 3:1.

2. Pss. 88; 142:1–2; Matt. 10:28–30; 1 Pet. 5:7. I recommend that you read the whole book of Psalms. The psalms are filled with the cries and laments of David and the other authors. They continually praise God and then, almost in the same breath, question His presence and His ways just like we can. Our hearts need to spend time in the psalms as they are narratives of our own joy, sorrow, thanksgiving, pain, and teach us how to reverently call for God's action while proclaiming confidence in God and His kingdom.

3. Dr. Timothy Keller, *Counterfeit Gods: The Empty Promises of Money, Sex, and Power and the Only Hope that Matters* (New York: Dutton, 2009). I drew much of the content for this section from Matt Chandler's sermon *Source and Surface Idols*, which is available at https://www.tvcresources.net/resource-library.

4. Phil. 4:8–9.

5. Rom. 8:29.

6. Rom. 1:29; Gal. 5:19; Eph. 5:3. These three verses are a sampling of many throughout the New Testament that include the Greek term *porneia*, which is a catch-all term that the Bible uses to describe any kind of unlawful sexual behavior. It is consistently applied to any sexual or marital relationship that does not reflect God's design for the lifelong covenant between one man and one woman, including a consensual, monogamous, romantic relationship between two members of the same sex.

7. See the book's Introduction where I state my biblical convictions about homosexuality with supporting Scripture.

8. Rom. 2:4; 2 Pet. 3:9–15.

9. Rom. 4:4–10; 2 Cor. 5:10; Rev. 22:12.

10. Phil. 2:12–13.

11. Isa. 42:8; Rev. 4:8–11.

CHAPTER 13 MY LIFE

1. I used this common phrase and portion of Scripture because to me it meant that I had tried really hard to do the right thing and it didn't work, so I could give up and it would be alright. The phrase actually comes from 2 Timothy 4:7 and the rest of the sentence says, "I have fought the good fight, I have finished the race, I have kept the faith." Maintaining our faith in Jesus Christ until death is what makes the fight worth it.

2. Matt. 18:15–17; 1 Cor. 5:9–11.

CHAPTER 14 BUILDING A STORYLINE

1. Dr. John Thomas (JT) English III, "Christian Story," www. thevillagechurchresources.net.

2. Jer. 2:13.

CHAPTER 15 MY ALLEGIANCE

1. I no longer loved or trusted God. I began to ascribe God's qualities to a person. She seemed more stable, more protective, and a better rescuer than God. I felt that loving her made me stronger and freer. Psalm 18:1–2 says, "I love you, LORD, my strength. The LORD is my rock, my fortress and my deliverer; my God is my rock, in whom I

take refuge, my shield and the horn of my salvation, my stronghold." The truth is that only God is able to be all these things all the time. Only He offers true salvation for eternity.

2.   See John 4:1–42.

CHAPTER 16 RESULTING WRECKAGE

1.   Rom. 6:1–14.
2.   Heb. 12:4–11.
3.   Matt. 25:31–46; Rom. 6:23.
4.   2 Cor. 7:10.
5.   Ps. 51:17.
6.   Eph. 2:1–2 (ESV); Heb. 3:7–18.

PART THREE GETTING OUT

CHAPTER 17 HIS RESCUE

1.   Matt. 27:45–52.
2.   Capitalization of certain nouns and pronouns stops here upon the reorientation of my highest worship.
3.   Luke 15:11–32.
4.   John 3:17; 1 John 1:9.

CHAPTER 18 RECEIVING TRUTH

1.   2 Cor. 5:21.
2.   Eph. 2:1–5.
3.   John 6:28–29.
4.   Matt. 7:9–11.
5.   Exod. 3:14–15.
6.   2 Sam. 22:1–20; Isa. 43:1–7; Rom. 7:24–25; 2 Cor. 3:18; 4:16; Phil. 1:6; 2:12–13.
7.   John 4:13–14; 7:37–39.
8.   John 4:25–26.
9.   John 6:35.
10. John 8:12.

11. John 10:9.
12. John 10:11.
13. John 11:25–26.
14. John 14:6.
15. John 15:1, 5.
16. James 1:17.
17. 2 Pet. 1:3.

CHAPTER 19 HIS RECONCILIATION

1. Ps. 23:1–3.
2. Matt. 18:15–17.

CHAPTER 20 BATTLING FOR WISDOM

1. Ps. 23:4; Matt. 28:20.
2. Prov. 9:10.
3. James 1:5.
4. Prov. 4:7.
5. Rev. 2:4–5.
6. 2 Cor. 5:17–21.
7. Jen Wilkin, "Women in the Church," Acts 29 Advance the Church Conference video, 05:17, 2017. www.acts29.com. Gen. 2:23.
8. 1 Cor. 6:18; 2 Tim. 2:22.
9. Gen. 3:23–24; Eph. 5:31–33.

CHAPTER 21 HIS RESTORATION

1. 2 Cor. 12:7–10.

CHAPTER 22 DECIDING TO FIGHT

1. Eph. 6:10–18; Heb. 3:12–15; 12:1–3.
2. Matt. 22:34–40.
3. John Piper, "God is Most Glorified in Us When We are Most Satisfied in Him," *Desiring God*. October 13, 2012, www.desiringgod.org.

4. John 14:15–17.

5. Melissa Kruger, "Sneak Peek Interview: Jen Wilkin," *The Gospel Coalition,* April 24, 2018, https://www.thegospelcoalition.org/blogs/melissa-kruger/sneak-peek-interview-jen-wilkin.

6. Gen. 19:23–26.

7. Exod. 16:1–3.

8. Rom. 8:17.

9. 1 Kings 14:22–24.

10. Prov. 4:26.

11. 2 Pet. 1:3.

CHAPTER 23 HIS PROMISES

1. Rev. 21:1–22:5.

2. 1 Cor. 13:12.

3. Isa. 26:3; Rom. 5:1.

4. 2 Cor. 4:16–18.

5. Isa. 53:3.

6. Gal. 5:22–23.

7. Mark 2:15–17.

8. Matt. 5:29–30.

9. Heb. 4:14–16.

10. Exod. 13:17–18.

11. Gen. 3:8.

12. Rom. 8:22–27.

CHAPTER 24 LIVING IN VICTORY

1. John 14:6.